Outsourcing Software Development Offshore

Making It Work

OTHER AUERBACH PUBLICATIONS

The ABCs of IP Addressing
Gilbert Held
ISBN: 0-8493-1144-6

The ABCs of LDAP: How to Install, Run, and Administer LDAP Services
Reinhard Voglmaier
ISBN: 0-8493-1346-5

The ABCs of TCP/IP
Gilbert Held
ISBN: 0-8493-1463-1

Building a Wireless Office
Gilbert Held
ISBN: 0-8493-1271-X

The Complete Project Management Office Handbook
Gerald M. Hill
ISBN: 0-8493-2173-5

Enhancing LAN Performance, 4th Edition
Gilbert Held
ISBN: 0-8493-1942-0

Information Security Management Handbook, 5th Edition
Harold F. Tipton and Micki Krause, Editors
ISBN: 0-8493-1997-8

Information Security Policies and Procedures: A Practitioner's Reference 2nd Edition
Thomas R. Peltier
ISBN: 0-8493-1958-7

Information Security Policies, Procedures, and Standards: Guidelines for Effective Information Security Management
Thomas R. Peltier
ISBN: 0-8493-1137-3

Information Security Risk Analysis
Thomas R. Peltier
ISBN: 0-8493-0880-1

Information Technology for Manufacturing: Reducing Costs and Expanding Capabilities
Kevin Aki, John Clemons, and Mark Cubine
ISBN: 1-57444-359-3

Interpreting the CMMI: A Process Improvement Approach
Margaret Kulpa and Kurt Johnson
ISBN: 0-8493-1654-5

IS Management Handbook, 8th Edition
Carol V. Brown and Heikki Topi
ISBN: 0-8493-1595-6

ISO 9000:2000 for Software and Systems Providers
Robert Bamford and William Deibler, III
ISBN: 0-8493-2063-1

Managing a Network Vulnerability Assessment
Thomas R. Peltier and Justin Peltier
ISBN: 0-8493-1270-1

A Practical Approach to WBEM/CIM Management
Chris Hobbs
ISBN: 0-8493-2306-1

A Practical Guide to Security Engineering and Information Assurance
Debra Herrmann
ISBN: 0-8493-1163-2

Practical Network Design Techniques, 2nd Edition: A Complete Guide for WANs and LANs
Gilbert Held and S. Ravi Jagannathan
ISBN: 0-8493-2019-4

Real Process Improvement Using the CMMI
Michael West
ISBN: 0-8493-2109-3

Six Sigma Software Development
Christine B. Tayntor
ISBN: 0-8493-1193-4

Software Architecture Design Patterns in Java
Partha Kuchana
ISBN: 0-8493-2142-5

Software Configuration Management
Jessica Keyes
ISBN: 0-8493-1976-5

A Technical Guide to IPSec Virtual Private Networks
James S. Tiller
ISBN: 0-8493-0876-3

Telecommunications Cost Management
Brian DiMarsico, Thomas Phelps IV, and William A. Yarberry, Jr.
ISBN: 0-8493-1101-2

AUERBACH PUBLICATIONS

www.auerbach-publications.com
To Order Call: 1-800-272-7737 • Fax: 1-800-374-3401
E-mail: orders@crcpress.com

Outsourcing Software Development Offshore

Making It Work

Tandy Gold

AUERBACH PUBLICATIONS

A CRC Press Company

Boca Raton   London   New York   Washington, D.C.

Library of Congress Cataloging-in-Publication Data

Gold, Tandy.
    Outsourcing software development offshore: making it work / Tandy Gold.
      p. cm.
    Includes bibliographical references and index.
    ISBN 0-8493-1943-9 (alk. paper)
    1. Computer software—Development. 2. Contracting out. I. Title.

QA76.76.D47G63 2005
005′.068′4—dc22   2004051023

Visit the Auerbach Publications Web site at www.auerbach-publications.com

© 2005 by CRC Press
Auerbach is an imprint of CRC Press

No claim to original U.S. Government works
International Standard Book Number 0-8493-1943-9
Library of Congress Card Number 2004051023
Printed in the United States of America 1 2 3 4 5 6 7 8 9 0
Printed on acid-free paper

DEDICATION

For Dan, my Beloved

TABLE OF CONTENTS

PREFACE

The Offshore Imperative

It is mid-December in 2002 in New York City, and only 11 days remain before Christmas. Despite the weather and the holiday, it is standing room only at an Executive Conference on Offshore Outsourcing, and most leading financial services and other firms are in attendance.

You've picked up the right book. Top experienced Offshore technology leaders — hands-on implementers of Offshore in the Fortune 50 — help to answer these and other questions:

- What is Offshore or Offshore Outsourcing?
- Why is it an IT Imperative?
- What does my firm need to do to successfully evaluate Offshore?
- If we do decide Offshore is right for us, what can we expect?
- How do we avoid the pitfalls?
- How do we respond to security and geopolitical risk?
- What is the best way to handle sensitive employee concerns?

This book was born out of simple necessity. In January of 2001, as Senior VP and Program Manager of the Offshore Program Office, I was handed the task of making Offshore a reality for a large New England financial institution. The challenges were enormous — the worst technology-related job recession in recent memory, a general lack of understanding of the Offshore model (which I shared), and a huge distrust of anything that might lead to even fewer jobs within the beset IT organization. Despite my years of successfully starting up and driving IT initiatives, I knew I needed to get smart — and fast.

I created the Offshore Interest Group, at the time of this writing, a group of over 50 Fortune 100 hands-on Offshore Program Managers. We have been meeting by phone monthly since early 2001, where we share ideas, challenges, and advice. This book is both a tribute to and a show of appreciation of the generosity, professionalism, and vision of these professionals.

ACKNOWLEDGMENTS

To the members of the Offshore Interest Group, including Phil Stanley, Lou Fox, Fran Karamouzis, and others too numerous to mention, thank you for sharing your thoughts as we learn together about this important new venture. I'd like to extend a special appreciation to Offshore Interest Group members who directly contributed to this book. To Sri Tanjore Swami Sridar, one of the pioneers of Offshore who educated me about the recent relevant history of India. My appreciation and thanks to the editors and writers of *ComputerWorld* magazine; it's been wonderful sharing our mutual and informed enthusiasm. To Sandy Kriensky, Rene Marcotte, Ramya Krishnamurthy, Tanasia Cespedes, Susan Ryan, and Nader Hooshmand, my colleagues over the years, thank you for your wonderful friendship. My love and gratitude extends to Laurie Baum, who embodies such warmth and light in this world, and my dearest friend Rosemary Cook Burke. To Bert Shaw and John Pierrakos, for sending me out into the world with so much love that words cannot suffice. Finally, to my father and mother, both my Master Teachers in every sense; my sister, fellow school bus rider and technical wordsmith; my darling cats Emily, Zoe, Basho, Punim, and Key West Charlie; and especially my husband, Dan — my deepest love and gratitude.

SECTION 1

THE OFFSHORE IMPERATIVE

This book is divided into three sections. First, we look at understanding the Offshore model — how it works, what the financials portend, and the leading players. Next, we look at the historical evolution of the Offshore service model, key to understanding the present. Finally, we look at the execution of Offshore Outsourcing, helping you to be forewarned and forearmed.

In this first section, Chapter One provides an overview of the recent growth of Offshore, the most compelling new IT trend. Chapter Two is a pragmatic overview of Offshore program initiation. Finally, Chapter Three concludes this section with a close look at Offshore vendor management, including the vendor choice process.

1

CRUNCHING THE OFFSHORE NUMBERS: WHAT THE FINANCIALS PORTEND

WELCOME TO THE DEFINITIVE GUIDE ON OFFSHORE OUTSOURCING

The individuals and firms in this book represent over 60 years of Offshore Outsourcing hands-on Fortune 50 experience, encompassing both solid track records of success to emulate, as well as missteps and bloopers to avoid.

Offshore Outsourcing, perhaps more than most complex and broad IT initiatives, can make or break individual careers, and even companies. At issue is often more than simply the viability of the Information Technology (IT) organization as an entity. To the extent that the IT function provides the firm's strategic or competitive edge, Offshore Outsourcing can be a determinant of the success or failure of the organization as a whole. Either way the stakes are high.

In this chapter, we introduce the overall concept of Offshore Outsourcing. We also look at the hard financial numbers behind the Offshore wave, and its phenomenal, seemingly recession-proof growth (see Exhibit 1.1).

SETTING THE STAGE: THE COMPELLING OFFSHORE STORY

Attend any conference on IT consulting services today and a whirlwind trend will come to light. It is called "Offshore" — and it is the fastest growing IT trend today.

What is "Offshore?" Breathtakingly simple in concept, it can be tricky to implement. The computers and data they hold generally stay in the

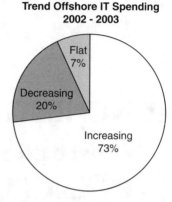

Trend Overall IT Spending
2002 - 2003

Flat
27%

Increasing
7%

Decreasing
66%

Trend Offshore IT Spending
2002 - 2003

Flat
7%

Decreasing
20%

Increasing
73%

Exhibit 1.1   Although 66 Percent of Companies Surveyed Show a Decreased Overall IT Spending, 73 Percent Show Offshore Outsourcing Spending Growing (Source: JP Morgan, Indian IT Services: CIO Survey, March 2002)

United States. The workers programming and providing technical maintenance and support services on those computers, however, reside in India, the Philippines, and a host of other locations. They log on to an international network, and perform these functions from the other side of the world. A small contingent — usually 20 to 30 percent of the overall team — stays in the United States to provide contact during normal U.S. working hours. In addition, the design and customer-interface functions usually remain in the United States. Offshore is truly a case of the IT function as a global melting pot — at the application team level.

Although Offshore Outsourcing has frequent coverage in the press as the ultimate threat to the information technology worker, the reality is that the Offshore Co-Sourcing model (20 percent Onshore, 80 percent Offshore) described above is usually applied to a maximum of 30 percent of applications — and even a smaller percentage of personnel — across any individual IT organization. There are many reasons, but one key concern is that most firms simply will not (or cannot, under regulatory scrutiny) allow remote networked consultants to have access to sensitive customer data. That limits the amount of Offshore Outsourcing pretty effectively in most industries. Most companies who are mature in Offshore Outsourcing — implemented the program three years or more — have shifted their perception from blind fear to an appreciation of the savings it can provide for that 30 percent, and serve to stave off an even bigger threat — that of being completely outsourced (the entire IT organization is replaced by an outside firm). The irony is while the popular press portrays Offshore solely as a threat to jobs, the reality is it just as often provides the savings and value to create more job stability and security.

Beyond the impact of jobs, the first question is usually — what about risk? 9/11 has only increased the Offshore Outsourcing trend further, as the illusion of U.S.-based safety was sadly brought home to us. The track record of early Offshore Outsourcing adaptors has shown that, even as the myth of U.S.-based "safety" has been debunked, the economics of Offshore Outsourcing has made war too expensive in terms of potential lost revenue. A recent *New York Times* article suggested, not completely tongue-in-cheek, that the question of whether recent skirmishes between India and Pakistan were leading to war was best answered by American Express — a reference to that firm's large investment in Offshore Outsourcing in India.[1] The article suggests that the best way to assess the likelihood of war is determined by asking the leadership of large companies with significant Indian investment, such as American Express. The article strongly implies that these countries are well aware of the potential cost of war in terms of negative economic impact. This economic threat serves as a big deterrent, the authors imply.

Why is Offshore so compelling? A master's-level computer scientist makes at most U.S. $14,000 per year in India, and is generally better educated and more enthusiastic than his $100,000 plus American counterpart.[2] Do the math, and the potential savings are staggering. Based on personal experience, those of the presentations at various conferences on Offshore, and discussions of the Offshore Interest Group members, most companies list their Offshore projects as the only ones that regularly demonstrate an IRR (Internal Return on Investment) well over 110 percent. Usually, quality and efficiency improve as well. By 2010, India may run out of workers, and newcomers such as China may take the lead.

A quick note about the author: as part of my role as Offshore Program Manager at a large northeastern financial institution, I created and coordinated a monthly Offshore Interest Group. This virtual group is made up of experienced Offshore Program Managers from leading Fortune 100 firms. Together we represent well over 60 years of Fortune 100 Offshore experience. This book is intended to be an executive toolkit on Offshore, a kit created from real-life examples and lessons learned from these experienced firms and individuals. Each chapter introduces a key set of concepts and illustrates them with real-world examples. Speaking from the two years of sharing monthly insight and practical experience with the Offshore Interest Group membership, this book focuses on pragmatic solutions proven in real life, not theories. This book is targeted at the senior technology and business executives who need to cut costs without reducing service, and want to learn from those who have proven success in meeting that objective.

First, we consider the macrocosm of what is at play across the technology industry as a whole. Newspaper coverage to the contrary, a deep understanding of the Offshore phenomenon is not possible via a sound bite. The disparity between public misconception and reality is wide, fueled by fear in a shrinking economy that particularly threatened the formerly secure jobs within IT. The record, year-over-year profitability of the set of leading Offshore Outsourcing vendors, coupled as it is with the recent lackluster financial performance of Traditional IT Outsourcing service providers, creates implications regarding the relative growth of Offshore Outsourcing that cannot be ignored. And indeed, are not overlooked by Wall Street and the global investment community, as the respective stock price history and other financial measures attest.

Later in Chapter Two, we look at Citigroup as a microcosm of the individual firm and the kind of savings generally at stake when considering Offshore. Along the way, we define our basic terms and concepts, creating a vocabulary of Offshore that can serve us as we dig deeper into the details of methodology and best practices in subsequent chapters.

OFFSHORE OUTSOURCING VERSUS TRADITIONAL IT OUTSOURCING

To understand the IT imperative that is the technology discipline Outsourcing, it is first important to make a clear distinction between it and what we will of Offshore call, for lack of a better term, Traditional IT Outsourcing.

The Traditional IT Outsourcing model is relatively clear-cut. An outside technology firm is hired to take over the IT function for the organization in whole or in part. The theory is that because managing technology is their primary business these large firms can provide more expertise at a lower price by leveraging economies of scale across many customers. So, rather than have a division of the firm perform technology functions, the organization looks outside for the entire function throughout the life cycle, from IT strategic planning, to systems analysis and design, and finally systems maintenance to retirement.

Although there have been success stories with Traditional IT Outsourcing, there is also a relatively high rate of visible and expensive failures.[3] Defining failure as the termination of a Traditional Outsourcing legal contract before the original agreed upon termination date, for contacts that had been in place for at least one year, D&B found that 25 percent of traditional outsourcing relationships failed.

In Traditional Outsourcing, what seems to occur is that the initial flush of savings and efficiencies in the long run become overshadowed by the inability to establish a close strategic and business partnership between the newly streamlined "foreign" IT organization and the management of the firm it is serving at the operational level. Over the long term, firms require a proactive technology partner able and willing to provide creative input and judiciously advise in investments in technology. Although top executive-level relationships don't seem to flag, middle-management alignments tend to disappear during Traditional IT Outsourcing, and as a result, the organization does not have a means of realizing the creative process in a manner that really integrates IT. Anyone who has worked in a major Fortune 50 firm knows that it is already hard enough to bridge the communication, personality, values, and priorities gaps between IT and its internal business customers. Add another layer — such as an outside firm providing IT services — and that relationship is usually all but dead. Yet it is this relationship, at the operating management level (not the executive), that determines how technology supports the creative heart of the organization.

In order to have valuable and meaningful input between the "line" (revenue generating) businesses, bread-and-butter functions, and IT, there is an ongoing need to continually work to bridge the gap between business and technology to allow these functions to work hand in hand. Key partnerships often are tenuous, forged on personal relationships over shared experiences that evaporate in today's rapidly changing and mobile environment. In the past, and in much of the present, that means that today's technology leaders need to take the time to understand their business counterpart's models and challenges intimately. Although this will change over time, today's business leaders in large Fortune 50 firms by and large have not grown up with technology and lean on their IT partners for guidance or at least proactive initiation.

The problem with Traditional IT Outsourcing is that this partnership is one of the services that goes by the wayside in the emphasis on cost cutting. Few large Traditional Outsourcing firms can afford to have an IT strategic planner follow the business leaders around just to tee up next year's potential partnership — yet this is exactly what is required when business and technology meet over the table to put a plan together. If the IT function is kept inhouse, the best and brightest of IT leadership have learned to do double duty in keeping a close relationship with their business peers while simultaneously leading the tactical execution of the existing IT strategy. Although this may or may not be acknowledged, even with the growing number of executive-level "relationship managers" that are springing up as part of IT services everywhere, it one of the key factors that enable the kind of technology deployment that truly provides competitive advantage.

Offshore Outsourcing is unique in that the strategic inhouse business partnership function is preserved along with the savings associated with

Outsourcing. Traditional Outsourcing occurs when the entire IT function is dismissed, and IT exists solely through the service provider. The co-sourcing model, explained below, enables companies to have the savings and efficiencies of outsourcing, while keeping key strategic functions of project/program management, and so on, inhouse. This is through a business model commonly called Co-Sourcing.

In Co-Sourcing, the geographic placement of team members is determined by their function. Offshore teams are often discussed in terms of percentages, such as "80/20" or "70/30." "80/20" means that, of a given IT application development or maintenance support team implemented with the Co-Sourcing model, 80 percent of the team is located Offshore (out of the United States) and 20 percent of the team Onshore (within the United States or the Americas). This occurs of course, with "70/30" or even "60/40" teams.

Whatever the percentage of the team that is Onshore, the functions of that team usually include maintaining the partnership and planning function with their business counterparts. Although the specifics vary from team to team and firm to firm, as a general rule of thumb, the Onshore positions maintain the strategic, planning, or architectural functions, and the Offshore positions usually require the most tactical execution. Exhibits 1.2 and 1.3 show the typical Onshore/Offshore mix of team functions across the systems development life cycle.

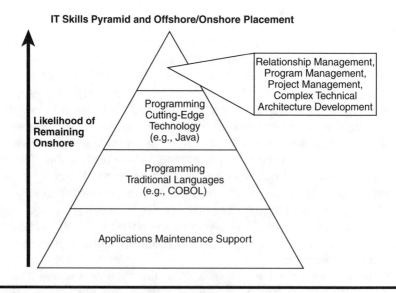

IT Skills Pyramid and Offshore/Onshore Placement

Likelihood of Remaining Onshore

Relationship Management, Program Management, Project Management, Complex Technical Architecture Development

Programming Cutting-Edge Technology (e.g., Java)

Programming Traditional Languages (e.g., COBOL)

Applications Maintenance Support

Exhibit 1.2   A Look at IT Job Impact across the System Life Cycle

Exhibit 1.3   A Look at Onshore versus Offshore for Each IT Stage

IT Life-cycle Stage	Primarily Onshore	Primarily Offshore	Equally Onshore and Offshore
Business partnership	X		
Overall IT strategy	X		
Application planning and design	X		
Business process planning and design	X		
Application analysis and design	X		
Application efficiency analysis/upgrades		X	
Application coding		X	
Application testing		X	
Application maintenance		X	
Application retirement planning			X

Benefits of Offshore Outsourcing

It is here that Offshore Outsourcing becomes clear as an imperative.

The typical Masters-level computer programmer with five years' experience in India commands a salary of roughly $12,000 U.S. These individuals are generally quality employees in every sense — they are generally enamored of American culture and are excited to be a part of it, however remotely. Their English language skills are excellent, and they are more than aware of the importance of these business opportunities to their country as a whole, as well as their immediate family.

A picture emerges, based upon the Co-Sourcing model, of an IT imperative that provides numerous benefits, with minimum of the costs — and the risks — associated with Traditional IT Outsourcing.

Of course, beyond illustration, there is often a gray line between Offshore Outsourcing and Traditional IT Outsourcing. For example, Traditional Outsourcing firms are now building extensive Offshore Outsourcing capabilities, and may blend the Offshore and Traditional Outsourcing models by Offshoring a Traditionally Outsourced function. But at the time of writing, it is unclear whether the Traditional IT Outsourcing companies, generally U.S.-based, will actually be able to catch up with the Indian-based Offshore companies. Although it is difficult to provide hard evidence as many corporate customers are legally prohibited from sharing information related to Offshore pricing or rates, strong anecdotal information points to the perceived gap of the value of Traditional Outsource providers who are late and smaller entries into the Offshore Outsourcing game. For example, at the Gartner Outsourcing Summit in July 2003 in Las Vegas, several in-the-moment audience polls asked the audience — generally more knowledgeable on Offshore than the average IT manager — of the comparative value of the Traditional Offshore companies now moving Offshore versus the Offshore Outsourcing companies who are based Offshore and represent the new wave. The results, poll after poll, came back that the Traditional Outsource companies are not really providing the same level of value in terms of price per services.

Thus far, the U.S. company market share of Offshore Outsourcing has been making fast inroads but is not keeping up with the plain vanilla Offshore Outsourcing firms. However, this is changing rapidly. Even though U.S.-based firms often can't match their India-based counterparts in pricing, the quality of the candidates, or the methodology sophistication of these companies, they often are the initial choice of many U.S. customers, who focus on what is familiar and perceived of as safe. Most Indian Offshore companies have attained CMM levels of 4.0 or beyond, whereas U.S. companies remain at 3.0 or less.[4] (CMM is one of several independent industry company certifications that evaluate the methodology and other processes relating to efficiency of IT execution — Level 5 is the highest rating.). However, this emphasis usually occurs just once, and upon contract renewal time, price is the focus, other firms are introduced, and value for dollar rather than "safety" is emphasized. Firm after firm in the Offshore Interest Group has shifted from U.S.-based to India-based firms, or decided upon a mixture of both with the requirement that the U.S.-based firms lower prices significantly. Therefore the financial trends outlined below are probably true for the long term, but may not hold as new vertical markets are introduced to Offshore for the first time and reach for the known quantity in an Offshore partner.

And just as India-based Offshore Outsourcing firms such as Infosys find it hard to compete with U.S. firms for top U.S. graduates, even the top U.S. firms here cannot compete with the top firms in India.

The press abounds with stories about how Offshore Outsourcing is following in the footsteps of other industries moving overseas in search of cheap labor, and the impact of these labor movements on an economy that will be made up of increasing levels of unemployment. It is the IT skills pyramid above that provides the key to the jobs retained here in the United States over time. As Offshore Outsourcing becomes more and more part of the mainstream, U.S. corporations will not be able to afford to keep the Offshore-appropriate jobs here in the United States, when these services are available at such inexpensive and high quality elsewhere. The landscape of Offshore sets the waves of change across the way we will structure our IT skill departments, our training, our colleges, and our career planning, far into the future. Note again, however, that there is a natural limit to the IT jobs that can be moved Offshore — the

Exhibit 1.4   Benefits of Offshore Outsourcing

Significant cost savings
Preserve the value of the internal IT organization
A competitive imperative
Ability to move U.S.-based employees higher up the IT skills pyramid
Hedge the availability of mainframe programmers, who are rapidly "aging out" in the United States
Leverage time differences to shorten system and product development life cycles
Not all time zone differences are challenges, and creative use of the fact that half the organization is sleeping while the other is awake can provide a compelling advantage
Support efforts related to cultural diversity and acceptance
Document and streamline those old application systems
Increase quality and efficiency in systems development as well as maintenance and support
Improved overall methodology and discipline

limitations of networked consultants' access to sensitive customer data. In the Offshore Interest group, as an example, most firms average about 20 percent of the IT organization in a Co-Sourcing model for Offshore. Usually external consultants are the first eliminated, minimizing the direct impact on employees.

Why Offshore? Let's take a look at the overall advantages (Exhibit 1.4) that the Offshore model provides:

- *Significant cost savings.* Most Offshore Outsourcing programs demonstrate an IRR well over 100 percent. IT projects are routinely approved with an IRR well under 70 percent. The savings generated by Offshore are difficult to match with other initiatives.
- *Preserve the value of the internal IT organization.* In mature organizations where Offshore Outsourcing is well understood across the organization, it is often credited with saving the jobs of the IT employees from the more drastic Traditional IT Outsourcing. So it may well be viewed as an integral part of keeping the IT organization intact.
- *A competitive imperative.* Most firms that provide advice and counsel on strategic direction of IT, such as Gartner, have marked Offshore Outsourcing as a corporate imperative, as a result of the myriad advantages it provides.
- *Ability to move U.S.-based employees higher up the IT skills pyramid.* Employees unable or unwilling to move into higher value positions are most at risk. For those that can, Offshore may actually serve

as a career boon. Moving the programming as well as the maintenance and support functions Offshore frees up the U.S.-based IT resources to do the more interesting and challenging efforts (and generally more highly prized and recompensed in the job market) such as new project development, systems architecture, and project management. The challenge for the firm going Offshore is in the fair and equitable treatment of negatively affected loyal and long-term workers. We discuss these issues in detail later in this book. But for the vast majority of workers who are spending a percentage of their time maintaining systems and would love a chance to be free of that — this is the opportunity for which they have been waiting. And the economics make sense — just given real estate costs of housing IT workers, it makes much more sense for the programmer and maintenance IT "seats" to be elsewhere — not the United States.

■ *Hedge the availability of mainframe programmers, who are rapidly "aging out" in the United States.* Offshore ensures that your firm will have continued access to mainframe programmers well into the next decade, despite the anticipated shortage. As Y2K vividly illustrated, despite the best of intentions, today's businesses do not always follow a predictable schedule in retiring old technology. New technology employees do not learn and train on yesterday's technology. Thus, the cost of maintaining technology may sharply increase as trained resources able to maintain and enhance these systems become scarce. Offshore Outsourcing will help to ensure that the old legacy systems are able to be maintained at a reasonable cost.

■ *Leverage time differences to shorten system and product development life cycles.* Although time differences must be managed carefully in Co-Sourcing to ensure efficiency, the positive is that while part of the team sleeps in the United States, the rest will be up and working, and vice versa. Productivity can theoretically double, or at least be significantly enhanced.

■ *Not all time zone differences are challenges, and creative use of the fact that half the organization is sleeping while the other is awake can provide a compelling advantage.* Thus far, the reigns of the development teams headed in the United States have not allowed this to become a de facto working mode, but there are examples of product development that were literally occurring around the globe and handed off via the Internet. Although newsworthy and in some sense proven as a working model, these are far from the norms. Most companies are still struggling with geographical and functional turf wars within the United States, never mind opening up possibilities to a true partnership overseas. One area where these false barriers have dropped is in the area of Business Process Outsourcing or BPO. Still a fledgling discipline within Offshore across the board, it has matured in the phone and help desk support arena. The chances that the individual you are calling on the toll-free number to get help resides within the United States are becoming less and less. Offshore firms provide local sports, weather, and other data to phone workers to maintain the illusion and are getting increasingly sophisticated over time in maintaining the front.

■ *Support efforts related to cultural diversity and acceptance.* Most IT organizations struggle with the realities of providing equal opportunity to all workers, especially in retention of quality diversity candidates. Executed correctly, Offshore can provide an invaluable learning opportunity to underscore the value and importance of acceptance of other cultures within the organization. Most large organizations today are committed to diversity, but all too often have a homogeneous IT staff despite best efforts. The first time a crowd of individuals in flowing saris walks the corporate halls to the local cafeteria usually leads to a double-take — even for those who helped to create it. A breath of fresh air, a new way of looking at the world for employees even over lunch, can result.

■ *Finally clean out the closets — document and streamline those old application systems.* For many firms, the process of moving old systems Offshore represents the first time these legacy systems are properly documented and processes streamlined. Most large firms have an enormous backlog of systems that are created off to the side of the official architecture, created on the fly for an emergency need, and possessing little organization, documentation, and structure. Offshore firms possess great ingenuity and abilities in these areas, and are able to quickly create order out of chaos by evaluating, combining, and making more efficient the maintenance effort. Many firms have their talented IT professionals maintain these systems "on the side" so they never get the full benefit of a once-over in terms of creating more efficiencies in their integration with other applications, the running of the application itself, or the way the system is maintained. Offshore firms specialize in transforming these old dinosaurs into leaner and meaner equivalents, streamlining the drag on maintenance and support as well as enhancements. This equivalent of cleaning out the old closets in the IT application suite can free up a surprising amount of wasted money, energy, and time, and decrease the fear factors related to dependency on the one or two individuals who know how to make it run.

■ *Increase quality and efficiency in systems development as well as maintenance and support.* Most IT professionals today have to wear many hats. Separating a team out to do the maintenance and support, or the applications development, often means increased efficiencies because the focus of those teams is streamlined. As projects are moved Offshore, processes that are not optimal must be eliminated, and creativity comes into play. These efficiencies can provide a measurable increase in the quality of services, improvement in time-to-market of systems, lower defects, and improved rate of response in internal or external user service-level agreements (SLAs).

■ *Improved overall methodology and discipline.* Offshore Outsourcing firms often have greater command of traditional IT quality disciplines such as CMM and Six Sigma. It is not uncommon for firms to leverage their capabilities to help these in-house quality initiatives move along at a faster clip inhouse.

Impact on the Individual Worker: The Hurdle of Offshore Outsourcing Is Not All Bad News

A growing trend in the Offshore Outsourcing world is secrecy and silence, even in larger firms. Many individual executives are instructed to maintain low visibility to avoid negative press. But the impact of Offshore Outsourcing within a Co-Sourcing model may not be completely negative.

Let's look at a typical scenario from an individual employee's perspective. Before Offshore, Susan, who is an IT programmer working in a large insurance firm supporting their Internet customer portal, spends 20 to 30 percent of her time maintaining her application, 20 to 30 percent dealing with internal user problems and issues, and the remainder of her time planning next year's enhancements with other team members.

A year later, Susan is now part of an Offshore team and has a different set of tasks as the Onshore representative of the on-site portal. She now spends only 10 percent of her time dealing with maintenance issues and user problems, primarily either dealing with issues that come up during the day that require immediate attention while the Offshore team sleeps, or providing additional information and support to the Offshore team in their maintenance efforts. A full 90 percent of her time is allocated to system planning and design, and as a result of the overall lowered costs of systems maintenance as well as the rapid progress of Susan and her design team, the new upgraded portal has been scheduled a year ahead of original expectations. As the Offshore team becomes more and more efficient, and their learning curve increases, the costs to Susan's firm for the portal will decrease even further. Susan is thrilled with the turn of her career, as she anticipates that her market value will allow her to move to her goal, that of project lead, a year sooner than under her old set of duties.

But every upside usually has a potential downside. Let's take a look at the typical pitfalls of Offshore Outsourcing.

CHALLENGES OF OFFSHORE OUTSOURCING

The heart of the challenge of Offshore Outsourcing is frequently the Achilles' heel of the organization. That is strategic planning relating to staffing. Strategic staffing is challenging on many fronts, not the least of which is difficulty in anticipating the level of business growth over any long-term period. Many firms have simply given up long-term planning, as anything planned past 6 months has little to no meaning in today's rapidly changing business environment. Planning for staffing growth over a 12-month period may be almost impossible if the business plans do not extend for that timeframe.

Yet Offshore Outsourcing, as the popular press underlines daily, is about dealing with the challenge of anticipating and managing the firm's IT skills mix up front. In the representative group of Offshore Interest Group Program managers, this is the single most difficult issue to negotiate, anticipate, and handle with grace as the program executes. Let's take a look at the various factors behind the press hype.

Strategic staffing planning means that we are in the realm of turf wars, and if there is an executive leadership gap, the Offshore initiative will often die or be postponed with the management team responsible for launching it. Usually six to nine months into the process it becomes clear that Offshore is working, not just well, but very well. The implications that not only line workers, but the ranks of IT management, can be thinned as the result become evident. Unless there is a firm hand from above monitoring the initiative, increasingly difficult in the best organizations that have spent years trying to align authority and decision-making responsibility close to the individuals who execute, the growth of the Offshore initiative may wane.

Are IT jobs at risk across the board? As Susan's example above illustrates, it depends upon whether the firm decides to reinvest the savings of Offshore into increased capability within the IT organization (getting more IT services for less investment), or it takes the savings from IT and applies it elsewhere in the organization (bigger marketing and sales budget, for example). Usually, firms do a combination of both. Certainly, if there is any strategic value to IT, reinvesting in employees such as Susan in terms of enabling them to provide higher value to the organization as they move up the IT skills pyramid is usually a forgone benefit. Susan was doing the higher-level skills job well prior to Offshore, and her ability to solely focus on those aspects of her job provided real benefit to the organization as well as higher job satisfaction for her.

So, the real potential negative impact is reserved for those unable or unwilling to move up the IT skills pyramid. The programmers unable or unwilling to become architects or project managers are the ones who will be left behind. Knowing and understanding this is the key to successful Offshore deployment, not only in terms of providing a soft landing for these employees in terms of training opportunities to operations or other U.S.-based jobs, or generous retraining programs, or both. Handling these challenges with grace, and protecting these usually loyal and long-term employees, means that the early turf fighting must be kept to a minimum, and the overall impact realistically assessed.

Thus, although the benefits may have you ready to sign up, also understand that Offshore is not for the faint of heart. Offshore Outsourcing is among the most complex cross-organizational initiatives a firm can undertake, and it is very important to enter into the process as fully versed as possible. All of the topics touched upon below are explored fully in subsequent chapters.

Critical Success Factors for Offshore Outsourcing

What are some of the critical components for successful execution of Offshore within Information Technology or IT? Exhibit 1.5 explores some of the most frequent challenges.

Exhibit 1.5   Critical Success Factors for Offshore Outsourcing

1. Upfront strategic staffing planning, especially regarding employee impact
2. Organized and fine-tuned communications
3. Upfront cost assessment and management
4. Network security architecture development
5. Knowledge transfer cost and quality management
6. Software vendor consent management
7. Funding the appropriate level of ongoing Offshore program office oversight
8. Top-down executive support
9. Risk management

1. Upfront Strategic Staffing Planning, Especially Regarding Employee Impact

Although Offshore Outsourcing will benefit the entire IT organization by bringing overall costs down, and therefore lowering the always-present threat of complete Traditional Outsourcing, it is almost guaranteed that even the mention of Offshore will bring fear and trepidation into the hearts of the IT staff. Know that half the battle to winning Offshore is to deal upfront with the tough people questions. All of your employees will be watching how those loyal hard workers are treated now that there are cheaper and more efficient labor sources available. Acquit yourselves with heart as well as intelligence by anticipating and executing an orderly transition so that your affected employees don't walk out with just a way to pay the bills for a short time, but have the opportunity to create alternative jobs or careers.

2. Organized and Fine-Tuned Communications

Botched communications can create a situation in which you lose your best people due to misunderstandings and fear. Handled well, Offshore can be understood to be the boon it truly is, or at the very least, have a neutral impact. As organizations go down the path of Offshore, the fear is replaced with a more realistic view of the benefit to the organization as a whole. Offshore Outsourcing also has a natural limit for security reasons. The companies that are willing and able to allow remote access directly into their systems handling sensitive customer data are few to none. Deployed correctly, Offshore Outsourcing is usually held to a maximum of 30 percent of the overall IT organization, frequently less.[5] Much of the time, the main focus is replacement of external high-priced contractors from the Big Four and other IT services consultants with Offshore resources. So, the fears that most jobs will evaporate are usually overstated, and it is not usual in companies that are mature (over three years experience) in Offshore for there to be a broad understanding that the shift to Offshore is a boon to the IT organization as a whole, by allowing it to provide more value with less investment, and supporting the career and skills growth of its members. However, there is a long road to travel before these firms reach that level of understanding. The way that communications regarding Offshore are handled can either be a calming or escalating factor in the perceived fear of the initiative. Later in this book, we delve deeply into this most important of potential pitfalls of Offshore.

3. Upfront Cost Assessment and Management

In discussing Offshore with peer Program Managers as well as vendors, the average break-even point for Offshore initiatives appears to be well over six months. Costs often include significant investment in network security, risk management, knowledge transfer (training the Offshore team in the applications they will be either developing or maintaining), and software vendor consents (obtaining the okay from software vendors that the existing licenses apply to external consultants acting upon the firm's behalf).

Although the costs of entry into Offshore can be relatively high, the return on those costs is usually so staggeringly positive that these concerns tend to evaporate over time. The opportunity cost of tying up staff to conduct knowledge transfer, and the investment in the network security architecture, are usually overshadowed by the fact that once these hurdles are overcome, the year-over-year savings that Offshore enables is very very high and usually only increases with time as the applications become more fine tuned and efficient.

4.   Network Security Architecture Development

It is unlikely the firm's network security team is familiar with the issues and challenges of Offshore. It is wise to anticipate both a learning curve and the legitimate need for a new architecture, as well as new equipment such as firewalls, to support that new architecture.

Eric Hacker, network architect at a major New England financial institution, a poet as well as an outstanding technician, describes most organizations as a "donut" with a hard outer crust and a "soft, chewy center." In other words, it's hard to get inside the network from outside, but once you are in, it's easy to go anywhere. Not a good design for Offshore, which requires the ability of the network to make a distinction between native and external consultants as they float about in the ether of the network. In particular, again, it is critical to ensure that external Offshore consultants get nowhere near sensitive customer data: thus the need for a new architecture, usually through a series of firewalls or more basic structural fortifications.

5.   Knowledge Transfer Cost and Quality Management

Knowledge transfer refers to the learning "shadow" period which is required when Offshore personnel come to the United States to train on the applications or systems they will be enhancing and supporting. New-comers may underestimate the time required to get Offshore personnel up to speed. Most experienced firms require Offshore vendors or service providers to keep knowledge transfer costs to a contractual fixed cost. Otherwise, to quote Ted Podest from Citigroup, you may "burn while you learn," supporting your Offshore vendor on unnecessary spending.

The challenge relating to knowledge transfer is really a more subtle one, and that is, how to align the IT planning cycle with the longer project cycles associated with Offshore. By the time the application has completed knowledge transfer, negotiated with software vendors for licensing rights for Offshore consultants, and executed the minimum requirements to shore up network security, it is not unusual for over six months to have elapsed. In the overall scheme of the return on investment where the savings are at least five years, often over ten years, six months' investment is not significant, but it certainly has a tendency to "blow" the current fiscal year's IT budget and staffing process. Most large organizations are teetering on the edge of a total crash when Offshore is introduced, because it upsets what is already a delicate balance of business interface, technical opportunity, and resource management. Knowing it gets easier does not make the initial pain go away.

6. Software Vendor Consent Management

Consents are required for Offshore personnel to obtain permission to access the system under your firm's original software licensing agreements. For example, if you run your HR systems on Peoplesoft and want to Offshore that application, Peoplesoft must agree there are no additional software licensing fees involved. Policy varies by vendor and most are cooperative, but many consider Offshore Outsourcing a "revenue opportunity" and obtaining access for your Offshore consultants may become a time-consuming and sometimes expensive process. Legally, because most existing software licenses do not anticipate individuals from other firms, located in different countries, working under those licensing rights, the driver's seat is firmly occupied by the software firms. Negotiating the rights to include Offshore consultants in future software licenses is a definite shift and a critical part of minimizing the future churn for Offshore, but many of these licenses are long-term and conceived many years before Offshore became a viable option.

7. Funding the Appropriate Level of On-Going Offshore Program Office Oversight

It is tempting for newcomers to declare early victory and assume that the more strategic Offshore vendors do not require the additional financial burden of a consistent, centralized program-level support and oversight. This can rapidly cause the firm to "snatch defeat from the jaws of victory." Even if the program office is left intact, all too often it is downsized in terms of visibility and focus after the initial flush of startup. All vendors' partners require constant, long-term oversight and management support — no exception with Offshore service providers.

The Offshore Program Office provides centralized risk management, vendor negotiations, performance monitoring, and reporting services. There is a delicate balance among ensuring the correct number of vendors in terms of providing a natural level of both competition and capabilities, allowing the firm to leverage strengths and weaknesses of different vendors, and keeping the number of vendors down so that volume discounts can be applied. Mature program offices provide an internal marketing and center of excellence for Offshore as well as create and maintain the correct balance between these two opposing influences.

8. Top-Down Executive Support

Almost a cliché, it is true nonetheless that Offshore will be dangerous to your career health without unambiguous support from the top. The initiative will have enough challenges from everyone else without having to run interference up above as well. Spend the time up front to get executive support and backing — if it is not forthcoming then let it go, or move to another company where the leadership is willing to truly lead.

9. Risk Management

Offshore usually requires all components of the firm's oversight function — legal, risk, compliance, and security — to work together to find solutions. Creativity and flexibility, while maintaining fealty to the requirements of their discipline, will be required of all team members.

Now that we have taken our first look at the benefits and challenges of implementing Offshore Outsourcing, let's look at the financials. One of the more interesting trends is the financial performance of the Offshore Outsourcing firms as compared to their Tradition Outsourcing counterparts. Finally, we take a close look at one of the leading Offshore firms, Infosys.

Who are the leading players in Offshore? Exhibit 1.6 shows the top Offshore Outsourcing firms based in India.

Exhibit 1.7 shows the macrocomparisons among a handful of Traditional Outsourcing firms (Accenture, CSC, EDS, and IBM) and the top five minus one Offshore Outsourcing firms (Infosys, Wipro, Satyam, and HCL) for the 2002 and 2001 fiscal years. The top Offshore Outsourcing firm, Tata Consultancy or TCS, is not included in the list because it does not break out the IT consultancy financials from the rest of the very large conglomerate. As a privately owned firm, Tata does not have to reveal its financials to stockholders. However, it would be reasonable to assume

Exhibit 1.6   The Top 20 India-Based and 10 U.S.-Based Offshore Firms, July 2002

	Top 20 India-Based Vendors		Top 10 U.S.-Based Firms Exporting Software to U.S.[a]
1	TSC	1	IBM (prior to merger with PWC in 2002)
2	Infosys	2	Cognizant
3	Wipro	3	Oracle
4	Satyam	4	Hughes
5	HCL Technologies	5	Hewlett-Packard
6	Patni Computer Systems	6	Digital Globalsoft
7	Silverline	7	Syntel
8	Mehindra British Telecom	8	Covansys
9	Pentasoft	9	PWC (prior to merger with IBM)
10	HCL Perot Systems	10	Orbitech
11	Mascot		
12	NIIT		
13	iFlex		
14	Mphasis		
15	Mascon		
16	Mastek		
17	Birlasoft		
18	Polaris		
19	LTIT		
20	Hexaware		

[a]Not all are vendors; some inhouse only.

Source: National Association of Software and Service Companies (Nasscom) — India's software regulatory board — www.nasscom.org., July 2002.

that TCS' financials match the rest of the Offshore Outsourcing groups in providing simply outstanding returns.

The 2001 to 2002 fiscal years represent a key time period, because it is the direct aftermath of 9/11 and if there would be a backing off of Offshore Outsourcing, one would assume it would be then. However, again, the financials speak for themselves. The Offshore Outsourcing firms are grabbing market share at an unprecedented rate despite the overall weak economic climate, and the Traditional Outsourcing firms are showing an overall weakness.

The handful of Traditional Outsourcing firms, even those who are rapidly establishing themselves as having an Offshore Outsourcing capability, showed an average revenue growth of less than 5 percent for 2001, and less than 12 percent for 2002. During that same time period, the Offshore firms demonstrated a whopping 65 percent revenue growth for

Exhibit 1.7 Traditional Outsourcing Firms (U.S.-Based) versus Offshore Firms (India-Based)[a]: Financial Comparison for 2001–2002

Traditional	Price ($)	2002 EPS ($)	2002 Revenue Growth (%)	2001 Revenue Growth (%)
Accenture	14	0.56	1.0	15.0
CSC	26	2.01	8.6	12.3
EDS	14	2.28	-0.2	12.0
IBM	77	2.10	-2.3	7.0
Traditional Average	33	2.00	1.78	11.58
Offshore				
Infosys	65	1.25	32.0	103.0
Wipro	30	0.74	5.2	25.6
Satyam	11	0.16	33.0	87.0
HCL	0	0.00	12.5	45.0
Offshore Average	27	1.00	20.68	65.15

[a] Tata or TCS not included since financials not broken out for Offshore services.

Source: Hoovers Online, www.hoovers.com. (Based on resarch of on-site data conducted Jan–March, 2002 and updated July 2002.)

2001, and over 20 percent for 2002. The revenue dollars are definitely moving — and in one direction!

What are the implications for Traditional IT Outsourcing firms? Wall Street has taken note and sentiment on the Street has weakened regarding Traditional IT Outsourcing firms.[6] Karl Keirstead, Senior Vice President, IT Services Equity Research, Lehman Brothers, in a presentation to the SIG Sourcing Leadership Group in Orlando Florida in 2002, noted that as a whole P/E multiples have compressed, revenue growth has slowed, bookings have slowed, and despite the news headlines seeming to the contrary, even megadeal signings have slowed for Traditional Outsourcing. Karl summarizes the impact factors as pressures from

■ Market maturity (inevitable pressures)
■ General soft demand increase pricing
■ New competition from Offshore vendors
■ New competition from bundled services with hardware vendors

Yet he notes that, to date, margins appear to be holding up well.

In general, Mr. Keirstead points out, the Traditional IT Outsourcing firms are very loath to disclose their financials to the extent that the Offshore firms meet voluntarily today. This can only hurt these firms in the post-Enron era.

According to a study by independent market research firm INPUT, "Growing at a projected rate of 22% annually, the U.S. market for IT outsourcing will reach $110 billion by 2003."[7] The *Atlanta Journal* reported, "The North American IT outsourcing market is projected to increase from $101 billion in 2000 to $160 billion in 2005, and 26 percent of firms already using offshore services plan to double their spending in this area within the next year, according to Gartner Dataquest."[8] India remains the leader.

The percentage of total billable employees Offshore for Traditional Outsourcing companies is usually still well under 5 percent, as opposed to a minimum of 50 percent Offshore for India-based Offshore firms. The National Association of Software and Service Companies (NASSCOM) shows the relative regional share of IT Service spending as follows worldwide: North America at 67.7 percent, Western Europe at 21.3 percent, Japan at 2 percent, Latin America and Rest of World at 5 percent, and Asia Pacific at 3.2 percent.[9]

What can Offshore Outsourcing actually provide in net savings? In a recent article in *CIO* magazine, Rita Terdiman of Gartner Inc. made the following estimates on the cost reductions afforded by Offshore Outsourcing:[10]

What percentage of savings should a firm expect from offshore outsourcing?

Rita Terdiman: There are so many variables, but I'd say 25%–50%. In outsourcing, not offshore, if your projection is to save less than 15%, then [the rule of thumb is] don't bother because of the cost overruns you could end up paying. For offshore, there are so many complexities that it should be another 10% [of savings] — unless there are huge numbers involved. If you have a $1 billion IT budget, and you can shave 20% off, that's $200 million — now you have a different story. Even if you can take 10% off, you might as well do it.

Offshore in Microcosm: A Look at the Payback of a "Typical" Offshore Program

On a micro level, what can the individual firm expect in terms of overall savings for Offshore? Although we explore this topic more fully under vendor management, even at this summary level of discussion it is important to note that resource management as a strategic function is gaining widespread acknowledgment as a critical strategic function. To this end, more and more "C" level positions, such as Chief of Resource Management, are being added to partner with the traditional CIO, CEO, and CFO functions. Offshore Outsourcing is best viewed within the overall context of a resource management strategy that is driven across the organization from the top down.

Why the top down? The last few years of widely fluctuating changes in the value of IT resources, from their peak prior to 2000, to the valleys of 2001 to 2002 and beyond, require a flexibility and organizational resilience to make the most of these potential savings. Most organizations, for example, when hiring on-site consultants, are very aware when the market prices for these resources increase, but don't manage the down-swing well when they decrease. To the extent a firm has myriad independent consultants, each with his own individual contract, as opposed to a central point of negotiation, these prices will simply not respond to the downward trend in the marketplace because there is no one who has incentive within the organization to enforce them. Individual project managers depend on the specialized skills of consultants and are loath to replace a successful contributor with a cheaper but still effective resource, or to renegotiate terms based upon market changes. Thus, without a centralized function, what usually occurs is these consultants either remain on indefinitely or are terminated outright. A central function can negotiate and leverage volume offerings, even for specialty firms or individuals, to ensure downwards pressures on on-site consultants' compensation are reflected appropriately within the organization.

What has this to do with Offshore Outsourcing? Often, the "lowest hanging fruit" for big savings is the replacement of on-site contractors with Offshore resources. The average on-site contractor is generally — at a minimum — $85 per hour. The average Offshore contractor is generally — at a maximum — $30 per hour. Even if you have significant one-time or ongoing infrastructure costs required to implement the Offshore model, it is unlikely that over a three-year period your Offshore hourly costs will rise above $35.00 per hour, including the costs for the percentage of the Offshore team that remains onshore within the Co-Sourcing model.

Let's look at the numbers if we replace 100 contractors at $85 per hour with Offshore resources at $35 per hour. Assuming the 100 consultants are working a 45-hour week, the total cost is $3825 per week for an individual or $382,500 for all 100. Over a one-month period the savings is $900,000, or $10,800,000 annually. This does not include increases in efficiency, quality, or reliability that usually accrue from Offshore Outsourcing.

Note that the numbers used in this example are, at the time of writing, extremely conservative. Most Offshore Outsourcing vendors are able to provide an overall resource cost of much less than $35 per hour, and most consultants are still charging well over $85 per hour. It is no surprise, with these figures, that Offshore Outsourcing is the first IT project type that regularly supplies an internal rate of return well over 100 percent.

Risk and Offshore: A Final Word

Now that we have established the potential savings, the question becomes, why isn't every firm Offshoring? Well, according to Gartner,[6] if they are not, they should be! The dramatic savings point to a likely scenario that pits early adopters against late ones and casts doubt on the long-term organizational viability of the late bloomers. Offshore Outsourcing is an imperative — a complex one, but nonetheless, it is an option no firm can afford to ignore.

Why do firms lag in adopting an Offshore model? My personal theory is that it challenges our comfort zone. Tellingly, less than 25 percent of Americans own a passport.[11] This means that less than 25 percent of us have traveled outside of Mexico, Canada, and the Caribbean. Although we consider ourselves global sophisticates, the reality is that we are as biased as the next country in terms of assessment of what is comfortable and familiar. In my own firm, even though there were competing financial services companies that were executing Offshore for over 14 years, at the beginning of the program many individuals would voice the concern that no direct competitors were implementing Offshore in the industry. It was only when the program office posted a laundry list of our competitors that showed virtually EVERY other competing firm was actively initiating or running an Offshore program that this kind of response quieted. It had no basis in fact but it "felt" right — we are often more comfortable with our illusions. Illusions about the capabilities and lives of those who live overseas still run us, despite facts to the contrary.

Those who do lag may do so out of what may seem legitimate concerns about global security. Certainly, post-9/11 America is one in which those concerns are headlined nearly every day. Yet these headlines seem to have little impact on the companies who are increasing their Offshore presence daily, and on demand for these services. Experienced Offshore Program Managers, with more than ten years in Offshore, view geopolitical risk differently. First of all, they point out, 9/11 happened here, not in India.[12] The days of a false sense of security based upon geography are, unfortunately, over. Second, rightly or wrongly, they believe that the value of Offshore to India is such that they will not risk war because it simply will have too high an economic price. In later chapters, we explore how India remains the clear leader today but there are many countries more than eager to provide similar savings and services to the United States, and the competition is heating up in newer areas such as Offshore Business Process Outsourcing which are still up for grabs in terms of country leadership. Finally, these experienced program managers have a sophisticated set of risk avoidance processes that lower the likelihood of catastrophic impact. In the Co-Sourcing model, generally the data and computers reside within the United States and stay there, so the impact is primarily in "knowledge transfer" cost or losing the training investment of the workforce overseas. There are many ways to establish redundancy up front and still reap the savings rewards of Offshore.

CHAPTER SUMMARY

The numbers don't lie — well, in this era we need to qualify that with "usually" — and here, in the context of extreme financial disclosure, the relative profit margins of the Traditional versus the Offshore Outsourcing firms are painting a compelling picture. The reason for this is evident in the hourly savings related to Offshore resources, demonstrating roughly $40 to $50 per hour lower costs for the same or better quality resources. Traditional IT Outsourcing firms are struggling financially, while at the same time — even within the context of post-9/11 America — India-based Offshore Outsourcing firms are growing exponentially and thriving financially. On a macro industry level or a micro individual company level, Offshore Outsourcing offers a level of savings that is quickly becoming an imperative for all IT organizations.

NOTES

1. Amy Waldman and David Rohde, "India and Pakistan: The dispute burns on," *New York Times*, October 22, 2002, p. 3.
2. Later in the book, I discuss how the present-day culture of India places the highest value on technology and math skills, almost like American doctors today. Schoolchildren are drilled in math and science for hours before and after school. The typical Indian college graduate is more like a Masters-level engineer in the United States in terms of skills and abilities as a result. It is well documented within international education studies such as TIMSS — Third International Mathematics and Science Study — that U.S. college technology and math students are well below their foreign counterparts in these particular skills. In the Offshore Interest Group, across the 50 companies that share ideas and experiences, there are many experiences describing the technology acumen of the Indian folks as "scary." To date, despite 20 years of work, there have been no high visibility execution failures in IT in India. Finally, a little-known fact is that the Indian people did Y2K — which put Offshore on the map — with no background in mainframe technology. By the time computers came to India in the 1970s, they were all UNIX minicomputers. They taught themselves mainframe technology "over the weekend" and came to work the next day knowing the technology. So although it is my opinion, there are many facts to substantiate this that I cover later in the book.

3. Dun & Bradstreet, *Barometer of Global Outsourcing, Business Wire,* February 24, 2000, pp. 1–3.
4. It is a well-known fact acknowledged within the Offshore and also the consulting community. The first companies to become CMM certified were the Indian-owned Offshore firms. None of the major so-called former Big Five consulting firms, such as IBM, Accenture, Bearing Point, and so on, are CMM certified at the corporate or organizational level, even though they frequently put themselves in the position of advising their U.S. customers how to achieve CMM, which I've always found very odd.
5. Most firms are well aware of the negative press relative to Offshore, and take the first option of eliminating consultants rather than employees if at all possible — this is common sense. Of the members of the Offshore Interest Group, only a small number have had layoffs directly due to Offshore, and these are relatively small in number. Most layoffs are related to the general economic conditions. Most companies do not publish or discuss these policies, however, so it will need to remain anecdotal.
6. Karl Keirstead, presentation to the SIG Sourcing Leadership Group, Orlando FL, 2002.
7. Daniel Nodes, INPUT market research report, March 7, 2001.
8. Anya Martin, "Offshore outsourcing grows," *Atlanta Business Chronicle*, April 18, 2003, pp. 1–2.
9. NASSCOM.
10. Ed Parry, "Gartner: Offshore outsourcing horse has 'left the barn,'" SearchCIO.com, July 8, 2003.
11. Phyl Gyford, "How many American's own passports?" 1/31/03, at www.gyford.com.
12. In later chapters I talk about the reason that India is leading so dramatically to date in Offshore Outsourcing. One of the underlying tenets of the book is that all countries are not equal when it comes to the cultural and historical factors that make them able to provide these services — India is unique in these factors. Many individuals in the United States tend to lump all countries outside the United States together — however, they are all very different in many ways, and one way is their ability to provide these services to U.S. companies. I do, however, spend one chapter looking at the other countries and compare them in salient characteristics for provision of Offshore services.

2

GETTING STARTED IN OFFSHORE

This chapter looks at one of the originators of Offshore Outsourcing, Citigroup, and what it takes to overcome one of the biggest hurdles — successful navigation of Offshore Outsourcing initiation. Topics covered include:

- The importance of executive support and clear communications
- Establishing the program office and executive oversight
- Setting appropriate expectations with the management team
- Defining the initial approach to Offshore
  - Do you need outside expert help?
    - How to hire help
  - ROI analysis
    - Estimating costs
  - Defining the parameters of that all-important, initial effort
    - To pilot or not to pilot
    - Conducting an overall readiness analysis of your IT application suite
    - Establishing a initial timetable for network security infrastructure
    - Management reporting

Finally, we end with a lengthy look at ethics in the workplace, shared with us by one of the experts in the growing field of evaluating and managing ethical business conduct.

EXECUTIVE SUPPORT AND COMMUNICATIONS: THE KEY TO SUCCESS

Starting an Offshore program without visible top-level support is a bit like climbing up a tall tree covered with Vaseline — you are guaranteed failure before you even begin the long slide down to the bottom. *It is only within organizations experienced in the Offshore model (three years or more) that there is an understanding that Offshore Outsourcing is key to the long-term health of the IT organization as a whole.* In the current economic and IT job environment, and the current press coverage of Offshore, the program is undoubtedly the center of controversy. Visible and unwavering executive support is central to success — without it the program will sink under the immediate and almost universal resistance across all levels of the organization.

Once the Offshore program has been implemented and the IT organizations have seen that the impact is not uniformly negative and in fact contributes to the viability of the IT organization over the long term, the visible solidarity of executive vision in concert with a comprehensive communications plan becomes less critical. However, as the technical complexity of the Offshore model is illustrated in the next few chapters, the lag time between commitment to Offshore and the actual implementation is usually at least 6 months, and may actually be 9 to 12 months out. So, it is important to brace the organization for a protracted and ideally well-crafted and proactive communications effort that by necessity will be organized and implemented in the face of fear, disapproval, and uncertainty.

The realities of the Co-Sourcing model recommend that the total impact be limited to no more than 30 percent of the IT organization, and within that 30 percent it most frequently is a specific subset of tasks that are generally outsourced. Ideally, part of the general message from the executive team will be to lay out the total strategy in terms of what work is affected (in terms of roles, not individuals), and what the organization is planning on doing in terms of supporting individuals who can be retrained to other roles within the organization.

The most likely scenario is that of the 30 percent or so of the organization that is affected, most will be able to move up the IT skills pyramid with some investment or training. Thus, maintenance and support will have a chance to learn the latest programming skills, and programmers will be able to train and work on the newer projects or become designers and architects. This could actually be a positive for many individual contributors.

The individuals most at risk are those who are unable or unwilling to make the transition up the IT skills pyramid. What to do with employees who have provided years of loyal service and are unable to adjust to the new skills required of them is the sorest point of Offshore. Here the scale of global economies becomes personal — the fact is that the work of the individual sitting here in the United States who performs maintenance and support or programming services cannot match the cost/value proposition of their counterpart sitting halfway around the globe available at one third the cost with equal or better performance.

Thus, executive support and communications planning is really a code word for establishing up front a humane and fair strategy for dealing with those individuals who will lose their current roles within the organization. As executive lead of the first Offshore Program at a large eastern financial institution, it was the "Offshore Opportunity Program" that served this function. The Opportunity program occurred within the overall context of multiple layoffs and a very dismal local economic climate in which newspapers consistently highlighted the employment blight now hitting local, formerly secure IT workers. Offshore was unpopular from inception.

The Opportunity Program members started working up the management chain to ensure that everyone who lost her position would have a place to go, even if it were to replace a series of temporary consultants. This became a highly visible standard across the entire IT management team, so that individual managers knew they and their staff would be subject to scrutiny if they did not work to find a place for the displaced workers where there was a skills match. A weekly meeting attended by management representatives with clout, human resources, and other stakeholders ensured focus continued. At these meetings the team utilized a database that matched the skills of the displaced workers with the available slots as well as the consulting roles across the organization. Overall, this effort was successful; at the time of writing this book, roughly three years after program inception, not one employee had been laid off as a result of the Offshore program.

It is even better if the organization can allocate upfront training dollars, or institute a no-hire policy to ensure additional jobs are available for these workers. Whatever the strategy, know that all the firm's workers are watching, and justly will reach their conclusions about both the organization and Offshore from the way you treat these most vulnerable of workers.

It is vitally important that these issues — of affecting workers unable or unwilling to be retrained — be discussed and managed up front. If you take nothing else from this book, adopt this principle. The overall excellence of execution, the sheer reliability of the Offshore services, strangely makes Offshore very different than most IT programs. IT organizations new to Offshore tend to rely upon what is fast becoming a completely outmoded set of business processes — those relating to hiring and managing individual contributor consultants. Although these older processes are within the organization's comfort zone, the business processes that are required for Offshore versus those needed for individual contributors or even groups of U.S.-based IT consultants are completely different. We talk more about this during our chapter on vendor management, but suffice it to say here that most of the emphasis in hiring U.S.-based consultants is focused upon the careful evaluation of resumes and skillsets. In fact, India-based Offshore firms have created their bread and butter on creating cultures of incredibly quick learners, who can pick up difficult systems, software language skills, and related items over a weekend where an IT engineer here may require months of training. In addition, usually contracts with Offshore vendors are structured as fixed price, so these vendors simply won't get paid if they can't do the work. Thus, poring over resumes listing years of experience for individual offshore resources becomes doubly irrelevant.

Rather than pore over resumes in a warmed-over retread of outmoded hiring practices, the program management team is much better off focusing and leading a comprehensive vision that involves understanding organizational restructuring and strategic skills management. These become the fulcrum around which the success of the Offshore program revolves. Human nature being what it is, these issues are most often ignored — they become the pink elephant standing in the middle of the room in every meeting. If the firm has not anticipated and built in the cost for a soft landing for their displaced employees, it is a disservice to their loyalty, the overall success of the program, and the overall health of the IT organization. My personal experience, as well as the majority of the members of the Offshore Interest group in our many discussions on just this challenge, is that it is this issue, and this one alone, that accounts for most of the delays and difficulties around implementation of Offshore.

Unfortunately, often the strategic IT skills plan cannot be executed effectively via middle management — this operationally focused team does not generally create a completely new organizational structure, which is the ultimate result of Offshore if done correctly. It is a delicate balance to decide exactly how much to Offshore over time, especially when the successful results, and huge savings, start rolling in. Overdo the percentage of Offshore allocation across the IT application suite, and the organization may realize early savings, but will eventually be crippled by the lack of internal intellectual capital and IT strategic partnership, as is the case in programs where IT is completely Outsourced. Minimize the percentage of the Offshore allocation, and over time the costs for IT will not remain competitive. These decisions must be aligned with the overall strategy of the organization. Firms that do not have maturity already in aligning IT strategy with overall business strategy — that, for example, do not have a true CIO function but still have IT reporting up to Finance or other administrative functions — will find themselves at a disadvantage in leveraging the full capability of Offshore as a strategic IT capability.

Even for those firms with the savvy to enable IT as a strategic partner in the organizational structure and processes, understanding the long-term skills requirements of an IT organization over time can be almost an impossibility given today's rapidly changing business environment. Business needs swing so rapidly that a 12-month plan may be almost meaningless, never mind the longer horizon required by Offshore.

In today's Fortune 100 culture, large corporate firms are often torn between two IT organizational structures, each with their advantages and disadvantages. One organizational model decentralizes IT, recognizing the need for IT to be light on their collective feet, and able to respond to the needs of a specific business unit to respond to rapid shifts in the business climate. Centralized IT, the alternative model, allows the organization to leverage standards to create savings across a large and well-entrenched IT function, and also to create a culture of rapid IT response through those standards. The key to successful Offshore management hinges on the ability to proactively manage and communicate the skillset requirements of the IT organization moving into the future, and to balance the availability of those U.S.-based skills with the Offshore component, even in the face of ongoing business climate uncertainty and change. Balancing the size of the Offshore program, along with the typical tensions between the decentralized and centralized IT organizational models, is the challenge. Creating and executing a successful proactive skills strategy moving into the future makes Offshore outsourcing one of the most difficult strategic challenges facing executive leadership.

A LOOK AT AN EXAMPLE OF ENLIGHTENED LEADERSHIP: HANDLING EMPLOYEE IMPACT AT A NORTHEAST UTILITIES COMPANY

It is important to note in this arena where the challenges are the most difficult and controversial — displaced, long-term, and loyal workers — there are examples of outstanding success. A large northeast utilities firm executed Offshore, and was very challenged in this area. Most of the workers tended to be clustered in age near retirement, that most vulnerable of times in employment, and had forgone years of higher salaries at competitive employers in return for what had been an unstated promise of stable employment. Although this particular utility was not publicly owned, it was highly regulated, and had many aspects of the corporate culture of a public utility. The CIO, then in his early sixties with years of experience (now retired), was a man of both vision and great compassion.

He, like many in this book, saw the chance to promote the long-term viability of the IT organization as an early adopter of Offshore. The first thing he noted to me was the outstanding flexibility and hands-on know-how of the Offshore service providers. This utility used the integrated software package SAP to manage many of its internal processes, software known for its sophistication as well as the associated complexity. Even though this utilities firm had individuals who were national leaders in their particular niche of SAP execution, the CIO shared that "these resources from India learned the technology cold in record time — better, deeper, and faster. My people actually found them scary."

His solution to the challenge of the individuals no longer required by the firm was creative, humane, and very popular. First, he successfully lobbied to include, as part of the upfront cost of the program, a choice of several indepth training plans for a variety of new positions. One I recall was PC technician for computer repair — there were others of a similar nature. It turns out, however, that none of the affected employees opted for any of these programs! The reason is that these employees were also offered an opportunity to become part of one of the Offshore partners that was U.S. based, a national consulting firm. Employees were guaranteed a minimum of one year's employment with that firm, with the understanding that subsequent to that year, they became employees at will (in other words, no guarantees of employment). Upon completion of that year, the individuals who took this option then became subject to the consulting firms' normal staff management evaluation and other human resources processes.

In the move to the consulting firm, employees had a more generous benefit package, more opportunities for advancement and training, and some had the option to enjoy these advantages while still remaining working at the utilities company in their former roles. When I discussed this with the CIO, the program had been in place for over seven years, and virtually every employee successfully made the switch. Many came by to thank him personally and tell him how happy they were working for the new consulting firm. Many had moved on to other work in the area through this consulting firm, and were enjoying a career renaissance.

WELL-PLANNED AND EXECUTED COMMUNICATIONS: A CRITICAL SUCCESS FACTOR FOR OFFSHORE PROGRAM INITIATION

What does the ideal executive communications program look like? The watchword is to communicate early, frequently, and as completely as possible. If it not possible to answer questions, such as those regarding the impact on a specific function or group within the organization, the best policy is one of honesty — this information is not yet available. Communicate that information as soon as it is feasible. Anticipate a negative impact on employee satisfaction in the form of annual surveys and other forms of feedback, and make sure that this is taken into account before the firm embarks upon Offshore.

In parallel, actively provide the organization with the facts. In particular, that Offshore is a critical means of avoiding that most dreaded of eventualities — the complete Outsource of the entire IT organization. Provide the key message that Offshore will affect less than 30 percent of the overall organization and in particular not involve any core competencies within IT, so that employees able to shift to those core competencies will be in a stronger position to contribute to the organization and to develop new skills to bring to their overall career path.

Ideally these messages are crafted, moved up the management chain for approval, and ultimately delivered initially by the CIO, then disseminated and re-emphasized multiple times at every level of management. One aspect of communication around Offshore is the understanding of the impact of the unknown and the anxiety it creates. Employees often need to hear the same message over and over to really understand and to believe there is no hidden subtext. Engaging an internal professional communications team, or hiring an outside expert, is highly recommended. The CIO of the utilities company cited above made a point of hiring — and recommending to others as they embark on Offshore — an outside communications expert.

Ideally, communication occurs regularly and across all internal channels. Some of these vehicles include the following:

- Creation of an Offshore Web site
- A series of internal gatherings initiated by an official program "kick-off" (Exhibit 2.1) meeting well attended by IT executive management
- An electronic newsletter
- A place on the agenda in all staff meetings

Include a time for question and answers — a blind e-mail box that allows employees to log questions and concerns anonymously is one good way to keep apprised of the general concerns.

These measures will not make the program more popular, or even build more trust — IT professionals are notoriously both pragmatic and jaded within the organizational hierarchy and as such believe only what is seen — but they can prevent a total anxiety meltdown. At heart, amidst the fear and concern, everyone understands that the world economy is no longer something individual workers can hide from, and that the future of the entire organization is dependent upon these seeming compromises.

Exhibit 2.1   A Sample Kick-Off Meeting Agenda for Offshore

Hosted by:	Head of IT organization and all direct reports
Facilitated by:	Head of Offshore Program Office
Attended by:	As many IT workers as is practical
Length of meeting:	3 to 4 hours (half day)
Goal of meeting:	Underscore executive commitment to Offshore; start organizational understanding and dialogue
8:00-9:00 am	Travel/coffee, etc.
9:00-9:30 am	Opening remarks, "Benefits of Offshore, and Why Now?" by IT Organizational Lead
9:30-10:00 am	[ideally] "Benefits Anticipated to Business from Offshore" by Business Lead or "The Case for Offshore (Savings at Stake)" by Offshore Program Manager
10:00-10:30 am	"Logistics of Offshore Program" by Offshore Program Manager 　　Breadth, depth of program 　　Applications included in program 　　Offshore Service Providers — who they are, how they were chosen 　　Critical Success Factors Timeline 　　Next Steps
10:30-10:45 am	Break
10:45-11:30 am	Staff Impact by Panel: HR, IT Management Team 　　Commitment to core competencies 　　Training programs 　　Impacts on consultants 　　No-hire policy 　　Roll-out of communications plan
11:30-12:00	Questions and answers — all topics okay If organization is interested in a day-long kick-off meeting, the additional topics below can be added
12:00-1:00	Lunch
1:00-2:00	Introduction to Offshore Service Providers by Offshore Vendors 　　Organizational introduction, including locations, experience, strengths 　　Success stories in similar organizations
2:00-3:00	Cross-cultural learning by Communications/Offshore Service Providers 　　Introduction to the culture of the Offshore provider — if U.S.-based, introduction to this capability within the U.S. partner firm

Exhibit 2.1 (continued) A Sample Kick-Off Meeting Agenda for Offshore

	Many Offshore firms have wonderful films of their facilities, etc.
	Working successfully with geographically diverse teams — methods and approach
3:00-4:30	Business Process Reorganization by Panel Discussion: Legal, Network Security, Compliance, Methodology, etc.
	Discuss ways organization will change as a result of Offshore program
4:30-5:00	Questions and answers — all topics okay
	Overview of communications moving forward, including places where workers can get more information as well as submit questions

Continuing employees in roles that no longer make economic sense puts the organization as a whole at risk, so that if the Offshore program can model a compassionate and equitable resolution visible to all, ultimately everyone is stronger.

This message is one that mature (over three years' experience in Offshore) organizations understand, and inviting these members into your firm can also be a compelling source of communications support in the difficult and delicate time of program inception. If possible, bring in architects to speak to architects, CIOs to speak to CIOs, IT managers to speak to IT managers, and especially security network consultants to speak to their peers. This is a very effective means of cutting through the blinders workers have fallen into, through no fault of their own. Most professionals have little time to cultivate peers outside their own department, never mind in different companies. Tunnel vision often results, and in times of change, a broader vision is absolutely required for success. Discussing a successful program implementation with external peers can be a very effective, calming influence.

ESTABLISHING THE OFFSHORE PROGRAM OFFICE FOR EXECUTIVE OVERSIGHT

Filling the role of Offshore Program leadership is one of the more critical decisions affecting program success. Most important, the placement of the program leadership role must be at least equal to the operational management hierarchy.

What does this mean? In every organization there is one, at most two, layers of management that essentially run things day to day — this layer serves as a filter for information between the majority of workers and the executive team. Below this layer, it is difficult to gain senior management access, and above there is mostly reporting of results, with little "hands-on" operational involvement. It is vital that the Offshore Program Manager be a minimum of a peer (usually it is difficult to make them senior) to that set of operational managers, whatever their official titles may happen to be.

The first job of the Offshore Program Manager is to force the organization to come to grips with the political cost of the program as outlined above, especially the difficult staffing strategy discussions, and to set into place an extensive and sophisticated communications strategy to reflect those difficult realities. Once this has been wrestled with and the organization is still willing to move forward, the actual implementation work begins.

What are the characteristics of a strong Offshore Program Office lead? It may be of use to share some of my personal experiences here. Despite many leadership opportunities in leading Fortune 50 firms over a 20-year career, it was the Offshore Program assignment where I learned, sometimes smoothly, other times not so successfully, to stand up and fight for what I believed. Early on in the Program I realized that I would need to take a firm and guiding hand, given the mix of upper management's workload and level of distraction (Offshore was of course just one of many high visibility initiatives), as well as the Big Four firm's entrenched senior executive relationships and stake in keeping their power base. In particular, if I didn't stand up for the rights of the employees of the firm throughout the Offshore process, they would have no advocate. I grew to believe that although not easy, success of the Offshore program was critical to the viability of the organization over the long term and, despite its challenges and complexities, was an organizational skillset that I needed to imbue in order to effectively protect the organization's long-term success. I knew these would certainly not be popular or easily explainable views. I also personally took on a vow to make sure that I would do whatever I could to minimize the negative impact of individual jobs where I could. In both, I was largely successful.

I don't believe that my growth as a leader is unusual for Offshore. One of the commonalities of this book, as we move forward to talk to individuals who have been involved in Offshore, is their commitment to finding new ways of solving old challenges, and their willingness to do first, and ask permission later.

In addition to a certain moxie, other characteristics required for success are the obvious abilities of excellence in program management, knowledge of systems, IT life-cycle methodology, infrastructure, business process reengineering, executive interface, and above all the ability to deliver on time, on budget, and to quality specifications. But willingness to advocate for the not so obvious or easy answer, and to protect as many individuals in the process, are the two more subtle characteristics I would recommend in a visionary leader. At one point or another, most Program leaders have found themselves putting their own jobs on the line for what they believe. Offshore is not for the faint of heart nor the politically naïve.

Once the leader is identified — even if you have to hire from outside the firm — then and only then is the time to engage in external consulting help. It is strongly recommended the firm put in place the individual Program Manager prior to engaging any consultative help in mobilizing an Offshore Program, especially if that strategic planning assistance is from one of the traditional Big Four or similar IT services firm that provides both strategic as well as tactical IT consulting support. Many organizations new to Offshore make the mistake of engaging their traditional strategy partners without fully thinking through the cost implications over the long term. Hiring the Big Four to head up an Offshore strategy effort is a bit like putting the fox in charge of the hen house. Although many of these strategic consulting firms have extensive experience in Offshore, to date it is not the basis of their profit model, which relies on the more traditional Onshore consulting. Often the Big Four perceive Offshore as a threat to their survival — and the economics of Offshore outlined in Chapter One imply the threat is not an empty one. The Offshore model essentially means that the days of the $300 an hour plus depth technical consultant are over, and these firms base their revenue on these relationships, not on Offshore (as yet!).

It is not unusual for the Big Four managers assigned as the Offshore consultative leads to be the identical cast of individuals that had been dedicated to the firm for many years. Often, this leadership team may not have even personally traveled to any of the Offshore locations or had any significant hands-on Offshore experience. Offshore is simply the latest in what was a series of positions that enable them to preserve their roles within the firm. Although the Offshore Program, under these circumstances, is usually outstandingly successful in the basics — a testimony to the robustness of the delivery model — a U.S.-centric leadership team may result in additional organizational delays, stress, and costs. Frequently, mature organizations (involved in Offshore over three years) invariably seem to have either minimized their dependency upon Big Four firms, or proactively control the Big Four pricing premiums by creating competition through other firms headquartered overseas so they must lower their prices to stay in the game.

One member of the Offshore Interest Group shared an interesting anecdote about his program (timing was third quarter 2002). One Big Four firm competitively bid upon a specific Offshore project with two other firms headquartered Offshore. Not only was the Big Four firm higher in price, it also was clearly less experienced. The Offshore-based firms were able to show resumes of individuals who had specific experience in that application in Offshore — the Big Four were not. Also, the Big Four firm charged for an effort deciding which standard modules should go Offshore and which stay Onshore. The Offshore-based firms said, "We already know what needs to stay Onshore and Offshore based upon our prior experience — we'll share our prior knowledge with you and expedite the design effort." Although it is difficult to generalize, these point experiences are helpful to illustrate that in the world of Offshore the stakes are high, and neutrality is never a guarantee. Thus, there are not so subtle reasons to avoid the typical strategic Big Four partner as the basis for objective advice in the inception of Offshore — they are often the least neutral and although they can tap legitimate depths of experience in their dedicated Offshore practices, the typical Partner-in-charge account structure may make it difficult for the traditional revenue relationships to be replaced with an Offshore-centric strategy, even if that is what the organization requires.

It is true, on the other hand, that many Big Four organizations have compelling and long-term positive relationships with IT executives, and in bringing a controversial program to the organization such as Offshore it may be tempting to hand them the keys to the kingdom from day one and say, "Tell us how to do this." As time goes on, many of these firms are expanding their knowledge and stake in Offshore almost exponentially. The potential cost, however, may be a much higher price point with less experienced day-to-day program oversight and staffing. Be aware and structure the relationship, term of contract, and services agreement accordingly, as relatively "safe" as the Big Four may appear. If a traditional Big Four partner or equivalent does help to decide on the first set of applications to go Offshore, for example — an effort they of course do very well and which plays to their traditional strengths — consider also engaging other non-U.S.-based vendors to execute the work once it has been identified, so the organization is also exposed to these alternative vendor cultures and they also can start to build credibility and relationships. Be particularly careful not to cede control of the fate or decisions regarding employee impact to any external partner, no matter how well they have served the organization in the past.

What Are the Steps and Factors Involved in Choosing an Initial Successful Suite of Applications to Offshore?

This is often an organizational culture question that is beyond the control of the individual Offshore Program Manager. Most Offshore Program Managers find that, with all of the controversy surrounding Offshore, the culture of the organization dictates the initial approach. Personally, the program I managed executed an Offshore program with one big jump — all 26 applications, 126 team members ready to go at once. This was simply the way that particular organization structured these initiatives. Often, the key to successful program implementation is simply to navigate as quietly as possible around any major barriers, and align as much with the cultural norms of large IT program execution as possible. Offshore has enough visibility and controversy without courting more.

However, in the rare case that there is an option, consider carefully first piloting a subset of IT applications for Offshore. Even with the long lead time of Offshore due to knowledge transfer, software license vendor consent negotiation, and network security architecture startup — which can easily take six months or more — an eternity in organizational time — the lessons the firm can learn from the initial projects are invaluable. Offshore is a high stakes, high reward game and the more educated the firm is going into it, the more easily the team can deliver on the program vision and goals.

This is particularly true because the length of the vendor contracts for Offshore tends to be a minimum of three years when a firm first starts down the path. This is because, early on, the firm has to rely on the vendor for much of the management reporting and even a portion of the infrastructure, to execute Offshore. Most firms find that, as part of the upfront cost for Offshore, there is a portion of each network that is vendor-specific. Usually the internal corporate network(s) tie into the Offshore service provider at a specific U.S. location that houses a large network conduit (of whatever form, a T1 trunk or satellite, or both). From this conduit on, the Offshore service provider then takes the responsibility for the network connection to its workers overseas.

As firms gain Offshore experience, if they are smart they enable more vendor independence by developing their own sets of metrics, reporting, vendor-independent network secure infrastructure, disaster recovery, redundancy, and other program processes. The difficulty and cost of knowledge transfer is often overemphasized early on, and this contributes to a perceived need for a lengthy vendor contract (e.g., if it takes them three months to learn my systems, that's three months I'm paying for both my people and the consultants, or six months' total cost — we need at least three years to recoup that cost from this vendor).

In actuality, the savings are so dramatic once the actual Offshore team is in place and running, and there are so many excellent Offshore vendors out there who are willing to support knowledge transfer for nominal upfront costs in order to win a contract, that it becomes clear that knowledge transfer costs are not as dramatic as they may first appear. The most experienced firms, such as Citigroup discussed later in this chapter, treat Offshore vendors as a marketplace, choosing the vendor based upon a list of criteria and creating a very competitive scenario with much lower overall price points for service delivery.

What Are the Characteristics of a Good Pilot for Offshore?

Here's an initial laundry list in order of importance — note that the "softer" issues such as staff openness are often more important than the technical match.

- *Application does not allow direct access by Offshore consultants to sensitive customer data* — this is always the bottom line that separates the acceptable from the unacceptable in Offshore.
- *IT staff are open to the Offshore model* and are not threatened to the point of sabotage. It can be very helpful if they are provided with a clear role that represents a new skillset they are interested in learning. For example, they understand that upon the successful transition to the Offshore firm, all staff will be transitioned to a project with relatively high visibility and higher career rewards compared to their current role.
- *Does not rock the boat in terms of security* — in addition to the customer data rule of thumb, the application represents data and systems that feel "safe" for overseas involvement (later, as Offshore gets going, that definition of safety will expand by leaps and bounds).
- *Well defined* in terms of success criteria and goals (such as clearly measurable service-level agreements or new project development timetable), and is at least somewhat reflective or representative of other applications that initially appear to be slated to go Offshore.
- *Not blocked by a difficult software vendor consent process.* (Third-party software vendors must provide the firm with permission to work Offshore under the original software license without additional licensing fees — many older software contracts do not include overseas consultants under their licensing umbrella).
- Involves a cross-functional team that includes the major stakeholders, yet is simultaneously small and light on its feet.
- Maintains enough visibility to prove the point while not engaging a core or business critical application.

We take a deeper look at the pros and cons of piloting for Offshore later in this chapter. Moving to a different facet of initiating Offshore, while the pilot is being launched, many companies often choose to do a parallel organizationwide analysis effort that looks at all applications to identify their suitability for Offshore. These efforts are most useful if there is a hodgepodge of systems, software, and hardware, simply because there is often no record of "what is out there." Most large firms these days have been through multiple mergers and acquisitions, creating a true Tower of Babel for IT. Or, they are just adopting a culture of discipline for IT, recovering from a "shoot from the hip" organizational approach that is no longer tenable given the breadth and depth of the IT function. Either way, there are probably multiple applications with little to no documentation. Often, there is also little to no quality assurance in terms of streamlined maintenance processes, systems retirement planning, and architectural integration. To the extent that the analysis provides a good "state of the state" summary of the various application suites, finally bringing those rogue systems that sit outside the typical architecture to light, an application inventory during Offshore pilot can be very useful.

As emphasized here again and again, however, Offshore is different from what is expected, and this is true as well for the initial application mix. It is not usually found that the overly complex criteria applied by the external consultant(s), with all of the associated fancy grids and management graduate school theory, quickly goes out the window. Although provided to the firm new to Offshore at great cost and even greater fanfare, most of the analysis separating applications into categories appropriate and not appropriate for Offshore is simply not relevant moving forward. Offshore works too well, customer firms become more sophisticated in terms of understanding risk, and the suite of applications that are considered appropriate usually broadens to the full 20 to 30 percent that represents the maximum. Spending a great deal of dollars on consulting fees relative to subtle differences of initial Offshore applications is not often a useful exercise over the long term — almost as fruitless as an expensive and exhausting country comparison (although not quite!).

HIRING OUTSIDE EXPERTISE: AN INITIAL LOOK AT GETTING THE RIGHT KIND OF HELP FOR OFFSHORE

In the very early startup phase of Offshore, the security, trust ("Can we really give them THAT to do Offshore?"), and political turf concerns tend to be somewhat overblown. Once experience has been gained, it is not atypical that a firm decides to move Offshore a whole class of applications that had earlier been ruled out as too central or strategically important to the firm, and conversely keep Onshore a set of applications that on first glance are in the opposite category. In particular, some applications are eliminated due to the underestimation of two items — first, the difficulty of obtaining some of the third-party vendor consents without a significant cash outlay and second, the difficulty of obtaining Offshore personnel that meet the experience criteria for the few really esoteric applications that absolutely demand years of experience.

Thus, although an initial analysis of applications for Offshore is helpful to put the house in order — it is especially helpful if not comforting to finally know the total scope of undocumented applications laying about in the dark closets — realize that Offshore is a journey, and like other journeys will require revision and recasting of experiences and views over time. Hiring an expensive "expert" in Offshore for lots of cash outlay to help you through the pitfalls of categorizing applications in detail as appropriate for Offshore is really not warranted — as implied above, the real challenge in Offshore is in strategic resourcing, and upfront handling of the negative impact on the people who can't fit into the new organization. Although ultimately that is not something an outside consultant can decide, there is a true strategic set of decisions there that most large firms are not organizationally structured to handle with foresight and grace.

Hiring a modestly priced consultant(s), however, who does not provide a lot of hype about decisions for your organizational lifetime about picking the perfect processes or systems to go Offshore can be useful. The true Offshore expert will work with you, emphasizing the hard political staffing decisions coming up, and supporting a solid communications strategy to enable those decisions, and can provide a light onceover of Offshore-specific vendor information in a truly neutral way, and, *above all, has real demonstrable and referenceable hands-on experience (always check references!).*

After the first year to two years this advice and counsel will no longer be needed, but the right outside help can provide an invaluable buffer to the sometimes culturally challenging experience of dealing with the vendors headquartered Offshore, although they are of course getting increasingly sophisticated in direct interface with U.S. executives.

One area where companies can get sucked into spending a lot of money and time is the debate as to where to move Offshore. This is one area of Offshore community discussion that is puzzling. The fact is that 80 percent or more of all Offshore consultants are concentrated in India.[1] Unless you are looking to "Build, Operate, and Transfer" — in other words, hire your own workers directly overseas and utilize a firm only to help you navigate the dangerous waters of getting your own legal permits and tax structures to do business directly overseas — hiring a consultant to provide you with the pros and cons of different countries is a waste of time and money. We explore this more fully in Chapter Four.

Other than the positioning of the Program Office as a peer of the layer of operating managers, and the careful choice of "expert" help as outlined above where the expertise is really in organizational restructuring and strategic staffing and planning, the structure of the Offshore Program

Exhibit 2.2   Myths versus Reality in Geographically Dispersed Teams (GDTs)

Myth	Reality
Geographically dispersed teams are not as effective as traditional teams where everyone is located in the same place.	GDTs can match or exceed the performance of other teams for some tasks. They provide an advantage in some areas. Some co-located teams, when brainstorming, lock in on a single idea too early. This happens less frequently with a GDT.
Co-located teams are always preferable.	Face-to-face interaction is not always the best approach. When there are cultural or personal differences, [the greater formality of] electronic communication may be more effective.
Team dynamics are the same.	Research has shown that GDTs develop differently than co-located teams and therefore have different dynamics. (Interventions or team-building processes may need to be different for GDTs versus co-located teams.)
Team members cannot develop trust.	Trust can develop just as quickly when there is high focus on communication and interaction, regardless of co-location or dispersion.
There is no accountability.	Accountability should be based on measurable outcomes. This means shifting to a results-oriented paradigm. Out of sight does not mean [lack of accountability].
When things go wrong it's because of [the supporting] technology.	GDTs fail more often due to lack of "soft skills," not due to lack of technology skills or function. GDTs can use technology to enhance relationship building and speed team development.

Office (PMO) as a unit is not that different from most Program offices that are responsible for the delivery of technically and organizationally complex IT systems, with the exceptions of the effects listed in Exhibit 2.2 on the myths of geographically dispersed teams. A typical Offshore PMO organizational structure is illustrated in Exhibit 2.3. More detailed explanations of the roles and responsibilities of team members can be found in Chapter Five.

Exhibit 2.4 compares the Offshore Program Office with other types of technically focused IT PMOs. The Offshore PMO is made up of a series of executive stakeholders or sponsors, which, as discussed above, must be highly visible and present at key program milestones (e.g., the kick-off meeting) and decision points in order for this controversial and complex

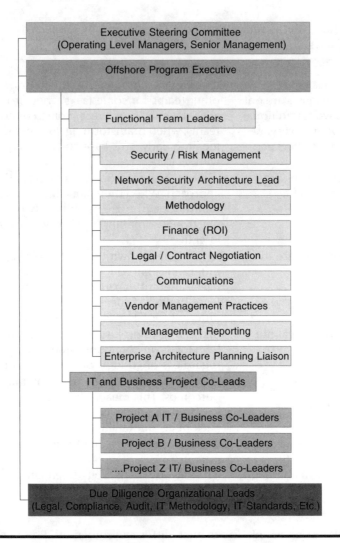

Exhibit 2.3   A Typical PMO Structure

program initiative to succeed. The typical Program Office is a matrix in nature, which means that while the Program Manager is leading the initiative, most of the team members are reporting up to their functional managers. For example, the project managers who work to execute the various projects work for the IT managers, the communications resource works in the communications department for the communications manager, and so on. All gather together to bring their collective expertise to bear upon the Offshore effort, under the guidance of the Offshore Program Office.

Exhibit 2.4   The Offshore Program Office versus the Typical Complex Technology Program Office

	Offshore PMO	Other PMOs
Usually comprised of a matrix (not direct reports) of project managers, architects, programmers, and other individual contributors across wide geographic and organizational boundaries.	√	√
Key to success is creating a structure so that the complex, multiple project timetables are met, within an overall program budget and to overall program quality standards.	√	√
Over time can change the way that vendor management is executed across the organization.	√	
Requires active participation of highest levels of legal, security, audit, compliance, and other due diligence organizations.	√	
Emphasizes cross-cultural training and awareness.	√	

Typically, the Offshore PMO runs relatively lean and mean in terms of staffing, as it is usually under scrutiny for expense and is considered pure overhead to the program. Nonetheless, most Offshore PMOs run anywhere from 3 to 12 dedicated resources (meaning they — unlike the other members of the program team — report directly to the Offshore Program Manager and have as their only focus Offshore-related duties).

The focus of the dedicated Offshore PMO resources is typically as follows:

■ *Management reporting* (see Exhibit 2.5 for a sample report): The Offshore PMO is the focal point for setting up and monitoring Offshore service provider performance, in particular service level agreements. SLAs are usually contractual minimum performance standards related to response to system downtime and other time-related performance measures such as bug fixes. They exist as a structured maintenance agreement that divides the potential errors into categories such as mild, medium, and severe across different categories of computer systems such as high, low, and medium priority — an SLA for a high-priority system may require an issue resolution in only hours, whereas a low-priority system may allow a timeline of days. Vendors are then measured by the percentage of SLAs they execute according to instructions within the agreed-upon timeframes.

General Update / Issues for Management Attention	Qualitative Results
•New vendor negotiations completed; contract signed on [date]. • Additional five (5) applications started knowledge transfer on [date]; completion anticipated in 3 months. •Project X delayed 2 weeks due to visa processing delays; no longer-term impact expected. •Employee survey listed Offshore as number one concern of IT workers.	• X percent of applications met 100% of SLAs (detailed on page 2 of this report). • Results of IT management satisfaction survey show that 90% are highly satisfied with their Offshore partner (4 out of 5); 10% are somewhat satisfied (3 out of 5) and 10% extremely satisfied (5 out of 5). • Etc., etc.
Program Growth / Application Mix	Financial Results
Total number of resources Offshore by application mix Planned Actual Notes Application A 10 8 Change order filed Application B 7 7 Application C 5 6 Change order filed Etc.	Program costs-to-date: $ Program savings-to-date $ Break-even anticipated 6 months or [date] Year over year savings $ Details page 3 of this report

Exhibit 2.5 Summary Page of a Sample Offshore Monthly Report to Management Team
Source: www.managementhelp.org.

- *Vendor negotiation:* It is only via a centralized PMO that the best prices can be negotiated on behalf of the organization. This is a complex topic, and we look at it in depth in Chapter Three. Suffice it to say here that vendor management is unlikely ever to be the same once the Offshore Program is launched.
- *Business process reengineering:* Often, leaders in the due diligence areas (such as legal, compliance, audit, industry oversight) need help to understand the impact of the Offshore program on their disciplines. The PMO can serve as the focal point for ensuring, especially during program inception, that the right individuals are speaking to each other and conferring upon the best way to solve organization problems and update business processes. For example, the head of security (networks) may need to work with the legal department to jointly determine the impact of the regulatory agency's decisions on acceptable levels of data access for Offshore consultants. The Offshore PMO can be the glue that brings these functional teams together, and provide valuable guidance and rules of thumb relative to decision making in what is usually a completely new set of challenges.
- *Methodology enhancement:* One of the biggest advantages of Offshore is in the shoring up of IT methodology in myriad ways. First, even in the most disciplined of organizations, there is a level of informality in the methodology when there are no geographic, time zone, and cultural boundaries (or these are relatively easy to supplement by face-to-face communications). When half the team is asleep when the other half is awake, or speaks a different native tongue, there is ample incentive to create greater levels of discipline. Offshore, therefore, can be the impetus to greater productivity across the entire IT team. Exposure to Offshore service providers, who invariably have the methodology discipline honed to a fine art, can be a wonderful influence even across those applications that never go Offshore. *Implied in all of this, of course, is the fact that most firms will need to undergo a revision and restructuring of their IT methodology in order to successfully execute Offshore.* The PMO usually works with the methodology owners and developers within the IT organization to serve as a focal point for information and support in updating the methodology for Offshore.

As illustrated in Exhibits 2.3 and 2.4, the project organization of the PMO is not significantly different from the team structures of other large, technically complex and geographically diverse IT programs. What differences there are reside in the breadth and scope of the business process reengineering that Offshore Outsourcing requires, and the team membership that must be present to reflect it.

Finally, one of the key functions of the Offshore Program Manager is to make sure that the representatives of all disciplines are heard and their concerns addressed, but that no *one discipline is allowed to create a permanent roadblock*. This is why the organizational equality of the Offshore Program Manager must be structured appropriately. At some point, the chorus of the popular view — that the current way is the only way — is silenced when the sheer numbers of companies that are doing Offshore in a big way come to light. It is difficult to maintain that security concerns are a permanent barrier to enable the program when the London Stock Exchange is run Offshore, as has been true for many years.

Getting the Most out of Expert Consultative Help in Initiating an Offshore Program: A Deeper Look

Now that we've taken a look at the Offshore PMO, it is easier to define the role of a useful expert consultant. Above, we touched briefly on how *not* to use expert external consultative help, as follows.

■ Do not perform or pay an expert consultant to do more than a cursory effort to "categorize" applications according to some so-called objective set of criteria that will ostensibly determine for now and the future what is appropriate for Offshore. Focus on learning through a pilot, and understand that the current views will change as part of the learning process. Alternatively, look to security and regulatory guidelines, and research on industry norms, for that information. A qualitative and thorough application inventory, however, is very helpful if the firm has a lot of "sidebar" applications that are outside the enterprise architecture. The greater the number of undocumented applications, the more helpful is such an application inventory.

■ Do not pay a consultant to evaluate the pros and cons of different countries. Generally, the choices for Offshore are either India-based Offshore services firms or the Big Four and their competition. The India-based firms speak for themselves — the Big Four have established Offshore services in a handful of countries outside of India, such as Accenture's base in the Philippines, or IBM Application Services Centers in Mexico and China. If you hire a Big Four firm, the locations of the Offshore services are generally predetermined, because they tend to cluster specific skillsets in distinct locations. So, for example, IBM today clusters its Seibel and SAP expertise in Bangalore, India. Although it is important to have a diversity of countries for risk mitigation purposes, working within existing top firms is by far the most reasonable and effective approach for newcomers to Offshore. Once the organization has cut its teeth, so to speak, then forays into complex country analysis may be helpful — not before.

There are, however, times when a paid expert consultant can be very helpful in initiating an Offshore Program. Navigating the many voices that come forth to offer paid help when the news is out — your firm is going Offshore — can be overwhelming. The lack of substantive written supporting material and the sometimes widely diverging opinions on key areas make it hard to distill and select advice and counsel.

■ *Do consider hiring expert communications and strategic staffing help.* These generally fall under the heading of organizational change management, and if I may indulge in a prediction, as Offshore enters the mainstream, the emphasis will shift from typical vendor management consulting (purporting to "rate the Offshore service providers/vendors," for example), to these kinds of more substantive and truly helpful support services.

■ Although *not strictly a function provided by an outside consultant, do consider a visit to India* very early on in the process of deciding when and how to go Offshore, and when and how to hire expert outside help. There is nothing quite like it — despite the physical challenges of the long flights — to create and build confidence in Offshore across both the IT and business management teams. Visits to India are almost always discussed in the hushed tones of the truly transformational experiences. The potential Offshore service providers will give you the royal treatment. It is important to expect the experience, however, to be typical of third-world travel — there is still a great deal of poverty and all that implies.

■ *Do* consider "outside the box" proposals from the many different types of creative business consultants and profit models that are rapidly building in Offshore. Where it does not hurt the business to completely outsource (e.g., in the growing BPO space, where already outsourced call centers are increasingly relocated Offshore), there are Offshore services firms that will pay cash up front to take completely a section of the business and run it Offshore. Many firms are switching their already outsourced call centers to India-based Offshore call centers for an immediate large savings and contribution to the bottom line, and a minimum of negative staffing impact. When firms are searching for an initial experience with Offshore, many first go with call centers because those applications are frequently already outsourced completely, so it's merely a switch from a U.S.-based to an India-based vendor. Not only is it is a good initial foray because the political difficulty is lessened because no direct employees are affected, but also it is often much simpler to execute; whereas staff needs to be trained in depth, the call center function is much more standalone and doesn't require the tight methodology ties to the U.S. software development team that is required for Co-Sourcing.

■ Depending upon the organizational culture, an independent consultant can help internally market the program and smooth the launch process. Why is this helpful? As we all know, in sales saying the wrong thing at the wrong time can break an early and tenuous relationship. Independent consultants can help the India-based Offshore firms steer clear of those snafus, and help them come up to speed in learning the culture of the organization to help position Offshore successfully. Although in many organizations this can most effectively be achieved by a set of internal champions, the political structure of some firms makes it easier if this role is played by an objective third party.

■ Finally, *do* consider bringing in program management tools, and the consultative help that often goes with them, to help with the large and complex task of detailed management reporting. Although dependency upon Offshore vendors for management reporting is not unusual in the first year or so of the program, for obvious reasons it is best to become independent as quickly as possible.

NEGOTIATING WITH OFFSHORE VENDORS FOR THE FIRST TIME

There is no area that renders firms engaging in Offshore for the first time more vulnerable than in the arena of vendor negotiation. There are several firms that specialize in providing advice and counsel. Are they valuable? As always, it depends upon what those individuals/firms are selling.

The reality is that all of the top India-based vendors are very safe choices, and will do an excellent job in providing Offshore services. We delve more into this in Chapter Three. Again, this is another example in which typical vendor management practices just don't apply to Offshore.

The emphasis in the United States in hiring IT help has always been in qualifying individuals as to whether they have skills. The India-based Offshore services firms tend to propose contracts that make that approach obsolete. The focus is on achievement of the SLAs or other quantitative performance measures without reference to hiring individual by individual. It is the Offshore Services firm as a whole that is being hired, and evaluated, and the India-based firms try to move the customer to seeing and trusting them as a whole entity. Usually, there is a consequent period of anxiety for the hiring firm. "If I can't review the resumes, then how can I ensure that applications will be managed, even if financially I won't have to pay?"

However, firms mature in Offshore, although they certainly utilize specific industry and application experience of the firm as a whole as one of myriad criteria in selecting a vendor, certainly don't focus on individual skillsets or the right to approve individual resumes, and usually trust the Offshore firm to manage their resources to achieve results. The Offshore services firms — large and small — generally treat every client and engagement as a make-or-break relationship for the viability of the company, due to the level of competition in Offshore. There is a sense of not having any room to make one customer unhappy for any reason, not in small part due to the still tenuous nature of acceptance of Offshore in the news media. One high-visibility failure could squash — if not the Offshore industry as a whole, now that it is so well established — that particular Offshore services provider's ability to win new customers, as nervous as new customers invariably tend to be. Offshore vendors are aware they are number two, and they are culturally structured to "try harder." With all of the coverage of Offshore, what is noticeably missing are the horror stories of execution gone bad.

Negotiation with India-based Offshore firms is very different from typical vendor negotiation with large U.S.-based IT consulting firms. For example, the publicly owned India-based Offshore firms are, as part of their corporate culture, much more open in sharing detailed financial results as well as customer references. Offshore consultants' expenses (travel, transportation, etc.) are rarely separated out and charged according to a formula specified in the contract, which is typical for U.S.-based vendors. The India-based Offshore services firms tend to include the majority of these expenses into an overall (very low) hourly rate. Both types of firms (U.S.-based and India-based Offshore services firms), of course, make a pricing distinction between Onshore and Offshore con-sultants, charging far more for resources who reside in the United States as part of the permanent Onshore contingent.

What's the net of all of these subtleties? The India-based Offshore firms have become increasingly sophisticated in learning new ways to make themselves more attractive to large U.S. corporations, and one way seems to be making it easier to negotiate and reach agreement. For example, not breaking out expenses in the hourly rates makes it that much easier for customers, as there is no longer a need to track and manage those details as part of their vendor management processes. As India-based Offshore services firms become more sophisticated, they are learning new ways to make the overall engagement process more accommodating to prospective customers. It is not unusual for an India-based Offshore services firm to be very flexible in order to win a new client, in terms of not only price but also fine points such as providing unpaid PMO resources for fledgling Offshore PMOs.

Another *key point of consideration is the length of the contract*. Although typical vendor services relationships may either focus upon and end after the duration of a specific project, or provide "blanket" savings subject to annual renewal, these may not appear sufficient. The relatively large upfront costs required to launch Offshore — knowledge transfer, software vendor consents, and security for network infrastructure — tend to push the minimum contract length to two years, with an average of three years. For an average program breakeven point that averages 9 to 12 months, anything less than three years may seem too risky.

Although the relationship with Offshore vendors is a long one (most Offshore relationships are at least seven years in duration — based upon an informal poll of the Offshore Interest group in April, 2003), it is useful not to contractually lock up that relationship for too long. The emphasis on the cost of knowledge transfer can be used by vendors to scare new clients into contracts of five years or longer, implying that is the only way to recoup the costs of relatively long and large knowledge transfer (100 consultants for 6 months is 600 months of upfront investment in Offshore, costly no matter how much the ultimate savings). However, signing any contract for five years is absurd — even three years is beyond the planning and business management horizon of many large corporations. It is important not to allow any vendor to scare firms new to Offshore into a contract length that normally would not be under consideration.

Isn't it true that Offshore's upfront costs justify a long contract? No, primarily because the level of competition among Offshore firms means that many of them will be flexible in sharing knowledge transfer and other costs associated with winning a new customer. It is also hard to overstate the India-based Offshore services firm's ability to learn quickly and make Offshore relationships successful, despite many odds. Beyond the leading ten or so Offshore firms, there is a growing subset of increasingly compelling "Tier Two" Offshore services firms who are even hungrier and more flexible. Given the overall culture of service explored in subsequent chapters, it is difficult to imagine any large firm that will not be able to flexibly manage their Offshore vendor relationships within the context of a reasonable timeframe (two to three years) for contracts.

APPROACHING THE MEASUREMENT OF ROI (RETURN ON INVESTMENT) WHEN INITIATING OFFSHORE

It is one of the facts of our measurement-oriented society that the easier a thing is to measure, the more meaningless the results.

So it is with Offshore. The real payback — keeping the IT department, or even the company, alive by getting to stay in the game — is too difficult to measure, yet that is the ultimate reason for Offshore. Analyzing the efficiencies of a handful of individuals now residing in remote locations is just the tip of the iceberg — usually Offshore brings many intangible benefits, not the least of which is a firm that has processes and methodologies well organized enough to function with radical geographical and cultural diversity. What is it worth to finally say the days of undocumented systems and dependencies on "stars" or technical cowboys — those individuals who create individual job security but organizational chaos through hoarding critical information — are gone for good?

Yet, even with these caveats, the savings associated with Offshore are stupendous (see the summary related to Citigroup later in this chapter), often representing over 10 percent of the operating budget of IT. This means the opportunity to deliver the same amount of IT services for 90 percent of today's cost, or reinvesting that to provide what would be worth 110 percent of services at today's cost. Figuring this savings year over year, and increasing it another 10 percent over time for increased efficiencies (as specialists and with all the energy and focus that implies, Offshore vendors usually are able to cut out the waste more quickly and deeper than before), Offshore means multiple millions of savings for even the smaller IT organization.

There's always a rub, and in this instance, the rub is that it takes a while for these savings to become evident. As mentioned above, there are a growing number of Offshore services providers who are willing to bet the farm on Offshore — using a business model in which they literally buy a capability from a larger organization, take that capability Offshore, and run it as a business charging back to the original firm. In this way, the larger firm avoids the complexity as well as the startup costs associated with Offshore. This can be a good option for firms who are so strapped for cash there is no other way, or for other strategic reasons cannot spare the resources to run their own programs, but there is a price to pay for this pain avoidance. That price is the lack of organizational knowledge in what is clearly the potential strategic advance of the decade — if not longer — so that the firm cannot opt to leverage that knowledge but must remain dependent upon this middle-man/intermediary. This is the organizational equivalent of allowing someone else to balance your personal checkbook — never a good idea, but certainly increasingly dangerous over time.

Breakeven for Offshore, in an informal survey conducted among members of the Offshore Interest Group, appears to average around 18 months. The initial costs to factor include:

- *Network security architecture* restructuring costs, such as firewall installation. We delve into this area in greater detail in Chapter 7.
- *Knowledge transfer,* or the costs of training to bring the Offshore firm up to speed on the particularities and peculiarities of the IT systems and related business processes to be moved Offshore. As mentioned frequently in this chapter, it is not uncommon for Offshore consultants to require three to six months shadow training with current IT resources in order to be effective (this includes time to document systems that are not currently documented).
- *Communications,* or the costs to effectively launch Offshore without an IT organizational meltdown. U.S.-based travel for face-to-face team building meetings (not so much required for Offshore execution as to help manage job impact communications and concerns) is usually not in today's trimmed-down budgets, but is often emotionally necessary for a demonstration of support by management, and to address the fears that the Offshore program may bring.
- *Travel,* including so-called marketing trips to India with internal business partners. The enthusiasm, professionalism, and sophistication one encounters on the modern campuses of the Offshore Service providers can make anyone a believer.
- *Expert legal counsel* may be a required safety net, particularly in highly regulated industries. Specialized legal firms have been established to provide advice to your internal legal counsel and may be helpful in getting through the first fine points of an Offshore contract. These can also provide advice on how to interact with regulatory agencies, who themselves may not be fully updated on Offshore and its implications for the industry.
- *Software vendor consent fees,* or the additional licensing fees existing software partners may legally require in order to allow Offshore consultants to work under current licenses. Unless the eventuality of Offshore is specifically referenced in today's license, third-party software vendors may view Offshore as a "revenue opportunity" in these lean times and request additional fees that may be significant. If they do so, in general the legal rights to do so are completely on their side.

- *Costs related to visa delays*, which are the most volatile of the vendor-related costs due to U.S. security in the post-9/11 world. Although Offshore personnel are not staying long term in this country (other than the very few who remain as Onshore team leads), for the knowledge transfer portion of the effort they must be granted a visa. Although most of the India-based firms take care of the direct fees per contractual agreement, delays due to security (on the U.S. side) are getting longer and longer, sometimes delaying the kick-off of the Offshore project. Many large India-based Offshore firms keep groups of visa-approved resources in a pool to avoid delays, but this strategy may not work for resources that require particular skills.
- *Training, severance, and other employee-based costs.* Ideally most employees will have another place to go within the firm, but some will not or cannot make the shift to a different role, and will need a well-deserved soft landing.
- *Corporatewide cultural programs.* Unfortunately, it is hard to over-estimate the lack of knowledge that most of the U.S. workforce has regarding cultures outside of the country. Other than the bits and pieces we pick up here and there, few of us have any formal education or even much indepth reading on the world at large. A light-hearted sharing of cultural norms, including a movie of the main workplace of the Offshore vendors, can be a serious support to the effort, and also serve as a formal welcome and acknowledgment of the Offshore team.
- *Business process reengineering* across many functional areas such as risk management, disaster recovery, vendor management, and enterprise architecture. These are treated in a separate chapter in depth, but note that Offshore Outsourcing often requires a restructuring of these processes across many levels.

Many firms that initiate Offshore programs have a short-term boost to their ROI for Offshore, which is the option to replace high-priced U.S.-based consultants with Offshore resources. This approach has many benefits, not the least of which is minimizing the negative impact on loyal, long-term employees. In the business case of Citigroup, below, the savings speak for themselves. Depending on how the ROI is positioned, the cost avoidance of these consultants can be viewed as a year-over-year return.

As implied in the discussion above, most firms assess the ROI of Offshore at a summary level. As firms mature in Offshore, the monitoring of the actual vendor costs gains greater and greater sophistication. Offshore's financial payback, however, is usually so great that it is not worth the anxiety to track the tiniest detailed impact.

The primary goal of those initiating Offshore then is to understand the nature of the initial fixed costs, listed above, so that they can be correctly reported to the management team in terms of setting expectations, and that they are not viewed as such a large hurdle so as to not engage in the program overall. Thus, proactive management of the list of expenses relating to Offshore, and ensuring that the firm maintains future flexibility by keeping the vendor contract as short as is practically possible, are the best steps to support a healthy ROI over the long term.

Before we leave the important topic of ROI, there are, of course, those external experts who make their living by helping firms with these calculations. A new suite of tools is appearing on the market, usually accompanied by nominal consulting fees, that support large firms in coming to terms with tracking and measuring the return on investment for Offshore. These command and control centers allow firms to utilize lower-tier, less expensive vendors because they provide the organization with the capability of detailed financial watchdog functions with minimal effort and oversight. This may represent the future of Offshore, and as the industry matures it is not unlikely we will see more and more of these capabilities and tools — and commoditization of Offshore services.

DEFINING THE PARAMETERS OF THAT ALL-IMPORTANT INITIAL PILOT: A DEEPER LOOK AT THE PROS AND CONS

What are some of the benefits of starting slowly, with a small pilot, in Offshore? Some of the pros and cons are listed below.

- ■ Pros
  - – A pilot allows the organization to more comfortably adjust to the timetable of Offshore for planning purposes. Most organizations will need to adjust the IT project planning and execution timetable to accommodate the long leadtime associated with launching Offshore programs and projects. Fortune 100 firms usually have an annual cycle of planning and execution relating to IT projects, and Offshore has a tendency to wreak havoc with those cycles. It is difficult to estimate and budget the initial staffing requirements and costs relating to knowledge transfer, especially when Offshore is brand new to the organization. In the tight world of IT where project funding and staffing allocation is always hard-won and hard-fought, having an extra three to six months of unanticipated time where IT staff is simply unavailable can be very difficult to incorporate into the typical project delivery schedule. A pilot can support a softer entry into the always difficult and complex staffing and budgeting process

across organizations, simply by providing more advance warning and greater advance knowledge.

- In today's complex matrix-management organizations there is usually a delicate balance in successful execution across geographically dispersed teams, building relationships between IT and internal business customers, and the politically charged use of consultants. The addition of Offshore and its complexities can push one or another of these aspects to the breaking point. A pilot can enable the organization to watch and incorporate the complexities of the Offshore timing and life cycle into the existing vendor management organizational structure.
- A pilot gives the firm more time to grapple with the difficult business process reengineering as it relates to the adjustments of methodology, contract negotiation, development of training programs, network design, and other organizational changes that simply require time to think through and implement.

▪ Cons

- Although a pilot has a lot of advantages in terms of allowing the firm time to adjust to the enormous shifts that an Offshore program implies, it also can be a negative. The biggest concern is that the pilot becomes a focus for employee dissatisfaction and fear related to long-term job security, and that the Offshore program is indefinitely weakened or postponed as a result. Postponement of the shorter-term hard decisions puts the overall IT organization at risk as it will be unable to compete at the price point of competitive IT firms that are Offshore-enabled. There is really no avoiding the harsher reality, and the sooner the organization enables Offshore, the more funding and therefore choices it will have not only for the compassionate retraining of personnel, but also for redirecting profits into the organization or reinvestment into additional IT services.
- Stating the obvious, the sooner one engages with Offshore in full throttle, the sooner the savings start rolling in and the sooner the organization starts to discern the reality behind the fear-based hype. The mature Offshore-enabled organization is almost unrecognizable from the new one. Gone are the exaggerated concerns relating to the uniqueness of the IT applications and the need for U.S.-based expertise to work them. In their place is a knowledge that not only is it possible to have an Offshore-enabled IT organization, but that organization brings multiple benefits in addition to startling savings. These benefits are described in detail in Chapter One, but include a general sense of improved structure and productivity related to IT effectiveness

across the organization — a more robust and well-understood systems development life cycle or methodology, a better appreciation and openness to other cultures and ways of doing things, a greater level of appropriate formality in keys areas such as documentation and software development, and achievement of measures of excellence such as SLAs.

– Finally, jumping in with both feet can be the differentiator for competitive advantage. In today's world of tighter and tighter margins, the returns on investment of an IT Offshore program can mean an IT expense rebate that provides a meaningful strategic advantage to the firm as a whole, depending upon how much of the firm's resources are invested in IT. There are opportunities for early adopters to raise the bar perhaps beyond the reach of the remainder.

ESTABLISHING AN INITIAL TIMETABLE FOR AN UPGRADED NETWORK SECURITY INFRASTRUCTURE

As explored in greater detail in Chapter 7, the creation of a workable Network Security Architecture is frequently one of the biggest challenges related to enabling Offshore.

This area is frequently a test of leadership for the Program Manager, and distinguishing between legitimate security issues versus entrenched thinking disguised by techno-babble can difficult. A key to success here is to bring stories of other companies to shake up narrow thinking. Connecting with other security architects at other firms farther down the road can be a source of creative problem solving, or at the least, squelch some of the casual or loud dismissals that it is not possible so that alternatives can start being considered.

Although it is difficult to be more specific as each network is different, the overall tone of problem solving is the most important first step. A pragmatic focus on the creation of immediate solutions with a minimum compromise of security is essential to move the team beyond endless debate. Executing a series of smaller bounded solutions rather than attempting to solve all issues from the start can be the difference between being stuck in limbo and starting down the path to resolution. As long as these more tactical solutions are executed within a long-term architectural context, no matter how fluid and changing that long-term picture may be in light of changes to the technology and business environment, this at least gets the program off the ground and creates a new way of looking at old problems. The presence or absence of key personnel with maturity, leadership, and a balanced view is the critical success factor for solving this particularly thorny challenge in Offshore. Leadership in this area is determined by the ability of the Program Manager to discern a qualified yet pragmatic security architect who can make reasonable compromises without putting the firm at risk.

CHAPTER SUMMARY

Here's a summary of key points in successful initiation of Offshore.

■ *Do try to keep your initial vendor contracts to no more than three years (two years is better).* Although the process of enabling Offshore may seem overwhelming at first, the dependency on the set of initial vendors may change dramatically once the organization has digested the experience of Offshore. Although the long life cycle associated with initiating and realizing Offshore will naturally seem to lend itself to a longer-term contract over two years, the shorter contract provides more pricing leverage and flexibility down the road. Year three seems to be the magic number when organizations awaken to the collective reality behind the hype of Offshore, and really take charge of their destiny.

■ *Do consider alternatives to the typical U.S.-based firm strategy advisory relationship for Offshore.* As outlined above, many of these vendors are not neutral and it is dangerous to treat them as such. This may be a difficult choice, because their political clout at high levels can be a valuable asset in helping to smooth the initial transition to Offshore. However, Offshore ultimately comes down to strategic staffing planning. A subtle but very real staffing war can result if staffing decisions are left to firms trying to cover their own revenue requirements.

■ *Do make sure your consultant has the skills and experience* in the heart of the Offshore conundrum — strategic staffing and communications. IT organizations tend to be filled with left-brain individuals who like to deal in black and white, and even executives in IT tend to lean towards endless analysis of factual data to avoid dealing with the tougher underlying issues. Conferences on Offshore IT tend to talk endlessly about the pros and cons of different countries, for example, when a deeper look clearly shows that India is where the majority of Offshore services are and will continue to be for the foreseeable future. Firms that start Offshore tend to be very focused on details of how closely the prospective vendors match their concept of an ideal background — with experience required in specific industries, applications, and even organizations — but the more experienced firms understand they are hiring general know-how and culture, and that applying credentials to Offshore firms in the same way that one hires individuals is a mistake. Thus, hire a consultant who won't pander to your natural fear of the unknown by supporting your organization's insistence on the minutiae of Offshore, indulging in detailed lists comparing vendors on small aspects of supposed organizational fit. These will be useless in a few years, but a well-executed and thought-out strategy relating to staffing and communications will be worth its weight in avoided conflict and in supporting employees to make a dignified transition.

■ As is true of all Offshore relationships, *do allow softer factors such as organizational fit and style to factor heavily into hiring decisions.* Can your organization's representatives "live" with the services providers for the long term? If you hire a consultant to help you, will that style be a good and reliable executive interface over the long term? In other words, all players' interpersonal styles need to be structured so that they can be played out for the long haul. The Offshore Interest Group often talks about the "marriage" of Offshore vendors. Structuring the contract so there are choices, one choice is the option to keep the relationship. Exhibit 2.6 is a Metagroup's snapshot of Offshore vendors as of early 2003.

■ *Do* remember that Offshore is one of those initiatives that somehow turn the old rules upside down and inside out. Anticipate the unknown and provide for maximum flexibility in as many aspects of decision making as possible.

BUSINESS CASE: A LOOK AT CITIGROUP (CITI), 17 YEARS AND COUNTING IN OFFSHORE

In this business case we profile Ted Podest. As we take a look at the first of several people and personalities who provide industry leadership, we gain a sense of what it takes to successfully navigate a large organization in the sometimes deep waters of Offshore Program management. Why look at Citi in a chapter on the successful initiation of Offshore? Read on, and find out how Ted, hired in 2000, successfully led cost containment for Wall Street high flyers.

Ted wasn't hired as the manager of the "Low Cost Development Group." The name of the group as well as the strategy came much later. Ted was working at a dot-com company for a few weeks in 2000 when he realized he'd "never be a dot-com guy." He called his old boss who was now the Chief of Staff and Controller for Citi. Ted accepted a job tracking metrics and reporting back to him regarding progress on a corporatewide Citi initiative to lower costs — rapidly and permanently.

Exhibit 2.6   The View from MetaGroup on Offshore Vendors

Leaders: TCS, Wipro, Infosys, IBM GSA

Challengers: Syntel, Satyam, EDS, CGI, Keane, CSC, Convansys, HCL, Accenture

Key Findings: High growth among offshore outsourcing firms has created a degree of confidence in this market. During the research process for this METAspectrum evaluation, more than 60% of vendors claimed to be market leaders and over 40% expected to be the number-one market leader. Although each of these firms does possess world-class skills and is a viable vendor, the current abundance of vendors has "raised the bar" for being a market leader. Pure-play vendors must extend beyond technical skills for project management and application development — such skills are "average" among leading vendors. Leading vendors are expanding vertical market offerings and improving the tools of doing business within the offshore model.

Leaders

Offshore leaders are larger pure-play vendors (TCS, Wipro, Infosys) and domestic vendors with well-established offshore practices (IBM GSA). Momentum is highest for these vendors, as IT organizations turn to them first when considering offshore strategies or as a benchmark against which to compare competitors. Success in offshore outsourcing is increasingly determined by business practices rather than technical expertise. Through 2005/06, market leaders will further extend global offerings/capabilities, package services into productized components, and converge with mainstream outsourcing markets.

Challengers

Market challengers are pure-play offshore vendors and domestic providers with offshore capabilities. Offshore vendors typically have higher technical capability (e.g., Capability Maturity Model Level 5). Domestic providers have greater name-brand recognition and more complete application service offerings (not just offshore). The close clustering of vendors in the METAspectrum graphic reflects the converging strategies of offshore and domestic firms. Through 2005/06, market challengers must develop brand names — offshore firms will focus on establishing brands, while domestic firms will work to be recognized for offshore capability. Vendors with successful brands will become dominant, and those that fall short in branding efforts will likely face consolidation/acquisition by 2007/08.

Followers

Hundreds of offshore vendors exist within India and dozens of other countries globally. Vendors are segmenting into three sectors: consulting/integration, information technology, and business process (primarily call centers). We believe that increased competition within the

---

Exhibit 2.6 (continued)   The View from MetaGroup on Offshore Vendors

offshore market and uncertainty about international stability will eliminate most pure-play offshore vendors from gaining significant market share without substantive competitive differentiators.

Bottom Line

Offshore outsourcing provides access to worldwide resources otherwise unavailable to most enterprises. Through 2006, offshore growth will continue to exceed outsourcing generally. Although hundreds of offshore vendors exist globally, only a handful have reached critical mass. Vendors included in this study will likely acquire firms as this market matures and consolidates. By 2005/06, most IT organizations will have an "offshore" strategy, despite the current efforts of domestic vendors to position "portfolio optimization" as an alternative global approach.

Business Impact: Application development and maintenance constitutes approximately 30% of spending for the average IT organization. Offshore typically reduces that expense by 30%, but introduces additional risks and challenges. We believe the average enterprise will ultimately outsource 60% of application work offshore (circa 2008/10).

Source: Offshore Application Outsourcing, A MetaSpectrum Evaluation, February 2003.

Ted had joined Citi after a wide and varied career across different financial management and technology leadership roles in and around Wall Street. When Ted joined Citi at the invitation of his old boss, he was to find it was a veritable melting pot of corporate cultures. Citigroup had most recently merged with Solomon, Smith & Barney, but this was the last in an ongoing series. And although Citi managers had lived with Offshore Outsourcing for many a year, the Solomon, Smith & Barney principals were both unfamiliar with the model and (as is typical) set against it. It didn't help that these were Wall Street salespeople at the top of their game, earning up to a million dollars and representing the front line of one of the cash cows for the organization. These strong-minded folks weren't used to *anyone* telling them to cut corners on expenses.

Ted spent the first six months maintaining a low profile, undertaking a detailed analysis of spending and costs across the entire organization. He interviewed a lot of the Citi managers who had been managing technology resources, and culled together the success and not-so-success-ful stories to create a good working knowledge of the organization's critical success factors. Ted didn't want to sell anything to these high flyers that wasn't solid.

As a result of his research, Ted was convinced that one of the biggest areas of expense management was in the way that Citi was overpaying its external IT consultants. The dot-com boom had left a big hole in the employment market, and starting salaries were reduced by as much as 20 percent since the salad days of 1999. But the costs of consultants had remained steady, primarily because there was no mechanism to lower costs within Citi's vendor management strategy. Ted was determined to create a program that would systematically open these costs to market forces, so that consultants were no longer overpaid as a result of simple organizational inertia.

Ted knew that creating the Low Cost Development strategy was just half the job. The other job was to sell it to the organization's high-profile managers. He started by publishing a series of stories that showed how success could be achieved via Offshore Outsourcing and other low-cost alternatives for IT staffing. He worked with his boss to institutionalize the program, tying the cost per head for utilization of IT resources of individual performance reviews and bonuses. Ultimately, each of the 18 managers in the organization needed to staff their IT projects with a minimum percentage of resources from this group to make their bonus and job performance goals.

In addition to the iron fist, Ted also used the soft glove. For those managers who were simply not ready to go to India for their IT resources, with all that implied, Ted expanded the definition of Low Cost Development resources to include on-site resources from India-based Offshore services providers. Low-cost consultants would be flown in from India, train on Citi's systems, and remain on site to provide services. This blending of on-site and Offshore resource management had a lot of advantages. First, it was much more enticing to gun-shy managers new to Offshore, because an on-site consultant was less of a change and less threatening. Second, if and when those managers decided they were ready to try the "real" Offshore model, their project's knowledge transfer costs were minimized because the on-site consultant was already trained. Third, it allowed Citi to aggressively leverage volume discounts, because the on-site consultants counted toward the total head count provided by the Offshore vendor. Finally, the administrative cost and overhead of managing hundreds of individual consultants as compared to a handful of Offshore vendors was dramatically lessened.

Ted's boss backed up his decisions on a consultant-by-consultant basis, as Ted went around replacing high-priced on-site consultants with Low Cost Development resources. As a result, after two years, the average price of Citi consultants dropped $300 per day, from $1100 to $800. The total number of on-site consultants not part of the Low Cost Development Group dropped from 1200 to 193. Bottom line savings? This program contributed, conservatively, $82 million in purse savings for fiscal year 2002 alone.

Most of the projects utilizing five consultants or more were moved Offshore, with the associated employees retrained to perform other, usually higher-skilled functions. Citi did not lay off any employees as result of this program. The Low Cost Development group was a hit.

Change this fundamental doesn't come easy to any complex organization. A story from early in the implementation of the program can provide an appreciation of Ted's creativity and determination. Ted and his boss were at a meeting with the trading sales managers, discussing one of the larger cash drains in the organization. The sales managers were subscribing to subscription information sources that were rarely used and extremely expensive, but of course when Ted suggested they be cut he met a lot of resistance. Ted turned it around by waving a bunch of $500 bills in their faces. Even though this was lunch money to these folks, it was a language they could understand. "Every time you cut an information source, your personal bonus goes up by $250." By handing out cash in real-time at the meeting, Ted and his boss saved $15 million in online access expenses. Ted had figured out a way to sell to the top salespeople in the world — on his own terms.

Ted will tell you that this MO — a long careful analysis followed by out of the box thinking — is typical of his career. In combination with superb salesmanship, Ted is creative with metrics and the meaning behind them. For example, lowering the hourly cost but also doubling the time to completion results in the evaporation of any savings. As a result of this kind of commitment to really sweat the details, Citi has a Low Cost Development command and control center that should be the envy of every organization. Ted was no greenhorn in monitoring costs through metrics. His former background in building a financial data warehouse for a leading bonds management firm was the background for a lot of his creativity and understanding. The financial data warehouse provided a consolidated set of reports that contained simple, accurate, and easy to understand metrics on profit and loss, sales credits, costs, and revenue for their government bond-trading business. Similarly, today's command and control center provides a point-and-click window into the current actual versus planned comparison of every aspect of each Offshore project, from timeline to staffing to project life cycle.

What is Ted's vendor management strategy for Offshore? Ted realized his vision in structuring his vendor management practices to maximize competition among Offshore services providers. Citi is a prestigious and large account, and volume discounts are expected as part of fair market value. Vendors are evaluated according to 18 criteria, which include quality measures, staff turnover, ease of audits, CMM level, and alignment with

Citi IT policies. One of the more interesting developments is Citi's increased use of Tier Two India-based software vendors, as opposed to Tier One and Big Four. Citi has been executing Offshore for over 15 years, so the level of organizational knowledge is deep, and a case can be made that it is that experience that allows Citi the ability to "reverse auction" and competitively bid Offshore work among a variety of vendors effectively. Citi, indeed, owns several firms that provide Offshore services directly, and has had successful public offerings for these firms.

Looking forward, we explore further the implications of these vendor management practices in Chapter Three. Before we turn to these in detail, however, it is time to look at that most current and timely of topics, business ethics management in the workplace

APPENDIX: A LOOK AT ETHICS IN THE WORKPLACE

This rather lengthy chapter endnote is a reflection of the new awareness regarding standards of business conduct that is emerging in the U.S. workplace. There is no initiative more on the ethical fork than Offshore. As U.S. business schools now add courses on ethics to their M.B.A. curricula, here too in this book, no discussion of Offshore is complete without a detailed reference to this most delicate of topics.

Below, Dr. Carter McNamara provides an excellent overview of this very pertinent topic to the initiation of Offshore. The author looks forward to the day when no Offshore Program is complete without a proactive Ethics Management program component implemented side by side, and hopes that in a small way, this interesting and extensive outline by Dr. McNamara helps to make that future a reality.

Ethics Management Programs: An Overview

About Ethics Management Programs[2]

Organizations can manage ethics in their workplaces by establishing an ethics management program. Brian Schrag, Executive Secretary of the Association for Practical and Professional Ethics, clarifies. "Typically, ethics programs convey corporate values, often using codes and policies to guide decisions and behavior, and can include extensive training and evaluating, depending on the organization. They provide guidance in ethical dilemmas." Rarely are two programs alike.

"All organizations have ethics programs, but most do not know that they do," wrote business ethics professor Stephen Brenner.[3] "A corporate ethics program is made up of values, policies and activities which impact the propriety of organization behaviors."

Robert Dunn, President and CEO of San Francisco-based Business for Social Responsibility in a 1999 interview with Dr. McNamara, adds: "Balancing competing values and reconciling them is a basic purpose of an ethics management program. Business people need more practical tools and information to understand their values and how to manage them."

Benefits of Managing Ethics as a Program

There are numerous benefits in formally managing ethics as a program, rather than as a one-shot effort when it appears to be needed. Ethics programs:

- Establish organizational roles to manage ethics
- Schedule ongoing assessment of ethics requirements
- Establish required operating values and behaviors
- Align organizational behaviors with operating values
- Develop awareness and sensitivity to ethical issues
- Integrate ethical guidelines to decision making
- Structure mechanisms to resolving ethical dilemmas
- Facilitate ongoing evaluation and updates to the program
- Help convince employees that attention to ethics is not just a knee-jerk reaction done to get out of trouble or improve public image

Eight Guidelines for Managing Ethics in the Workplace

The following guidelines ensure the ethics management program is operated in a meaningful fashion.

1. *Recognize that managing ethics is a process.* Ethics is a matter of values and associated behaviors. Values are discerned through the process of ongoing reflection. Therefore, ethics programs may seem more process-oriented than most management practices
2. *The bottom line of an ethics program is accomplishing preferred behaviors in the workplace.* As with any management practice, the most important outcome is behaviors preferred by the organization. The best ethical values and intentions are relatively meaningless unless they generate fair and just behaviors in the workplace. That's why practices that generate lists of ethical values, or codes of ethics, must also generate policies, procedures, and training that translate those values to appropriate behaviors.
3. *The best way to handle ethical dilemmas is to avoid their occurrence in the first place.* That's why practices such as developing codes of ethics and codes of conduct are so important. Their development

sensitizes employees to ethical considerations and minimizes the chances of unethical behavior occurring in the first place.

4. *Make ethics decisions in groups, and make decisions public, as appropriate.* This usually produces better quality decisions by including diverse interests and perspectives, and increases the credibility of the decision process and outcome by reducing suspicion of unfair bias.

5. *Integrate ethics management with other management practices.* When developing the values statement during strategic planning, include ethical values preferred in the workplace. When developing personnel policies, reflect on what ethical values you'd like to be most prominent in the organization's culture and then design policies to produce these behaviors.

6. *Use cross-functional teams when developing and implementing the ethics management program.* It's vital that the organization's employees feel a sense of participation and ownership in the program if they are to adhere to its ethical values. Therefore, include employees in developing and operating the program.

7. *Value forgiveness.* This may sound rather religious or preachy to some, but it's probably the most important component of any management practice. An ethics management program may at first actually increase the number of ethical issues to be dealt with because people are more sensitive to their occurrence. Consequently, there may be more occasions to address people's unethical behavior. The most important ingredient for remaining ethical is trying to be ethical. Therefore, help people recognize and address their mistakes and then support them to continue to try to operate ethically.

8. *Note that trying to operate ethically and making a few mistakes is better than not trying at all.* Some organizations have become widely known as operating in a highly ethical manner, for example, Ben and Jerry's. Unfortunately, it seems that when an organization achieves this strong public image, it is placed on a pedestal. All organizations are comprised of people and people are not perfect. It's the *trying* that counts and brings peace of mind — not achieving hero status in society.

Six Key Roles and Responsibilities in Ethics Management

Depending on the size of the organization, certain roles may prove useful in managing ethics in the workplace. These can be full-time roles or part-time functions assumed by someone already in the organization. Small organizations certainly will not have the resources to implement each of the following roles using different people in the organization. However, the following functions point out responsibilities that should be included somewhere in the organization.

1. *The organization's chief executive must fully support the program.* If the chief executive isn't fully behind the program, employees will certainly notice — and this apparent hypocrisy may cause such cynicism that the organization may be worse off than having no formal ethics program at all. Therefore, the chief executive should announce the program, and champion its development and implementation. Most important, the chief executive should consistently aspire to lead in an ethical manner. If a mistake is made, admit it.

2. *Consider establishing an ethics committee at the board level.* The committee would be charged to oversee development and operation of the ethics management program.

3. *Consider establishing an ethics management committee.* It would be charged with implementing and administrating an ethics management program, including administrating and training about policies and procedures, and resolving ethical dilemmas. The committee should be comprised of senior officers.

4. *Consider assigning/developing an ethics officer.* This role is becoming more common, particularly in larger and more progressive organizations. The ethics officer is usually trained in matters of ethics in the workplace, particularly about resolving ethical dilemmas.

5. *Consider establishing an ombudsperson.* The ombudsperson is responsible to help coordinate development of the policies and procedures to institutionalize moral values in the workplace. This position usually is directly responsible for resolving ethical dilemmas by interpreting policies and procedures.

6. Note that one person must ultimately be responsible for managing the ethics management program.

Ethics Tools: Codes of Ethics

About Codes of Ethics

According to Doug Wallace of the Falcrum Group, "A credo generally describes the highest values to which the company aspires to operate. It contains the 'thou shalt's. A code of ethics specifies the ethical rules of operation. It's the 'thou shalt not's." In the latter 1980s, The Conference Board, a leading business membership organization, found that 76 percent of corporations surveyed had codes of ethics.

Some business ethicists disagree that codes have any value. Usually they explain that too much focus is put on the codes themselves, and that codes themselves are not influential in managing ethics in the workplace. Many ethicists note that it's the *developing* and *continuing dialogue* around the code's values that is most important.

Occasionally, employees react to codes with suspicion, believing the values are "motherhood and apple pie" and codes are for window dressing. But, when managing a complex issue, especially in a crisis, having a code is critical. More important, it's having *developed* a code. In the mid-1970s, Johnson & Johnson updated their credo in a series of challenge meetings. Bob Kniffin, Vice President of External Affairs, explains in a 1998 interview by author Dr. Carter McNamara in San Francisco, "We pored over each phrase and word. We asked ourselves, 'Do we still believe this?' Our meetings resulted in some fine tuning, but basically we didn't change the values. The meetings infused the values in the minds of all of us managers." Many believe this process guided them in their well-known decision to pull Tylenol bottles off the shelves and repackage them at a $100 million expense. Kniffin offers some sound practical advice. "In a crisis, there's no time for moral conclusions. Get those done beforehand. But also realize there's no substitute for sound crisis management. For example, have a list of people with fundamental knowledge, such as who transports your products where and when."

Developing Codes of Ethics

Note that if your organization is quite large, for example, includes several large programs or departments, you may want to develop an overall corporate code of ethics and then a separate code to guide each of your programs or departments.

Also note that codes should not be developed out of the human resource or legal departments alone, as is too often done. Codes are insufficient if intended only to ensure that policies are legal. All staff must see the ethics program being driven by top management.

Note that codes of ethics and codes of conduct may be the same in some organizations, depending on the organization's culture and operations and on the ultimate level of specificity in the code(s).

Consider the following guidelines when developing codes of ethics.

1. *Review any values needed to adhere to relevant laws and regulations.* This ensures your organization is not (or is not near) breaking any of them. (If you are breaking any of them, you may be far better off to report this violation than to try to hide the problem.

Often, a reported violation generates more leniency than outside detection of an unreported violation, particularly per the new Federal Sentencing Guidelines.) Increase priority on values that will help your organization operate to avoid breaking these laws and to follow necessary regulations.

2. *Review which values produce the top three or four traits of a highly ethical and successful product or service in your area,* for example, for accountants: objectivity, confidentiality, accuracy, and the like. Identify which values produce behaviors that exhibit these traits.

3. *Identify values needed to address current issues in your workplace.* Appoint one or two key people to interview key staff to collect descriptions of major issues in the workplace. Collect descriptions of behaviors that produce the issues. Consider which of these issues is ethical in nature, for example, issues in regard to respect, fairness, and honesty. Identify the behaviors needed to resolve these issues. Identify which values would generate those preferred behaviors. There may be values included here that some people would not deem as moral or ethical values, for example, team-building and promptness, but for managers, these practical values may add more relevance and utility to a code of ethics.

4. *Identify any values needed, based on findings during strategic planning.* Review information from your SWOT analysis (identifying the organization's Strengths, Weaknesses, Opportunities, and Threats). What behaviors are needed to build on strengths, shore up weaknesses, take advantage of opportunities, and guard against threats?

5. *Consider any top ethical values that might be prized by stakeholders.* For example, consider expectations of employees, clients/customers, suppliers, funders, members of the local community, and so on.

6. Collect from the above steps, the top five to ten ethical values that are high priorities in your organization (see item 7 for examples).

7. *Examples of ethical values might include:*[4]
   a. *Trustworthiness:* honesty, integrity, promise-keeping, loyalty
   b. *Respect:* autonomy, privacy, dignity, courtesy, tolerance, acceptance
   c. *Responsibility:* accountability, pursuit of excellence
   d. *Caring:* compassion, consideration, giving, sharing, kindness, loving
   e. *Justice and fairness:* procedural fairness, impartiality, consistency, equity, equality, due process
   f. *Civic virtue and citizenship:* law abiding, community service, protection of environment

8. *Compose your code of ethics; attempt to associate with each value, two example behaviors that reflect each value.* Critics of codes of ethics assert that they seem vacuous because many only list ethical

values and don't clarify these values by associating examples of behaviors.

9. Include wording that indicates all employees are expected to conform to the values stated in the code of ethics. Add wording that indicates where employees can go if they have any questions.

10. Obtain review from key members of the organization. Get input from as many members as possible.

11. *Announce and distribute the new code of ethics* (unless you are waiting to announce it along with any new codes of conduct and associated policies and procedures). Ensure each employee has a copy and post codes throughout the facility.

12. *Update the code at least once a year.* As stated several times in this document, the most important aspect of codes is developing them, not the code itself. Continued dialogue and reflection around ethical values produces ethical sensitivity and consensus. Therefore, revisit your codes at least once a year — preferably two or three times a year.

13. *Note that you cannot include values and preferred behaviors for every possible ethical dilemma that might arise.* Your goal is to focus on the top ethical values needed in your organization and to avoid potential ethical dilemmas that seem mostly likely to occur.

14. *Examples of a code of ethics:* This example code was developed by The Management Assistance Program for Nonprofits[5] in St. Paul. The code is geared specifically to guiding relations among staff.[6] Note that you may be better off generating your own code of ethics from scratch rather than reviewing examples from other organizations. All ethical values are attractive to include in a code; however, you are most interested in those that provoke behaviors needed in your organization at this time. You may want to include quite different ethical values next year.

Ethics Tools: Codes of Conduct

About Codes of Conduct

"Codes of conduct specify actions in the workplace and codes of ethics are general guides to decisions about those actions,"[7] explains Craig Nordlund, Associate General Counsel and Secretary at Hewlett Packard. He suggests that codes of conduct contain examples of appropriate behavior to be meaningful.

The Conference Board found that codes of conduct are increasingly sophisticated and focused at lower levels in companies. Departments frequently have their own codes. Be careful, though. An organization could be sued for breach of contract if its practices are not in accord with its policies. That's why legal departments should review codes of conduct and other ethics policies. Also, that's why it's critical for organizations to review their policies at least once a year to ensure they are in accordance with laws and regulations.

Developing a Code of Conduct

Note that if your organization is quite large, for example, includes several large programs or departments, you may want to develop an overall corporate code of conduct, and then a separate code to guide each of your programs or departments. Consider the following guidelines when developing codes of conduct.

1. *Identify key behaviors needed to adhere to the ethical values proclaimed in your code of ethics,* including ethical values derived from review of key laws and regulations, ethical behaviors needed in your product or service area, behaviors to address current issues in your workplace, and behaviors needed to reach strategic goals.
2. Include wording that indicates all employees are expected to conform to the behaviors specified in the code of conduct. Add wording that indicates where employees can go if they have any questions.
3. *Obtain review from key members of the organization.* Be sure your legal department reviews the drafted code of conduct.
4. *Announce and distribute the new code of conduct* (unless you are waiting to announce it along with any associated policies and procedures). Ensure each employee has a copy and post codes in each employee's bay or office.
5. Note that you cannot include preferred behaviors for every possible ethical dilemma that might arise.
6. *Examples of topics typically addressed by codes of conduct include:* preferred style of dress, avoiding illegal drugs, following instructions of superiors, being reliable and prompt, maintaining confidentiality, not accepting personal gifts from stakeholders as a result of company role, avoiding racial or sexual discrimination, avoiding conflict of interest, complying with laws and regulations, not using organization's property for personal use, not discriminating against race or age or sexual orientation, and reporting illegal or questionable activity. *Go beyond these traditional legalistic expectations in your codes — adhere to what's ethically sensitive in your organization, as well.* (Note that, as with codes of ethics, you may be better off generating your own code of conduct from scratch rather than reviewing examples from other organizations.)

Ethics Tools: Policies and Procedures

1. *Update policies and procedures to produce behaviors preferred from the code of conduct,* including, for example, personnel, job descriptions, performance appraisal forms, management-by-objectives expectations, standard forms, checklists, budget report formats, and other relevant control instruments to ensure conformance to the code of conduct. In doing so, try to avoid creating ethical dilemmas such as conflicts of interest or infringing on employees' individual rights.

2. *There are numerous examples of how organizations manage values through use of policies and procedures.* For example, we're most familiar with the value of social responsibility. To produce behavior aligned with this value, organizations often institute policies such as recycling waste, donating to local charities, or paying employees to participate in community events. In another example, a high value on responsiveness to customers might be implemented by instituting policies to return phone calls or to repair defective equipment within a certain period of time. Consider the role of job descriptions and performance appraisals. For example, an advanced technology business will highly value technical knowledge, creativity, and systems thinking. They use job descriptions and performance appraisals to encourage behaviors aligned with these values, such as rewarding advanced degrees, patents, and analysis and design skills.

3. *Include policies and procedures to address ethical dilemmas.* See the section, Ethics Tools: Resolving Ethical Dilemmas, to select a method that is most appropriate for your organization's culture and operations.

4. *Include policies and procedures to ensure training of employees about the ethics management program.* See the section, Ethics Tools: Training.

5. Include policies and procedures to reward ethical behavior and impose consequences for unethical behavior.

6. Include a grievance policy for employees to use to resolve disagreements with supervisors and staff.

7. *Consider establishing an ethics "hotline."* This function might best be provided by an outside consultant, such as a lawyer, clergyperson, and so on. Or provide an anonymous "tip" box in which personnel can report suspected unethical activities, and do so safely on an anonymous basis.

8. *Once a year, review all personnel policies and procedures.* If yours is a small organization, consider including all staff during this

review. Take a full day for all staff to review policies and procedures, and suggest changes.

Ethics Tools: Resolving Ethical Dilemmas (with Real-to-Life Examples)

Definition of an Ethical Dilemma

Perhaps too often, business ethics are portrayed as a matter of resolving
conflicts in which one option appears to be the clear choice. For example,
case studies are often presented in which an employee is faced with
whether to lie, steal, cheat, abuse another, break terms of a contract, and
so on. However, ethical dilemmas faced by managers are often more real-
to-life and highly complex with no clear guidelines, whether in law or
often in religion.

As noted earlier in this document, Doug Wallace, Twin Cities-based
consultant, explains that one knows when one has a significant ethical
conflict when there is presence of (a) significant value conflicts among
differing interests, (b) real alternatives that are equality justifiable, and
(c) significant consequences on "stakeholders" in the situation.

An ethical dilemma exists when one is faced with having to make a
choice among these alternatives.

Real-to-Life Examples of Complex Ethical Dilemmas

"Our company prides itself on hiring minorities. One Asian candidate fully
fits the job requirements for our open position. However, we're concerned
that our customers won't understand his limited command of the English
language. What should I do?"

"My computer operator told me he'd noticed several personal letters
printed from a computer that I was responsible to manage. While we had
no specific policies then against personal use of company facilities, I was
concerned. I approached the letter writer to discuss the situation. She told
me she'd written the letters on her own time to practice using our word
processor. What should I do?"

Three Methods to Resolve Ethical Dilemmas

Organizations should develop and document a procedure for dealing with
ethical dilemmas as they arise. Ideally, ethical dilemmas should be resolved
by a group within the organization, for example, an ethics committee
comprised of top leaders/managers or members of the board. Consider
having staff members on the committee as well. The following three
methods can be used to address ethical dilemmas. Methods include an
ethical checklist, a ten-step method, and a list of key questions. (Note

that the Golden Rule is probably the most common method to resolve ethical dilemmas. The rule exists in various forms in many of the world religions.)

Method One: Ethical Checklist

Twin Cities-based consultants, Doug Wallace and Jon Pekel, suggest the following ethical checklist (see Exhibit 2.7) to address ethical dilemmas. If necessary, revise your decision and action plan based on results of the test.

Method Two: Ten-Step Method of Decision Making

Wallace and Pekel also provide the following ten-step method (see Exhibit 2.8).

Method Three: Questions to Address Ethical Dilemmas

A list of questions may help managers address ethical dilemmas.

Ethics Tools: Training

The ethics program is essentially useless unless all staff members are trained about what it is, how it works, and their roles in it. The nature of the system may invite suspicion if not handled openly and honestly. In addition, no matter how fair and up to date a set of policies is, the legal system will often interpret employee behavior (rather than written policies) as de facto policy. Therefore, all staff must be aware of and act in full accordance with policies and procedures (this is true whether policies and procedures are for ethics programs or personnel management). This full accordance requires training about policies and procedures.

1. Orient new employees to the organization's ethics program during new-employee orientation.
2. Review the ethics management program in management training experiences.
3. Involving staff in review of codes is strong ethics training.
4. Involving staff in review of policies (ethics and personnel policies) is strong ethics training.
5. One of the strongest forms of ethics training is practice in resolving complex ethical dilemmas. Have staff use any of the three ethical-dilemma-resolution methods in this guidebook and apply them to any of the real-to-life ethical dilemmas also listed in this guidebook.

Exhibit 2.7   Method One: Ethical Checklist

Circle the appropriate answer on the scale; "1" = not at all; "5" = totally yes

1.	**Relevant Information Test.** Have I/we obtained as much information as possible to make an informed decision and action plan for this situation?	1	2	3	4	5
2.	**Involvement Test.** Have I/we involved all who have a right to have input or to be involved in making this decision and action plan?	1	2	3	4	5
3.	**Consequential Test.** Have I/we anticipated and attempted to accommodate for the consequences of this decision and action plan on any who are significantly affected by it?	1	2	3	4	5
4.	**Fairness Test.** If I/we were assigned to take the place of any one of the stakeholders in this situation, would I/we perceive this decision and action plan to be essentially fair, given all of the circumstances?	1	2	3	4	5
5.	**Enduring Values Test.** Does this decision and action plan uphold my/our priority enduring values that are relevant to this situation?	1	2	3	4	5
6.	**Universality Test.** Would I/we want this decision and action plan to become a universal law applicable to all similar situations, even to myself/ourselves?	1	2	3	4	5
7.	**Light-of-Day Test.** How would I/we feel and be regarded by others (working associates, family, etc.) if the details of this decision and action plan were disclosed for all to know?	1	2	3	4	5
8.	**Total Ethical Analysis Confidence Score.** Place the total of all circled numbers here.					

How confident can you be that you have done a good job of ethical analysis?

Source: Used with permission from copyright holders: Doug Wallace and Jon Pekel, Twin Cities-based consultants in the Fulcrum Group (651-714-9033; e-mail at jonpekel@atti.com). Do not copy without reference to copyright owners. Not to be used for commercial purposes.

6. Include ethical performance as a dimension in performance appraisals.
7. An excellent ethics trainer, Bill Goodman, Chief Human Resource Officer at Aveda, begins, "We start our training even in our job ads," then adds, "but the best trainer is the behavior of our leaders."[8]
8. Give all staff a copy of this free "Complete Guide to Ethics Management."

Exhibit 2.8 Method Two: Ten-Step Checklist

STEPS	NOTES		
	Alternative 1	Alternative 2	Alternative 3
1. What are the known FACTS in the situation?			
2. Who are the key STAKEHOLDERS, what do they value, and what are their desired outcomes?			
3. What are the UNDERLYING DRIVERS causing the situation?			
4. In priority order what ethical principles or operating values do you think should be upheld in this situation?			
5. Who should have input to, or be involved in, making this decision?			
6. List any alternative and action plans that would: (a) prevent or minimize harm to stakeholders (b) uphold the priority values for this situation (c) be a good solution to the situation			
7. Build a WORST-CASE SCENARIO for your preferred alternative to see how it affects the stakeholders. Rethink and revise your preferred alternative if necessary.			
8. Add a PREVENTIVE ETHICS component to your action plan that deals with the underlying drivers causing the situation listed in Step 3.			
9. Evaluate your chosen decision and action plan against the checklist on the reverse side.			
10. Decide and build an action plan, and implement and monitor it.			

Source: Used with permission from Copyright holders: Doug Wallace and Jon Pekel, Twin Cities-based consultants in the Fulcrum Group (651-714-9033; e-mail at jonpekel@atti.com). Do not copy without reference to copyright owners. Not to be used for commercial purposes.

NOTES

1. Frances Karamouzis, "A look at India for Offshore sourcing options," Research Note AV-18-8057, Gartner, Waterford, CT, July 29, 2003.
2. Source: Carter McNamara, MBA, PHD, available at www.managementhelp.org.
3. See the *Journal of Business Ethics*, 1992, 11: 391–399.
4. This list is the "Six Pillars of Character" developed by The Josephson Institute of Ethics, 310-306-1868.
5. Available at http://www.mapnp.org/library/ethics/teamvalu.htm.
6. Also see Samples of Corporate Codes of Ethics (Center for Applied Ethics) at http://www.ethics.ubc.ca/resources/business/codes.html.
7. Source: Professor Tom Cannon, "Corporate, Occupational and Management Codes: Issues and Challenges," White paper, The Centre for Business Relationships, Accountability, Sustainability & Society, Cardiff University, July 28, 2003, p. 13.
8. Interview of Bill Goodman by author Carter McNamara, San Francisco, 1998.

3

CHOOSING AN OFFSHORE VENDOR: A LOOK AT THE OFFSHORE MATURITY MODEL

The largest challenge of Offshore is not necessarily the execution of the project goals. The challenge of Offshore is proactive intelligent management of IT human resources across the organization, with an eye to organizational agility. This involves viewing resource management as a critical component of strategic positioning, just as important as market positioning or any other competitive strategy. Human resource management is elevated above operational management levels to the executive office, and is as much of a focus as any other strategic plan. Reflecting this new reality is the increasing number of "C" level positions, such as Chief Resource Office (CRO), positioned as organizationally peer to the CTO (Chief Technology Officer) or CEO (Chief Executive Officer).

In this chapter we look closely at the implications of vendor management for Offshore. As is typical of Offshore, many of the old principles in vendor management are turned upside down and inside out. Some of the topics we look at are:

- What are the differences between Offshore vendor and other IT consultant resource management?
- Organizational structure and span of control: Where does Offshore vendor management belong?
- What to look for in an Offshore vendor:
  – Automated RFP tools — do they work?
- Negotiating an Offshore vendor contract — Do's and Don'ts.

■ The Offshore maturity model — anticipating organizational Off-shore vendor needs over time.
■ Strategic view — integrating the Offshore vendor within an overall context of resource management.
■ Summary: Keys to success in Offshore vendor management.
■ And finally, an end note — looking ahead — the view from Gartner.

We now take a look at several illustrations of how this interesting topic lives and breathes within an actual corporate environment.

GROUND RULES: A SNAPSHOT OF THE CURRENT VENDOR MANAGEMENT CULTURE OF THE FORTUNE 100

Offshore for IT is usually limited to the Fortune 50 or Fortune 100. Why is Offshore generally limited to the larger firms? To date, Offshore is a volume business. Offshoring a percentage of the resources for an IT department of much less than 1000 individuals is not cost effective for the customer nor attractive to Offshore firms seeking to establish early, high-visibility credibility in the United States. The Co-Sourcing model usually limits Offshore starts with 10 percent of the IT department, up to a maximum of 30 percent, for concerns related to risk management security and preservation of intellectual capital. Most Offshore firms require at least 100 individuals' potential (after the pilot) to make the exercise worthwhile. This landscape may or may not be true of the future, but for today, it is relatively rare to find a medium or small firm engaging in Offshore for IT.

Roughly 95 percent (depending upon to which analyst firm you sub-scribe) of current IT Offshore is performed in India. We defer this very important topic to look more closely at country differences in Chapter Four.

Although there are many potential vendors, most well-established vendors in the Offshore service arena fall into one of two categories, India- or U.S.-based firms. The India-based Offshore firms are outlined in Chapter One, and have within the last five years moved from the unknown to relatively safe choices with an impressive list of Fortune 50 clientele. These India-based firms are generally listed in tiers, with Tier One vendors comprising a list of ten or so top firms, and Tier Two comprising the up-and-coming firms, who are generally less well established in the United States and have an even lower price point than Tier One vendors. The second category of vendors are U.S.-based, including Accenture, IBM, EDS, and others. These vendors are working hard to establish leadership in the Offshore arena, and are often the first choices for U.S.-based companies seeking a known quantity and relationship for these services.

What Are the Differences between Offshore and Other IT Consultant Resource Management?

The vast majority of Fortune 100 firms have an IT vendor management organizational structure that is very decentralized in terms of the decision making relative to hiring individuals, but centralized in terms of contractual relationships. This is because traditional IT consultant hiring has been, of necessity, a two-step process. First, the organization identifies and executes a central contract for consulting services. This has a variety of advantages, including volume pricing and enforcement of cross-organizational standards ranging from legal requirements to management reporting.

Once that set of IT service providers or vendors is identified and a contract is established, it is usually up to the individual hiring IT managers to screen and approve the specific IT consultants that are to be assigned to their particular project. For many large firms, it means that despite the centralized negotiation of contracts, there is such a panoply of diverse options for filling both individual as well as project consultant "slots" that the contracts may not have much significance in terms of actual revenue or hiring for the consulting firm. For most small- and medium-sized IT projects, at times even the large and highly visible ones, hiring decisions for the great majority of consultants occur at the sole discretion of the operational, program, or project manager directly responsible for application performance.

So, for example, a typical Fortune 50 firm has a relationship with one or more U.S.-based firms who aid with strategic planning as well as myriad IT services, and a range of smaller-sized consulting firms and individuals. A snapshot of most firms in the late 1990s, before the dot-com bust, would probably reveal hundreds and perhaps even thousands of contracts, with individuals, small boutique firms, medium size, large, and finally strategic firms that also may staff across the full IT skill spectrum. These latter usually cultivate many-year relationships with the CIO and other executives, and may follow a CIO from one job to another, or even help place them there. It is not uncommon for departments to cultivate special relationships with consulting companies (of any size) or individual consultants that are very centered upon long-term trust built over time with a particular individual, and that when that individual leaves, the new opportunities for additional consulting work leave with them.

It is also not uncommon for a particular department to have no visibility or information as to the specifics of utilization — where, for example, a particular consulting organization may be working across different departments. There is little to no incentive for the pragmatic, busy IT manager to take on the relative risk, real or perceived, of partnering with a new services partner. Thus, despite the size of the Fortune 100 firm, most use consultants within very distinct department, geographic, or other silos. The typical IT manager knows very little about cross-organization trends or utilization, and is simply focused on the success of the handful he or she is managing on behalf of the individual application suite.

Information on exactly how the consulting firm is used across these huge organizations is usually presented by the new potential partner only when vying for new business, as a way to show knowledge of the customer; once established, there is little emphasis in keeping track of the cross-organizational consultant relationship ups and downs. High-visibility wins and losses aside, there is usually a feeling of relative chaos alongside fierce and hidden competition across individual spheres of influence where the normal rules of business differ greatly from one department, or even project, to another. IT managers dig their heels in; the risk of job loss relative to bringing on a new consulting partner that does not work out is seen as higher than the relative benefits of trying new ways or saving incremental costs across the organization. IT consultant relationships are usually well entrenched, hidden, and most everyone likes it that way — until the true cost of those hidden relationships is revealed.

While we are painting a picture here that most IT members of large firms will recognize, note too that the culture of decision making by individual managers is completely upended by the Co-Sourcing Offshore model, which derives its savings from taking the decision making for individual team members from local technology managers. Launching an Offshore program usually means that some, if not most, managers who are used to driving these hiring decisions will now be opted out of the decision-making process. Why? Most Offshore contracts, especially with India-owned firms, tie achievement of goals (such as service-level agreements or internal customer satisfaction ratings) to compensation, or contract renewal, or other financial incentives. This has become a de facto standard, a tried-and-true way of selling the relatively unknown India-based firm to a new account. U.S.-based firms were, early on, loath to match those terms, although most of them now have adopted this practice for Offshore contracts.

IT relationships in large firms, as we have noted before, are typical pressure-cookers, involving endeavors of great organizational, political, technological, and business process complexity. IT serves the business, and frequently the perception of IT management is one of many demands, with little to no control or power to create a way to reasonably meet those demands. To many IT managers, taking away their last vestige of control — regarding who they bring on board from outside the organization to augment the skills on hand — elicits a sense of incredulity.

Much of that sense of disbelief in this new model, however, is based upon the paradigm of vendor management that is described above.

Although individual spheres of influence may appear to provide greater repeatability and reduced risk, related to trust built over many years between individuals representing the consultants and the hiring firm, in actuality this is extraordinarily inefficient and expensive. A case in point is the recent dramatic reduction in the costs associated with consultants in the post-dot-com boom. Many large firms continued to pay very high prices, with no reflection of the new market conditions, simply due to inertia. At times the consultants have been in place for many years, and have more organizational clout and engender more loyalty than employees. The sheer overhead of trying to reduce the cost of what is usually hundreds of individual consulting contracts makes it impractical for many firms to ensure that prices go down, as well as up, to reflect market conditions. The ability to ensure that the right resource is in place, and that the firm is not overpaying them or keeping them on due to political influence, is greatly diminished. Even if there is no bias due to these factors — and remember that these consultants are usually paid a premium for the privilege of dismissing them at hand when they are no longer needed — the lack of central tracking and the complexity of that tracking make it very difficult in practice to reduce the hourly rates of existing consultants, spread as they are throughout the individual spheres of influence.

The feeling of chaos and personal influence also contributes to a lack of standardized methodologies that plague many companies. When execution is a mish-mash of individuals and many firms, even if there is a firmwide standard that is supposedly adopted by the various external consultants, the actuality of creating that common interpretation and understanding is very challenging. Having a published methodology is not sufficient — years of training and fine tuning are usually required in creating an organizational culture truly reflecting the documented methodology. There are many keys to the effective use of technology life cycles or methodologies, but certainly one of them is an organizational IT culture that has a common view and understanding of the definition of deliverables and their overall flow within the project. For example, a programmer in Des Moines needs to define the process and the deliverables associated with "opportunity assessment" or "regression test" in the same way as his or her counterpart in California, or else these project peers are required to spend valuable time negotiating and clarifying exactly what is meant by process and execution. This is time that could otherwise be spent actually working on the project deliverables themselves rather than bantering back and forth about what they consist of, in what order they occur, how they connect with each other, and who's responsible.

This is exactly where many of the India-based firms excel, and the U.S. firms are still catching up. CMM and Six Sigma certifications aside, when there is simply no option to "drop by and chat" to reach a common ground, clarity of methodology becomes paramount. Establishment of a crystal-clear, organizationwide systems life cycle is the bread and butter of the India-based Offshore firms. It is also not something achieved overnight.

Offshore is known for creating fervent converts. It's a bit humbling, to say the least, because many IT managers pride themselves on the value of the resume review in establishing an appropriate team, and leaving that level of control to an unknown individual halfway around the world may seem utterly absurd. Yet the model works incredibly well, and frequently firms report that there is a level of consistency of delivery as well as a reduction in cost that just is not seen outside the Offshore Co-Sourcing model. This is due in large part to the deep and well-established methodology discipline that resides in the India-based Offshore firms. There is also a sense by these firms that failure is simply not an option — when projects do get in trouble, there are so many people resources thrown at them that the situation is reversed quickly.

The sense by these India-based firms that one high-profile failure will be extremely damaging is probably a realistic assessment. There are so many excellent firms, and fierce competition between them, and there is still such a level of distrust of Offshore and negative press waiting for a failed project poster child, that even though it is unlikely that the Offshore model itself would be permanently damaged at this point, a company reputation certainly could be. One high-visibility failure would probably be all it takes for many India-based firms to be off the "short list."

In summary, as is typical of Offshore, the principles of good vendor management are really turned upside down. First of all, the more centralized the vendor management function is, the better for the organization. There are many reasons for this, but the key one is pricing. Offshore vendor pricing varies dramatically with the total volume of Offshore resources. This is a critical factor limiting Offshore vendors to large Fortune 100 firms to date.

Second, it is critically important to work as centrally as possible to minimize this traditional two-step process. The most effective Offshore contracts have built in some sort of validation of service that is independent of the individuals assigned to do the work, usually based upon an SLA. These SLAs specify the minimum requirement for timing of problem resolution and other system maintenance functions. For new product or project development in IT, a fixed price deliverable plan is agreed upon prior to project start. For either type of effort, it is up to the Offshore vendor to manage risk. *Offshore is essentially executed via a fixed-priced contract, and because it is not feasible to interview the majority of team members located in India (certainly project managers and interfaces across teams may be interviewed and approved), the old vendor management paradigm just doesn't apply to Offshore.*

Finally, centralized management of Offshore supports increased discipline, and decreases the typical chaos relative to managing hundreds or even thousands of individual contractor contracts. Offshore is frequently a double "win" for large firms who utilize Offshore to replace many individual, high-priced consultants. Not only are the price points dramatically different, but also employee impact is nil, and the administrative overhead of managing those contracts is eliminated. An added bonus is the relative ease of creating methodology standards by reducing the overhead and other complexities associated with working with myriad consulting partners.

As we've touched on in earlier chapters, Offshore tends to be so very challenging not due to technical execution, but because it upsets and restructures existing organizational boundaries. Vendor management is one key area — and here, the stakes can be very high. Sorting out which of the several parallel vendor organizations are set up to manage Offshore in an area where they do not already have established relationships with IT managers can add to the overall difficulty of the internal positioning and selling of the Offshore program.

ORGANIZATIONAL STRUCTURE AND SPAN OF CONTROL

Where Does Offshore Vendor Management Belong? Or, to Mandate or Not to Mandate, Offshore Outsourcing?

A centralized project management office is a critical success factor to most organizations in implementing Offshore. Although we deal in depth with the Offshore PMO in later chapters, establishing the strength and breadth of the Offshore PMO is required, if for no other reason than many regulatory agencies (who notoriously in large part have not yet caught up with it) will in the future require one for risk oversight, management, and reporting.

Most of the members of the Offshore Interest Group have a dedicated Offshore PMO that serves as a more traditional PMO (in other words, is an "influencer" and center of knowledge and excellence, rather than direct power to implement such as Ted's group in Citigroup, where management bonuses are directly tied to usage of Offshore and other low-cost IT services).

As firms become more experienced with Offshore and see the success it engenders, there are two reactions. One, strangely enough, is to stop the growth of the program, maintain steady-state, and assess the impact on the organization moving forward, in preparation for a more strategic implementation. The other is to formalize the power of the Offshore PMO to have more clout than just to suggest, sell, and facilitate. Let's look at two organizational examples. Sometimes Offshore is perceived as such a threat that the program is kept to a minimum for purely political reasons — not every executive in IT is altruistic.

Ward Holland is the creator of the Offshore PMO at Wachovia, one of the nation's top regional banks. Ward "grew up" in banking, and is one of the reformed skeptics turned enthusiast when the first project he was dragged into going Offshore outshone all prior performance. Like many peers within the Offshore Interest Group, Ward found the toughest part of his job to be selling the concept internally, despite the fact that the back-office systems he moved Offshore provided better results in terms of consistency, reliability, and quality as well as a dramatic decrease in cost. Ward limited Offshore IT to new project development, feeling maintenance and support were too complex for the time being in regard to assuring security of the network and other factors.

Wachovia's PMO is structured as many are within the Offshore Interest Group. Although he has the support of senior management, when Wachovia was merging with a recent acquisition, the decision was made by his senior management team not to use Offshore consultants during the merger. Now that the merger is near completion, however, Ward is finding "his phone ringing off the hook."

The implication here is that Ward needs to find willing participants, and indeed that participation in the program is driven by the choice of the individual(s) responsible for the new project development. Ward's PMO serves as a center of excellence, and performs the functions listed in Exhibit 3.1.

In the context of this discussion, what is notable about the list above is what is missing. That is the ability to require a minimum level of program involvement (and therefore savings to the organization). Offshore is rather unique across most large organizations in that it is by far and away structured to be voluntary participation. There are only one or two

Exhibit 3.1 "Typical" Offshore PMO Functions

Vendor selection
Contract negotiation (shared with Legal and other functions)
Influence and internally sell the Offshore program
Establish centralized reporting to senior management
Educate organization on Offshore processes
Serve as focal point for communications, often focusing on cross-cultural education (introduction of one culture to the other)
Serve as focal point to minimize negative job impact on employees

members of the Offshore Interest Group that have Offshore PMOs empowered to do more than suggest, provide expertise, and, when appropriate, facilitate. What is interesting about Offshore is that the organizations new to Offshore, such as Wachovia, tend to go more tentatively. As organizations see the results of Offshore, the commitment becomes stronger and stronger.

Offshore is often singled out as a source of employee disgruntlement and concern. We treat this more fully in other chapters, but often when firms mature in Offshore back away from a mandate it is due to employee perceptions, fear that is fueled by the constant negative media coverage.

Ted's story in Chapter One shows another side of the Offshore coin. Citigroup has such a history with Offshore, and a comfort, that putting a mandate as part of the power of the Offshore PMO was perceived as the next logical step. Although there is still internal selling involved in Citigroup Offshore PMO, tying individual bonuses to the use of the "Low Cost Alternative" group means that IT managers come to the PMO looking for its services, rather than the PMO going to the managers looking for volunteers. The implications for cost savings are great — in an organization with many hundreds of consultants, if not more, there is generally no reason not to mandate Offshore once it becomes more well understood and accepted, especially if employee impact is minimized (i.e., impact to consultants not to employees). Then the efficiencies of methodology, the reduction in overhead, and elimination of the individual spheres of influence become additional plusses to the very significant cost savings.

Why would mature firms move from an influencing to a more empowered, centralized PMO with the power to mandate involvement in Offshore? If you recall, in the Citigroup example, a merge of cultures — some familiar with Offshore, others not — created a situation where some IT managers needed to be brought within the Citigroup norms very quickly. Citigroup decided not to make it optional, but also limited the numbers to roughly 10 percent of all resources, so there is significant individual discretion as long as the manager meets the minimum quota.

In the world of IT, with so many complexities requiring a daily balancing act, smart senior management is wisely loath to micro manage. Putting their hand in too often has burned most senior managers. IT culture, within organizations, is one in which individual leadership credibility is won one project at a time. The higher the visibility, the more complex and the more strategic an IT project, the more charismatic personalities seem to be a determinant of success and failure. Much of the import of having a charismatic leader for a complex IT initiative is the ability of that individual to use personal persuasiveness and force of personality to bring consensus to what would otherwise be a contested strategic aim or vision.

All this shows that "mandate" is generally not in the IT vocabulary. It will be interesting to see if the strength of the Offshore model will overcome that traditional reticence. Certainly some organizations will never fully embrace Offshore without the mandate. In our discussions on this topic in the Offshore Interest Group, many hold the opinion that the only way to fully experience the benefit of Offshore is through a mandated minimum such as Citigroup.

A final note on organizational structure and span of control — some organizations have seeded the Offshore PMO in the procurement wing of the organization rather than under IT vendor contract management. This is very challenging because many times procurement individuals are better versed at buying widgets than crafting contracts to manage people, never mind the extra subtlety required to negotiate an Offshore contract. Offshore is probably unique in IT vendor service management in that a centralized procurement function may serve equally well as a touchpoint — as long as there is an IT PMO along for the ride. Procurement serving the administrative and vendor negotiation function, and the PMO providing the meatier negotiation advice such as tying SLAs to performance, and transition of methodology, and so on, are in some ways the best of both worlds, because procurement may be more objective in their evaluations. We take a much deeper look at the role and functions of the Offshore PMO in Chapter 5.

WHAT TO LOOK FOR IN AN OFFSHORE VENDOR

We've touched on vendor management differences as they apply to Offshore in a variety of contexts. Below is a quick summary of the points relating to Offshore vendor management. The bottom line is that the old vendor management model does not apply to Offshore in many ways. Why?

■ Today IT vendor management usually centers on a hiring model focusing on skills evaluation of individual team members through resume review, and phone or in-person interviews. Individual-by-individual hiring is still part of some Offshore programs, but most experienced firms have abandoned this practice as time consuming and not really relevant to the success of the program. This is due to the fixed price nature of the typical Offshore contract, the general excellence of the services provided, and the commitment of Offshore services firms to work through any problems very aggressively in order to maintain customer satisfaction. Although this is the very point that many IT managers will fight hardest against, *the reality is that Offshore works, and the IT applications that most IT managers consider so very special and difficult are in fact pretty routinely learned and executed via Offshore consultants.*

■ The other aspect of vendor management that is difficult to fully process and comprehend is the culture of operational excellence of the leading Offshore firms, frequently resulting from years of investment. As one measure of excellence, note the relative CMM maturity index. Most Offshore firms are at least two levels (out of a possible five) beyond their U.S.-based customers. This is the reason that visits to India are so powerful — the discipline associated with a common culture of excellence is almost palpable in these firms' modern campuses. Offshore firms have leveraged the typical highly educated and technically skilled labor pool in India, and achieved a kind of trump in their creation of a corporate environment with a level of consistent IT productive excellence spanning cultures and geographies. Although the U.S.-based vendors are working to achieve CMM levels, to date they tend to have the certifications limited within their individual Offshore service centers and have not achieved them across the entire organization.

■ *There is frankly little difference in services quality across the leading dozen or so Tier One India-based firms.* They are all excellent as long as they are deployed appropriately. As Fortune 50 and above mature in Offshore, the service relationship increasingly becomes an interchangeable commodity. We explore this concept of the maturity model relative to Offshore below.

If the old model is no longer relevant, what *is* material in the selection of an Offshore vendor? *The length of Offshore contracts is much longer than the typical consulting contract* (usually a minimum of two years, and more frequently three years or more). The upfront infrastructure costs relative to implementing Offshore are a strong contributing factor. As a result, the Offshore vendor is more of a marriage, as compared to the typical vendor relationship. The implications of the length of the connection, coupled with the general excellence of the India-based Offshore providers that are usually better at IT execution all around, is that the typical checklist-based evaluation is the cart dragging the horse.

Rather than drowning in the details, focus on the nature of the relationship and the general organizational fit in choosing an Offshore vendor — can you "live" with this vendor for the next three years? Although the quality of service execution of India-based Offshore firms tends to be relatively equal (excellent), the on-site representatives ensuring quality of services can vary — in terms of their fit to your particular organization's culture and needs. One area where the firms can show differences in capability, for example, is in executive management-level communications — not in terms of management reporting, but in the more delicate face-to-face executive interface. Generally, the higher the ranking of the India Offshore provider, the more adept at interfacing with higher management. Piloting a small project as a means of testing the relationship waters is never a bad idea.

For risk mitigation, choosing vendors that easily allow you to establish a geopolitical spread is a key component of your strategy. Let's be clear what we mean by risk here for Offshore. In the Co-Sourcing model adopted by most organizations, the data and systems physically reside in the United States, and the "investment" in knowledge transfer is the primary risk. Although the risk of war has been ever-present in the last 15 plus years that U.S. companies have Offshored in India, this has not stopped the large growth nor affected the projections for future growth. Geopolitical risk is perceived as part of the "price" that Offshore engenders. One major bank, for example, routinely moves documentation (systems knowledge), data, and application systems across five locations — two in India, one in the Philippines, and two in Europe — three times a day. Choosing a vendor that has an established base in several global locations can simplify this key success factor for Offshore. Look for a balance of Offshore firms showing demonstrable experience across governmental relationships, hiring of the local labor force, visa processing, legal, taxation, currency, and technical/communications infrastructure across a variety of countries as well as regions in India. Don't overlook the fact that risk across India varies significantly with the region. India is a large country, and Northern and Southern India, as an example, are likely to have different risk rankings across different points.

> *Although sweating the details between vendor 2 and 3 in the list may not be a critical success factor, the large decisions are not necessarily obvious. Deciding on the number of service providers can be a challenge in Offshore. The smaller the number of vendors the larger the volume discount, and the lower the complexity due to administrative overhead. The larger the number of vendors the easier it is to balance risk mitigation — and to maintain lower prices due to vendor competition. Finding a good balance can be tricky, especially at first.*

Taking a specific example, assume an organization with 1000 FTE (Full-Time Employees) in IT. The natural limit to Offshore represents roughly 300 FTE maximum. Assume an initial target of roughly 100 FTE for the first set of contracts. As leader of the PMO, the ideal would be to expose the organization to three levels of service — a Tier One India vendor, a Tier Two India vendor (to experience the lower price and consequent lower level of acclimatization to the U.S. culture), and a U.S.-based firm for its strength in strategic analysis and existing relationships among the management team. Each type of firm has its strengths and weaknesses, but it is a very important early advantage — if the volume supports it — to have an experience with each type of vendor to ensure the most knowledgeable and flexible vendor deployment moving forward.

A final point is to note that although the culture of operational excellence, based upon an organizationwide methodology that is the result of millions of dollars and years of investment, is not so easily replicated by U.S.-based firms, it is also true that the India-based firms are not so easily going to establish a presence in providing executive-level strategic advice and counsel. Although the India-based firms like to speak as if nothing is beyond their limitation, to date, the services have been volume business and coding/testing/support in focus. It will be interesting to see how these shift over the coming years, and how these large giants sort out the marketplace. Exhibit 3.2 outlines the strengths and weakness of the different vendor categories.

AUTOMATED RFP TOOLS: DO THEY WORK?

Although it is all well and good to advise to the contrary, it is also clear that 99 percent of the typical Fortune 50 firms will indeed focus on the vendor details, and ignore the true challenges and harder decisions such as strategic resource planning, when initiating their first Offshore program. These activities are what passes for good practice in vendor management in most large firms, and gaining agreement for Offshore is difficult enough without also taking on recasting the process of initiation. A good way to limit the cost and complexity of what is essentially a relatively irrelevant exercise in any real detail — comparing in detail the top India-based firms in terms of capability — is to purchase an automated RFP tool to collect the details. This way, valuable learning time (or consulting dollars) is not spent in sifting sand when it first is important to look at the size and position of the beach.

What can you expect from these automated RFP tools? Questionnaires are published and accessed via a secure Web site, and data collected by responding to those questions. Although time consuming to respond on the vendor's part, most tools have nifty and efficient reports that allow the user to analyze the results very easily based upon a variety of criteria such as geographic locations, specific applications or industry experience, average level of education of their employees, and all the other due diligence factors that make up an Offshore vendor profile. Just don't make

Exhibit 3.2   What Are the Relative Strengths and Weaknesses of the Different Types of Vendors?

Vendor Type	Strengths	Weaknesses
U.S.-based/ Big Four	Customer political connections	Lack of CMM/process excellence
	Executive interface	Harder to get best of Offshore labor pool
	Known quantity/familiar	Account leadership usually doesn't have direct Offshore experience
	Strategic thinkers	Can use undue influence in staffing decisions
	Perceived as "safe"	More expensive/less capable at coding/testing and similar low-end IT services
Tier One	CMM/process excellence	Cultural differences impede strategy efforts
	Inexpensive	May be ineffective in direct executive interface
	Coding/testing/ support	May be perceived as threat or unknown by IT rank and file
Tier Two	Same strengths and weakness as Tier One, but less expensive, and less able to interface with executives. The lower the Tier, the less expensive, and the more tactical the skillset. Most large firms experienced in Offshore use Tier Twos for their coding, testing, and support needs because they already have existing processes in place for executive interface, strategy, and management reporting.	

the mistake of deciding on your vendor (or seriously limiting your vendor choices) via these factors. Take the time to meet with the Offshore vendors in small groups with key individuals and see what kinds of organizational communications synergies (or lack of) occur; without exception, all the leading Offshore firms specialize in rapid learning and execution across a broad variety of industries and applications. The value of the overall culture of learning an Offshore vendor brings, rather than the specific experience in their industry or application suite, generally becomes more important over time, due to the general level of excellence in execution of the Offshore firms.

Although we delve into this in greater detail in Chapter Four, an historical illustration relating to the flexibility and abilities of the India-based Offshore firms may be helpful here. The time period that established beyond the shadow of a doubt the reliability of the Offshore model were the years before 2000, during Y2K. Y2K involved, as most readers know, the changing of the hard-coded date checks in software — code that evaluated the correctness of the year as starting with "19xx" instead of "20xx" as is required relative to the new century. Most of the Y2K code was written in COBOL, the most prevalent business language, on mainframe computers.

There simply were not enough mainframe COBOL programmers, so Offshore entered the mainstream. What is not generally well understood, however, is that most of the computer infrastructure that existed throughout India was established well after the mainframe era, in the 1980s and 1990s. These computers were mostly UNIX-based, and this is still the typical computer found in Indian classrooms and businesses. Most Indian nationals had never seen COBOL, or a mainframe computer, in their lives.

How could we hire Indians, by the thousands, to come and help us in a very complex language, computer system, and operating system they did not know? And how could they be so successful? The reason is revealed by a look at India itself. Within the culture of India, technical knowledge is more highly prized than any other, equivalent to the medical profession here in the United States. Every son and daughter wants to be a computer scientist as the most revered profession, and starts at a very early age to learn skills, drilling for hours at a time in math and science before school well before our equivalent to high school.

We were, and still are, essentially hiring the equivalent of Masters-level engineers to do our coding for us. These Indian workers could easily take home and learn mainframe technology — the languages, the operating systems, and all of the other aspects relating to mainframe COBOL — in a weekend. The equivalent U.S. worker — not a master's-level engineer in knowledge — would probably take much longer for that same level of learning. The typical U.S. customer has yet to come to terms with what we are really "buying" when we contract for Offshore skills in India, or understand the general level of skills that the average technology worker can demonstrate, for so little relative recompense.

This story is one of many that illustrate then, how outmoded the focus is on evaluating the details that distinguish these firms. All of the top India-based firms hire these outstanding workers, and they are all capable of executing whatever challenges we give them — because they have been training for just such an opportunity since the tender age of seven or eight. We delve more into the particular culture of India in Chapter Four.

NEGOTIATING THE OFFSHORE VENDOR CONTRACT: DO'S AND DON'TS

The Offshore Vendor Contract has several areas where they differ from the typical contract.

■ *Length of contract*: Due to the investment in getting Offshore up and running, many customers lean towards a minimum two-year, usually three-year, contract with Offshore vendors. These may become smaller over time, due to the fact that most firms new to Offshore are dependent upon the Offshore service providers for a great deal of knowledge, not to mention management reporting capability, as they get their first Offshore PMO up and running.

■ *Expense handling*: Most consultant-related expenses are folded into the hourly rate. As is usual with any IT consulting contract calling out different levels of cost, the hourly rate is based upon the category of skill and experience the individual consultant represents. Usually there are three to five categories, where differences in education, role, and experience lend themselves to different pricing. All other expenses, including professional training, cost of promotions and transferring in new individuals to replace those being promoted, on-site security administration, and so on, are normally included in the hourly rate for the India-based company. One major India-based Offshore firm, for example, has only one expense that is listed separately — not included in the hourly rate. This is round-trip airfare related to bringing the consultants over from India for the knowledge transfer period. For U.S.-based companies, on the other hand, associated expenses traditionally have been separately billed, either with a per diem (daily set limit) or according to other preset guidelines. This can make it difficult to compare actual costs across vendors. If possible, request that expenses be part of the hourly rate for all vendors, including the U.S.-based firms providing Offshore services, as it makes for much less effort in endless validation of receipts and the like, as well as comparing vendor price/performance. The cost of administering out-of-pocket expenses for dozens of consultants, even with a per diem, can be surprisingly high.

■ *Typical price ranges* can be anywhere from $15 per hour Offshore to twice that for more specialized coding resources. The $15+ can be compared to internal resources, which are usually at least $70 per hour (loaded with benefits) and may easily be three times that in large U.S. cities when costs for expensive office space are included. On-site resources from Offshore firms are usually 50 to 70 percent of the typical on-site consultant's cost. For the handful of consultants that reside in the United States permanently as the "Onshore" contingent of the Offshore program, these may be anywhere from 50 to 70 percent of the typical hourly rate of U.S.-based firms. Anecdotally and unsurprisingly, those members of the Offshore Interest Group who had more than one vendor seemed to have prices on the lower end of the spectrum. However, because virtually every firm was saving millions of dollars a year through Offshore, the relative benefit of looking at competitive pricing was overshadowed by other concerns. As an example, one very large insurance company, in particular, established a vendor strategy in which only one Tier Two vendor provided all services. Their executive leadership decided to have that firm totally committed as one of their only large customers, the proverbial big fish in a small pond, rather than deal with relatively less-committed service partners. This, in turn, may open up other risk factors (i.e., the wisdom of going with just one Offshore provider due to risk related to financial stability, for example). Thus, there may be factors, such as risk management, that may play a relatively large role in Offshore, offsetting emphasis on pure price.

■ *Fixed price*: India-based Offshore firms, especially when they were breaking into large Fortune 50 firms for the first time, made the relationship attractive by taking on most of the financial risk associated with these services. What does fixed price actually mean within IT Offshore? Usually, there is no impact on hourly rate as long as the Offshore services provider meets objective performance criteria. These criteria are usually in several categories:

  – *Service-level agreements*: For maintenance and support of applications, SLAs specify the turnaround time for fixes associated with different levels of systems priority. As an example, high-availability or high-priority systems may specify a solution workaround within a matter of hours, minutes, or even seconds; for lower-priority or background systems that run in batch mode, the acceptable time to respond to a problem report with a fix may be hours or days.

  – *Project delivery*: New systems development usually means the layout of a specific timetable, and achievement of deliverables according to quality and timeliness standards. Quality checks may include interim code reviews with formal acceptance signatures, and other forms of checkpoint, as well as the typical unit, regression, and systems interactions testing throughout the system's life cycle.

  – *Resource management*: Because the services provided by Offshore firms are only as good as the individuals providing them, it is not unusual for contracts to specify quality measures relative to resource management. These look at the workers' frequency of training, certifications, overall level of experience, and in particular, measures relating to staff turnover. Although most India-based Offshore firms include expenses relating to staff turnover as their contractual and financial responsibility — for example, by introducing a team member at no charge that mirrors the training of the employee leaving or being promoted for a sufficient time so there is no noticeable impact — a high staff turnover can be indicative of other more subtle issues in the way that the Offshore firm is managing. High staff turnover may mean the Offshore vendor is not keeping up with peers relative to salaries, benefits, or overall reputation. These are usually a point of investment and pride for all Tier One India-based firms, however, in dealing with Tier Two firms with less financial resources, adding objective studies of average salary per worker education and skill/experience level may be helpful to include in the formal contract. Beware here, too, not to make an assumption that dealing with the top U.S.-based firms means they have access to the best Offshore resources. The ability for even well-known U.S. firms to attract Offshore resources may vary widely in different countries. One frequently mentioned perception by locals, for example, is that there is a relatively low ceiling via which they can professionally grow as Offshore contributors, whereas the sky's the limit in native-owned firms.

– *Infrastructure ownership*: Most firms clearly delineate what is their responsibility via network and other infrastructure. Usually Offshore customers are responsible for maintenance and other network costs up to a single hub, beyond which the vendor (India- or U.S.-based) is responsible for the network infrastructure to the Offshore country. There is more subtlety than meets the eye here, however, as network throughput via these large trunks may be based upon a set of other customers with very different needs in terms of speed and throughput. This is one area where a pilot can be very helpful, because network access has so much complexity associated with it, and with so many variables that actual performance is truly the only ultimately reliable test. It is not uncommon for the network infrastructure costs to accrue to roughly 10 percent of the original savings anticipated by Offshore. So that, for example, a typical large firm will anticipate a 30 percent overall reduction of costs for Offshore, but 5 to 10 percent of those savings may be wiped out by the network costs, resulting in an overall reduction of 20 to 25 percent instead of 30 percent. Careful inspection and actual piloting of network performance, showing the actual interaction between the customer and the service provider's network, is the only way to determine whether the additional costs are even higher (in the case that the standard infrastructure provided by the Offshore vendor does not meet the throughput or other requirements of the Offshore applications). In addition, it may be somewhat challenging to incorporate Offshore representatives into the firm's enterprisewide e-mail and calendaring systems. At times, fast and reliable download and review of documents outside of the typical application coding and maintenance is most affected by real-time network performance.

– *Risk management*: Risk management is an area of much confusion. Certainly it is important that the Offshore vendors show a capability related to the typical Disaster Recovery Plan, including a set of fail-over hardware facilities (if that is relevant). The best risk mitigation strategy is to spread knowledge transfer learning across several different locations in India, and across other countries. As such, these are issues beyond the individual contract. It may be prudent to put in a clause requesting that if the service vendor changes strategy by removing itself from a country, that the customer has at least a year's notice.

– *Financial risk management*: Most IT managers will confirm that avoidance of delay is the biggest aspect of keeping IT costs down. Most if not all costs relative to IT project development and maintenance are about keeping the project on schedule. It does no good to have the hourly rate diminished, even dramatically, if the length of the project or the time on maintenance tasks extends accordingly. There are several relatively subtle sources of potential cost and delay that are unique to Offshore, discussed next in this list.

– *Knowledge transfer*: One of the biggest logistical challenges is the need to train Offshore personnel on the firm's systems. This is usually called Knowledge Transfer, and literally involves the Offshore resources shadowing the current systems personnel, sometimes for as long as 12 to 16 weeks. This may be delicate, to say the least, in terms of employee relations, cross-cultural communications, and employee satisfaction if job security remains uncertain. Clear communications and ethical management of employee opportunities are of paramount importance here. There is nothing quite so bitter as the employee writing a newspaper about having to train the person that will eventually replace her. Avoiding that overt cruelty is clearly an ethical goal of most Offshore programs. Due to these considerations, and the cost implications of the length of the shadow learning period, executing Knowledge Transfer may be perceived as so difficult that it may become a barrier to fair consideration of alternative Offshore vendors at the end of the initial Offshore contract.

However, this would be a mistake. There are many Offshore vendors who would make the investment in Knowledge Transfer to win new business, so no customer needs to live with an unsatisfactory service provider for long.

- It is important to note that Knowledge Transfer, which we deal with in far more depth in Chapters Four and Five, is a significant added cost, in that those employees training the Offshore personnel have quite a bit of their time allocated to the Knowledge Transfer process. Costs relative to Knowledge Transfer are one of the key reasons that the Offshore Programs show an average breakeven point at well over 6 months, sometimes up to 18 months, because resource costs are literally doubled for the period of Knowledge Transfer. What's the impact on the contract? Identify the potential roadblocks for staying on schedule for Knowledge Transfer and, at a minimum, structure the contract to share those risks. These are explained in greater detail below, and include potential delays related to vendor consents, visa processing, employee turnover (from Offshore vendor as well as inhouse employees), infrastructure challenges, and regulatory roadblocks. Of course, in the overall scheme of things, it bears repeating that the greatest barriers to moving forward in Offshore invariably are not these factors, but the lack of preparedness to address upfront strategic resource planning across the organization. More pragmatically, the contract should clearly specify who is responsible for all types of costs relating to Knowledge Transfer. Citigroup, in particular, manages Knowledge Transfer very tightly, and avoids what Ted calls the "learn while you burn" syndrome by carefully allocating fixed price and time allotments to Knowledge Transfer. This may not be practical for the firm new to Offshore, however, there should be at least an outer limit on time and knowledge — verifiable by some measure, preferably objective — expected by the end of that time period.

- *Vendor consents:* Unless the third-party software contracts in the firm already include provisions for Offshore, this may be a roadblock to the start of Knowledge Transfer and therefore to the start of the Offshore Program. The law is on the software vendors' side in terms of deciding whether the existing software licenses are applicable to Offshore consultants or limited to direct employees. Delay means added costs. The Offshore vendors should be able to provide you with a list of vendors known to be more difficult than others. Establishing an Offshore pilot with a software vendor that readily agrees to Offshore can buy you valuable time to work through the issues with other software vendors. In my personal experience of management Offshore, it was a long six months before the majority of vendor consents were achieved, with a handful requiring a significant outlay in cash. This is because any time legal departments must somehow get together to agree within large corporations, time moves slowly. The great majority of vendor consents, however, are not exploited as "revenue opportunities" and are resolved within the first three months. The primary point here is to ensure that the timing of these consents doesn't contribute unnecessarily to the overall cost of the program by taking the PMO by surprise. As far as the contract goes, there should be some flexibility in the delineation of the actual projects included in the Offshore program to account for unforeseen vendor consent issues.

– *Visa processing*: As Offshore becomes more and more popular, and travel to the United States by nonnationals comes under increasing scrutiny, yesterday's informal governmental relationships easing visa restrictions are becoming harder and harder to establish. Delays are increasing across the board as this book is being written. The larger Offshore firms deal with these by having a pool of ever-ready candidates on hand; some are better at managing these pools than others. It is important to put maximum acceptable visa processing time periods and expectations in the contract, and to specify the vendor will have a flexible approach to staffing, in order to stay on track for the Offshore program. My personal experience is this is where the U.S.-based vendors, with their traditional emphasis on the skills and hiring of individuals rather than competencies, can add significant costs and delays to the Offshore program.

– *Management reporting:* It may be surprising to see a passive activity, reporting of program results, in the list relating to financial cost management. However, the Offshore program is frequently so beleaguered in terms of popular understanding that it is critically important to get accurate, easily understood, and widely disseminated results out quickly. Then the general negative buzz dies down to reality — not all jobs are disappearing, Offshore works and works well, and for most workers, the opportunities for skills enhancement and advancement within IT are stronger than ever before. It is important to have clearly stated, within the vendor contract, the role and expectations regarding management reporting of program results, with timeliness and due dates defined up front. It is not a bad idea to specify to vendors the role they need to play in shoring up the new Offshore PMO, until that structure is fully formed, and to be responsible for all management statistics in a weekly report until the Offshore PMO can take on that responsibility.

- *Regulatory requirements related costs*: Because regulatory agencies are in their infancy in terms of requirements for Offshore, it is important to build into the contract some wording that requires a fair division of financial responsibility if reporting or network security requirements change significantly during the terms of the contract.
- *Intellectual capital ownership*: As is standard in any vendor contract, language preserving competitive advantage through confidentiality is important.

IMPORTANT LEGAL NOTE: A comprehensive review of all software contracts for legal language relating to Offshore Outsourcing, and a firmwide policy requiring this language as a part of all standard contracts signed in the future, is highly recommended. Beginning this review and establishing this policy, perhaps with expert legal help on retainer, while the vendors are being selected or the Offshore Pilot is unfolding can save a great deal of time and effort later in the program, and serve as a reliable guide for eliminating immediate pilot options.

THE OFFSHORE MATURITY MODEL: ANTICIPATING VENDOR MANAGEMENT FOR THE ORGANIZATION MATURE IN OFFSHORE

As firms gain experience in Offshore, the almost fearful dependency on vendors tends to evaporate. Three to five years' experience in Offshore seems to be the magic number — somewhere in that time period, the controversy and fear relating to employee perception seem to become much more reality-based (if handled ethically and with appropriate communications).

What are the functions that need to be shifted from vendor support to customer control — usually the Offshore PMO — as soon as practical?

- Management reporting: For obvious reasons, it is not a good practice for vendors to produce (as opposed to contribute to) evaluative reports of their own work. Yet this is one of the more challenging aspects for firms new to Offshore to implement in a comprehensive way. Ideally, the following content is included in an interactive tool or report. This minimal information is available by project, ideally with summary rollup capability:

- Team membership by project
- Percent Offshore/Onshore by project
- Team turnover by project
- For new development
  - Project deliverables schedule and on time/late status
  - Project quality measures
- For maintenance and support
  - Description of service level agreement
  - Level of attainment of SLAs (percentage)
- Financial costs planned versus actual by project
  - Hourly actual versus planned costs
  - Vendor consent project-specific costs
  - Distributed costs from program (networking infrastructure, PMO costs, legal costs, risk management costs)
- Strategic importance of project and where it fits within overall IT plan

Although the field is new, it is easy to anticipate that there eventually will be myriad tools helping to provide these kinds of interactive reporting and monitoring capability. For the present, there are few options to developing this capability inhouse, which is difficult and time consuming. Usually a three-year window is required to fully understand the implications of Offshore and the strategic advantage it can provide, and to fine tune the reporting to focus on those key factors.

- *Build, Operate, Transfer:* Many firms, having braved Offshore and won the battle, so to speak, are ready to go to the next step and eliminate the middle-man. Several firms in the Offshore Interest Group have successfully negotiated Offshore and are ready to try it for themselves, especially in less technically complex areas such as call center operations, which are frequently outsourced anyway. Build, Operate, Transfer means engaging with other firms that set up Offshore operations only to finally transfer ownership. Unlikely as it may seem at first, many firms are confident enough to move to this operating model within four years of initiating Offshore.
- *Risk management:* This area is discussed more in Chapter Seven, but oversight by a vigorous PMO is recommended to ensure an updated and effective risk mitigation strategy.
- *Methodology:* Offshore vendors, especially the India-based service providers, are much more disciplined and ahead of the curve in terms of methodology and discipline as evidenced by their superior CMM and Six Sigma ratings. It is important to manage those

differences proactively and to utilize these capabilities to raise the overall competency of the organization. Frequently, eliminating hundreds of individual consultants and replacing them with Off-shore vendors can aid in helping to create a common approach to methodology. It is important, despite the advantage in culture that vendors bring, for the PMO or equivalent to remain fully in charge of the process of Offshore as it relates to methodology. This topic is discussed in detail in Chapter Five. No IT organization can remain vendor-neutral while essentially allowing the vendor to drive the process — this is one of the key responsibilities of the Offshore PMO.

The Offshore Maturity Model is a theory developed as a result of many conversations with Offshore PMO leaders. The theory is a simple one — as firms gain experience and confidence in the Offshore model, their dependency on vendor know-how diminishes, and price/performance becomes paramount. Thus, when first embarking on Offshore, customer firms require a great deal of support and advice to realize the vision. Advice and counsel on management reporting, network architecture, knowledge transfer, and the best way to approach a difficult vendor consent agreement — all of these are needed and appropriate.

After the first three years, often sooner, the mechanics of the Offshore program become rather rote. The management reporting is in place, the knowledge transfer process is old hat, the network up and running, vendor consents achieved or abandoned, and the risk management program implemented. What many firms tend to do then is to Build, Operate, Transfer and go into business for themselves. Simultaneously, many start looking at Tier Two firms who offer a better price point but are often a bit rough around the edges. These Tier Two firms provide a sort of "no frills" skills support, often because they are so thinly staffed, or simply inexperienced in interfacing with executives, or both. But the services the best of them provide are excellent, as usual, and if a company no longer needs the extended support to make Offshore work, these Offshore skills truly become a commodity. It will be interesting to see if the Offshore Maturity Model indeed is predictive of how the industry will mature over the next five to seven years, which represents the timeframe in which most large firms should reach this level of experience. A recent member of the Offshore Interest Group described a process in which an online RFP, conducted after the initial Offshore contracts expired, resulted in roughly a 20 percent decrease in overall costs. This involved both the addition of new vendors, as well as the reduction in price for some existing vendors.

STRATEGIC VIEW: INTEGRATING THE OFFSHORE VENDOR WITHIN AN OVERALL CONTEXT OF RESOURCE MANAGEMENT

What are the key conceptual points to moving beyond a tactical approach to resource management of IT talent? If the India-based firms have taught us anything, it is the value of establishing a truly disciplined corporate culture of technology execution — with all of the investment that implies — in corporatewide standards touching upon everything from master data in reporting systems to training and mentoring of new talented recruits. Of course, discipline starts at the top.

Looking back at the Infosys interview, it is striking that even with a young and vigorous management team of many talents and a well-established working relationship, it is the CEO and his team who are directly teaching the next layer of up and coming leadership. Although this is changing, many large U.S. firms still cling to the CEO as celebrity, with the ego and the protection of personal political standing this implies. Direct mentorship of new executive leadership, involving orderly planning of management succession years in advance, while not unknown in the United States, is not the norm. To put it bluntly, as is typical of most strategic IT opportunities requiring discipline and creativity, Offshore has demonstrated that there is little room for ego brandishing.

In the recent past, discipline meant avoiding the "cowboy" technologists who cut corners in IT methodology with impunity, establishing bases of power based upon the fact that they were the only ones who could unravel their own "spaghetti code." In the delicate balance between personalities and legitimate need for charismatic leadership, the IT culture is one of personal credibility, won one hard-fought project success at a time. *It may be the very balance between the charismatic individual as represented by the old paradigm, and the execution of the invisible and interchangeable group as represented by Offshore, that represents the true underlying cultural struggle — and future direction — of IT.*

CMM and Six Sigma preach standardization and the unstated elimination of the charismatic individual. Individual spheres of influence are replaced by organizationwide methods and centralized processes more akin to the predictability and measures of software as factory piecework than the result of creative hacking. Elimination of the IT cowboy culture has its advantages — in addition to the increase in timeliness, reliability, and quality of overall IT effort, there is more time available to establish true partnership with the internal customers or business counterparts. The key challenge of strategic IT sourcing is not just identifying the right mix of Offshore, regular consultants, employees, and critical skillsets for the future — it is actively creating an organization that is seamless in its ability to understand and leverage the IT advantages that Offshore brings across the business environment, by finally enabling communication and joint creativity.

Although creativity between IT and business remains the realm of individual relationships, the newest generation of business leads are now computer literate and can be expected to actively understand the value and role of technology. Freeing up talented project, program, and relationship managers from the difficulties inherent in charismatic as opposed to mechanistic IT development has the ironic result of allowing more strategic leveraging of technology across the organization. This is the true opportunity inherent in Offshore. Here is a summary list of other considerations in overall vendor and staffing management for Offshore. All of these support the underlying principle of strengthening standards — hiring, methodology, and management — across IT.

- *Eliminate the administrative overhead* with multiple contracts of single consultants. The costs of managing multiple legal contracts, tracking expenses, and the consequent chaos can be minimized by replacing the many with a handful of Offshore contracts, all with these included in the base hourly consultant price. *Create an organizational mechanism to ensure the consulting fees reflect downward market prices* and don't remain artificially high due to simple inertia or complexity.
- Create a center of excellence, *a dedicated related PMO focused on the investment and training to achieve a strong, organizationwide, common methodology.* This is one area in which the India-based Offshore firms can really be of help. Ideally, each IT employee should feel as if the Offshore program enables her to grow in ways that were unfeasible before, by eliminating the more rote and repetitive tasks associated with IT.
- *Clearly communicate the core skills that IT employees are encouraged to develop* as part of the new IT organization. These are generally related to the "softer" skills such as relationship management, program and project management, methodology development, and IT architecture design. *Also communicate the natural limit of the size of the Offshore program,* as made prudent by preservation of intellectual capital as well as security concerns relating to exposure to customer data.
- *Commit a percentage of the savings from Offshore to create a soft landing* (substantial retraining) for long-term, loyal employees unable to move successfully to adopt the skills required by the new organization. Remember, all employees are watching how

these individuals are treated on behalf of the firm. Establishing an ethical and fair business practice standard may be the most important one of all.

▪ Structure the entry into Offshore, once the initial learning curve is successfully negotiated, so that IT managers have many choices — Nearshore, Offshore, and even dedicated permanent Onshore resources from Offshore firms. Rather than have the PMO fight to win everyone over with the most extreme form of Offshore — moving the application or maintenance effort to India or other remote locations — structure the program so that the "Nearshore" locations such as Canada and Mexico are considered part of the Offshore win. As these IT managers gain experience, they can move their areas of responsibility to remote Offshore locations over time.

Most important, in industries where technology is a factor of competitive advantage, establish a "C" level position, such as Chief Resource Officer, that focuses purely on the skills mix and incubation of a positive technology organizational culture.

SUMMARY: KEYS TO SUCCESS IN OFFSHORE VENDOR MANAGEMENT

▪ *Balance* across three factors: (a) the number of Offshore vendors to maximize the volume discount (less vendors), (b) country/geographic risk (more vendors), and finally (c) the encouragement of pricing competition (more vendors).

▪ Know and *leverage the strengths of the different vendor types*. The lower the "tier," the lower the price is, and generally the more tactical the skillset. Anecdotal evidence points to higher pricing in U.S.-based firms, but these may be useful as part of the vendor mix nonetheless with their measure of perceived safety and existing relationships among IT managers.

▪ Be careful about not allowing any vendor, however effective in other strategy service roles, to drive by default the organization's overall strategic decisions relative to IT sourcing by handing them the director's role in Offshore. Ensure that employee jobs are not jeopardized as a result of long-term, high-level consulting relationships that position their consulting revenue over the rights of long-term and loyal employees as the number of Onshore coding and testing jobs shrink as a result of Offshore.

▪ For risk mitigation, choosing *vendors that easily allow you to establish a geopolitical spread* is a key component of your strategy.

- Contracts for Offshore have unique components, and expert advice may be a good investment for the first one.
- *Offshore vendor relationships are more of a long-term commitment than a resume review exercise*, and evaluating the soft factors such as organizational fit is much more important than the typical checklist evaluation in vendor selection.

APPENDIX: THE VIEW FROM GARTNER

Frances Karamouzis is a leading knowledge source from Gartner consulting, frequently referenced in articles on Offshore.

Frances spends her time advising large firms on the Offshore process, and during her frequent trips to India, looks with a discerning eye to report on the newest trends and patterns. Originally from a Big Five consulting firm, Frances is one of the leading breed of new consultants able to winnow through the typical marketing hype on Offshore. Frances has a bachelor's degree in international business and accounting as well as a master's degree in business administration with a concentration in finance, both from New York University.

Below is an article Frances wrote for Gartner on vendor assessments for which we were able to obtain permission to publish as part of this book.

A Look at India for Offshore Sourcing Options[1]

In 2002, Gartner published the following Strategic Planning Assumption:

> *By 2004, more than 80 percent of U.S. executive boards will have discussed offshore sourcing and more than 40 percent of U.S. enterprises will have completed some type of pilot or will be sourcing IT services through a global delivery model, such as nearshore and offshore (0.7 probability).*

According to a *BusinessWorld* article published in March 2000, General Electric (GE) adopted an outsourcing rule of thumb called "70:70:70." This approach was that 70 percent of GE's work would be outsourced. Of this amount, 70 percent would be done in offshore development centers. And of this amount, about 70 percent would be done in India. This ultimately would result in about 30 percent of GE's work being sourced in India.

In 2003, Gartner declared its "80/80/80 Discuss, Analyze, Act" prediction for the growth of global delivery models (nearshore and offshore):

Through 2004, despite the potential human resource backlash, 80 percent of U.S. executive boardrooms will have discussed global delivery options (nearshore and offshore); of those, 80 percent will pursue an analysis of global delivery options (nearshore and offshore) and 80 percent of those enterprises using global delivery models will act by increasing their level of people resources (nearshore and offshore) by as much as 30 percent (0.8 probability).

Bigger Is Not Necessarily Better

The largest vendors with significant scale are not always the best option for customer enterprises. Small and midsize ESPs that operate in India are viable sourcing options (see "Small/Midsize Offshore ESPs: Application Outsourcing Vendors" and "Small/Midsize Offshore ESPs: Packaged-Application Focus"). These ESPs are grouped into three categories:

- Generalized application service providers — Birlasoft, HPS America, and Mastek
- Providers that focus on financial services offerings — i-flex and Mphasis BFL
- Providers that focus on packaged applications — Hexaware Technologies, iGATE, Intelligroup, and L&T Infotech Ltd.

This list is not inclusive of all small and midsize ESPs that operate in India. We applied key criteria to select which ESPs to analyze:

- Received (by Gartner analysts) the largest number of inquiries and requests for information from buyers in the United States and Europe
- Achieved revenue from offshore services of $50 million or greater

NOTES

1. Source: © 2003 Gartner, Inc. or its Affiliates. All Rights Reserved.

SECTION 2

A HANDS-ON OFFSHORE PROGRAM MANAGEMENT TOOLKIT

Before we dive into Chapter Five, a detailed checklist for the Offshore Program Manager, we need to take a detour. Chapter Four provides a look at the historical evolution of the Offshore service model, key to understanding the present, and the unique factors behind the vast difference in Offshore market share between India and the rest of the world.

4

CHOOSING LOCATIONS FOR OFFSHORE: COUNTRY PROS AND CONS

What are the factors separating one Offshore location from another? Let's summarize the context of this question from our exploration in earlier chapters.

- *Paying a consultant to perform a heroic and detailed analysis of how different countries' cultures and features map to your organization's needs is generally a waste of time and money.* Although the percentage of Offshore services market share may vary slightly in the available studies and literature, the minimum estimate generally shows at least 70 percent of the Offshore market is in India and going strong. The continued outstanding financial growth of India-based firms, based as it is upon principles of maximum disclosure and the certainty of multiyear contracts, is a good indicator that India will dominate the market for at least the near future (three to five years).
- *Multicountry presence is a key factor in one key area — risk management. It is important to build in a multigeographical presence, and the easiest way to do that is to be sure to implement with vendors that offer a well-established presence (in the labor market, understanding the legal environment, emigration requirements, etc.) in several different alternative countries.* The most flexible India-based vendors also provide options for Nearshore consulting in locations such as Toronto, Canada, as an example. Chapter Seven treats the subject of risk management in greater detail.

For most firms new in Offshore, then, the emphasis on analyzing different countries is very much misplaced and frankly, often serves to derail the initial Offshore program effort from more important topics. To put the debate to rest, however, we explore briefly here some of the different countries now vying for Offshore investment dollars. Far more important, in this chapter we discuss the characteristics of the culture and history of India to gain a deeper understanding of the unique phenomenon that seeded the initial Offshore services industry.

COUNTRY STRENGTHS AND WEAKNESSES: A LOOK OUTSIDE INDIA

Country comparisons as analyzed by Gartner are outlined in Exhibit 4.1. Exhibit 4.2, courtesy of the Citigroup Program Office, compares different countries relative to their political system, infrastructure, English-language-speaking skills, technical skills, cost, strengths in Offshore, and time zone differences with the United States.

Exhibit 4.1   Managing Risk: Country Specific Factors[a]

Factor	High	Medium	Low
Governmental support	India, Ireland, China	Canada	Russia
English proficiency	India, Israel, Ireland, Canada, Philippines		China, Russia
Educational system	India, Israel, Russia, Ireland, Canada, China		Philippines
Telecommunications infrastructure	Israel, Ireland, Canada		India, Russia, China, Philippines
Cost advantage	India, Russia, China, Philippines	Israel, Ireland, Canada	
Availability of skilled resources	India (for now!), Russia	Israel, Canada, China, Philippines	Ireland
Cultural differences with US	India, China	Israel, Philippines	Ireland, Russia, Canada

[a] India dominates with at least 80% of total offshore development revenue. Political stability, marketing skills, and bureaucracy/regulations are also key country-based factors.

Source: Gartner Strategic Analysis Report 9/24/2001

Exhibit 4.2   Country Comparison[a]

India

Political: Democracy

Business: Strong legal system, modern banking system, relatively mature capital and money markets. Markets are free of government intervention and SEBI (Security Exchange Bureau of India) — a body similar to SEC in the U.S. is involved in the governance.

Salary of Graduates U.S.$ p.a.: $2400

Total Number of Graduates p.a.: 2,000,000

Education System: English as primary language

Software Exports: U.S.$6 billion

Infrastructure: State of Art — most development centers have some of the best infrastructure in the world, including hardware, software, recreation facilities. Privatization in the telecomm sector has exponentially improved the bandwidth and prices have reduced over 60% in last year alone. However, power shortages in certain regions create bottlenecks.

Time Difference Based on EST: 9:30–10:30 hrs ahead based on DST/ST

Notes: India is still by far the destination of choice, however, with due course of time Philippines and China may catch up. Philippines more so than China can compete globally with India. With respect to cost both Philippines and China will be more competitive than India, but poor infrastructure, relatively immature software processes, poor quality initiatives, and lack of good project management skills may hamper growth. In the case of India, the questions that will be always raised are possibilities of conflict with Pakistan and dominance of few large companies. With respect to Pakistan, the threat is real, but it has been there for over 50 years and the saber-rattling maneuvers between the two new nuclear powered nations will go on. Most Indians and Pakistanis don't think there will be a nuclear war and as long as a U.S. presence is there on this subcontinent things will not get out of hand. With respect to the Indian software scene being dominated by few large companies, it is true that more than 60% of India's overall software export is done by a top few Indian companies. However, more and more clients are realizing the need for individual attention and personalized service and time-to-market issues and moving business to the second and third tier companies in India.

China

Political: Communist

Business: State dominated and controlled. Most major sectors including telecomm and foreign investments in technology are heavily regulated, and there are heavy tariffs on the import of computers and semiconductors, etc. However, with China's entry into the WTO most of these issues may be mitigated. China has already announced that it will participate in the Information Technology Agreement and eliminate most

Exhibit 4.2 (continued)   Country Comparison[a]

of these tariffs by 2005. With the entrance of China into the WTO, it is hoped that software piracy will be reduced (it is currently one of the biggest industries in China — see comments) and tougher laws protecting intellectual capital and patents/copyrights will be instituted.

Salary of Graduates U.S.$ p.a.: $2000

Total Number of Graduates p.a.: 950,000

Education System: Chinese/English as secondary language

Software Exports: U.S.$1 billion

Infrastructure: Is trying to emulate India. There are pockets of good infrastructure, specially in areas around Hong Kong, Shenzhen, and Beijing and in the newly created technology parks. Getting telecomm and right connectivity is still an issue; everything is highly regulated and government owned, therefore it takes time to get things approved. Software has suddenly become a government priority, therefore it is expected that the bureaucratic licensing process will be eased.

Time Difference Based on EST: 12:00–13:00 hrs ahead based on DST/ST

Notes: China is trying hard to emulate India's success in software, however it has a long way to go. The biggest hurdles in its path are related to infrastructure, language, quality, project management skills, and most important, protection of intellectual capital. China's track record in the areas of enforcing software piracy and patent laws has historically been very poor. Because all business is government owned and enabled, issues relating to ethics of the Chinese government may be more of a concern in post-Enron world. Companies like Cisco and Lucent have lost billions of dollars to Chinese factories that have replicated their products and are selling them at 1/10 the price. Despite China's sure entry, until laws are passed to protect intellectual property and respect patents, it is going to be tough for China to compete in the global market for software. Case in point is that China's software piracy industry is double the size of its legitimate software exports — for example, you can buy almost any major software product on the streets of Beijing and Hong Kong for under $100.

Vietnam

Political: Communist

Business: Vietnamese government has taken the unprecedented step of singling out software development as a key plank of its modernization plans. Targets have been set to generate $500 million in software exports by 2005. A draft of incentives and reforms are already in place to provide the preconditions to realize this aim. Vietnamese government is drafting new licensing procedures, tax incentives, labor cost, and infrastructure reforms, all of which once in place can truly position Vietnam as an emerging destination for software outsourcing.

Salary of Graduates U.S.$ p.a.: $1200 (NOTE: This salary number is only for Mainland China and does not include Hong Kong and Macau.)

Exhibit 4.2 (continued)   Country Comparison[a]

Education System: Vietnamese/English as secondary language

Total Number of Graduates p.a.: 15,000

Software Exports: U.S.$78 million

Infrastructure: Infrastructure is a hot issue in Vietnam right now. Telecomm sector is set for far-reaching liberalization that could provide a launch for IT services in Vietnam. Until this liberalization takes place, Vietnam is a difficult country to operate in, and except for Ho Chi Minh City there is no other city with the right infrastructure and connectivity.

Time Difference Based on EST: 11:00–12:00 hrs ahead based on DST/ST

Notes: Vietnam is an upcoming country especially in the Far East software market. Most of the clients that are doing software development are from Australia and Japan; there is a definitive cost advantage over countries like India, however there are issues like political stability, ability for the government to press forward with the promised reforms, language, lack of project management skills, and formal quality assessment initiatives.

Indonesia

Political: Democracy

Business: Indonesia is relatively an easy country in which to do business. Historically it has been known for tourism, but lately government has provided considerable incentives to export and special focus is being given to software and IT. Bali, the ultimate tourist destination, is fast emerging as a local hub for software development.

Salary of Graduates U.S.$ p.a.: $3500

Total Number of Graduates p.a.: 2000

Education System: English

Software Exports: U.S.$15 million

Infrastructure: Bali in Indonesia is an upcoming IT technology hub. A number of smaller software companies have opened operations there due to good infrastructure and telecomm facilities.

Time Difference Based on EST: 11:00–12:00 hrs ahead based on DST/ST

Notes: Indonesia is one of the brightest and upcoming stars in the software environment of Far East. It is the largest country in the ASEAN region, and it has one of the largest populations after China and India (approx. 250 million). The educational system is English-language based, and government is pushing forward considerable reforms to encourage software export. Challenges relate to lack of maturity of the local software firms in executing large complex projects, lack of formal quality initiatives in place, and in some regions (especially in the North) political disturbances (over 98% of the country is Muslim and lately there has been quite a lot of anti-American feeling). But over time all of these can be overcome, and after the Philippines, Indonesia is by far the best alternative in Asia Pacific.

Exhibit 4.2 (continued)   Country Comparison[a]

Malaysia

Political: Constitutional Monarchy

Business: Malaysia has always been one of the most investor-friendly countries, and has been a leader in hardware and telecomm outsourcing. Interference from government is negligible and there is strong support for any form of export from the country. Intellectual capital is protected by tough laws and software piracy is not a major issue.

Salary of Graduates U.S.$ p.a.: $7200

Total Number of Graduates p.a.: 30,000

Education System: Malay/English

Software Exports: U.S.$250 million

Infrastructure: Excellent infrastructure and telecomm facilities. Bandwidth is easily available and no bureaucratic approvals are required.

Time Difference Based on EST: 12:00–13:00 hrs ahead based on DST/ST

Notes: Malaysia has considerable expertise in embedded software (because of large investments by giants like Motorola and Intel), and in Packaged Application Implementation (SAP, etc.); in areas of application development Malaysia is not given due attention. However, these days almost all Far East countries are trying to achieve the same success that India has achieved in software and so a lot of attention is being paid to software export. The rates in Malaysia, however, are not in the ballpark of India and other players in that area, therefore ROIs are difficult to justify especially in a country that is new to the game.

Singapore

Political: Democracy

Business: Again one of the easiest countries in which to do business. Strong support for business and legal structure to support rights of foreign investors. Tough laws against software piracy and protection of intellectual capital.

Salary of Graduates U.S.$ p.a.: $16,000

Total Number of Graduates p.a.: 12,500

Education System: English

Software Exports: U.S.$2 billion

Infrastructure: State of Art — May be one of the best in the world.

Time Difference Based on EST: 12:00–13:00 hrs ahead based on DST/ST

Notes: Singapore logically is one of the top choices for any kind of software development. Infrastructure is excellent and quite a few very good quality software firms have centers in Singapore. However, due to the rates being high and difficulty in hiring and retaining staff, it is not a favored country for software development. However, lately it has become a popular place for COB (continuity of business) and backup and recovery centers.

Exhibit 4.2 (continued) Country Comparison[a]

Philippines

Political: Democracy

Business: One of the largest trading partners with the United States in Asia, the Philippines is also the source of maximum number of Asian immigrants in the United States. Predominantly an open country with over 90% of the population being Christian, however, there are a number of barriers to setting up subsidiaries for foreign companies, and the presence of a local Philippine partner is mandatory. Protection of intellectual capital and software piracy is a major problem. Several Big Five U.S.-based firms have established rapidly growing facilities.

Salary of Graduates U.S.$ p.a.: $2900

Total Number of Graduates p.a.: 380,000

Education System: English

Software Exports: U.S.$1.2 billion

Infrastructure: Good infrastructure, connectivity is still an issue and is government controlled. However, the thrust is towards liberalization and government is inviting foreign investment to expand its infrastructure capabilities and compete globally.

Time Difference Based on EST: 12:00–13:00 hrs ahead based on DST/ST

Notes: After India, the Philippines would be the best choice for software development in Asia. It has a good education system, good infrastructure, and abundance of technical resources. However, the main areas of drawbacks are political instability, lack of good resources in emerging and newer technologies (Philippines has tons of mainframe programmers, but when it comes to J2EE,.NET, etc. ,one has to really struggle), and lack of companies with mature software practices. Most software companies are controlled by two or three major families in one form or the other (two main ones are Lopez and Marcos).

Thailand

Political: Constitutional Monarchy

Business: Investor-friendly country with a strong legal system and a good track record in protecting foreign investments. Relatively straightforward to set up and run export business out of Thailand.

Salary of Graduates U.S.$ p.a.: $3200

Total Number of Graduates p.a.: 1500

Education System: Thai/English as secondary language

Software Exports: U.S.$20 million

Infrastructure: Pockets of good infrastructure, especially around Bangkok and adjoining areas.

Time Difference Based on EST: 11:00–12:00 hrs ahead based on DST/ST

Notes: A few good companies have brought Thailand on the software map, still their practices are small and not very mature (typical software

Exhibit 4.2 (continued)   Country Comparison[a]

company size would be under 200 employees — nothing in comparisons to the 1000s in India); however, their rates are good and it is a good place for small size units.

Sri Lanka

Political: Democracy

Business: Investor-friendly country, has been a front runner in attracting investments in the areas of manufacturing (especially garments). Strong legal system with protection to copyrights, patents, and against software piracy.

Salary of Graduates U.S.$ p.a.: $2800

Total Number of Graduates p.a.: 9000

Education System: English

Software Exports: U.S.$12 million

Infrastructure: An upcoming country that is trying to emulate India's success. A few good technology parks have opened in Colombo, and Candy and telecomm infrastructure exists for considerable expansion in these parks.

Time Difference Based on EST: 9:30–10:30 hrs ahead based on DST/ST

Notes: Again an emerging country in S.E. Asia, because of the British influence, good education system and decent infrastructure. Problems are more in terms of political instability and terrorism.

Israel

Political: Democracy

Business: Modern legal system, easy to do business and foreign investments.

Salary of Graduates U.S.$ p.a.: $25,000

Total Number of Graduates p.a.: 10,000

Education System: English

Software Exports: U.S.$1.8 billion

Infrastructure: State of Art — may be one of the best in the world.

Time Difference Based on EST: 7:00–8:00 hrs ahead based on DST/ST

Notes: Israel along with Ireland are the original countries with whom outsourcing started. Extremely good talent and infrastructure. However, the rates have increased considerably; in addition it is difficult to retain talent (major brain drain to United States) and ever-present security concerns are the main drawbacks.

Ireland

Political: Democracy

Business: Modern legal system, easy to do business and foreign investments.

Exhibit 4.2 (continued)   Country Comparison[a]

Salary of Graduates U.S.$ p.a.: $19,500
Total Number of Graduates p.a.: 43,200
Education System: English
Software Exports: U.S.$8 billion
Infrastructure: State of Art — may be one of the best in the world.
Time Difference Based on EST: 5:00–6:00 hrs ahead based on DST/ST
Notes: After the United States, Ireland continues to be the largest exporter of software in the world. Ireland has considerable points in its favor. For example, it has a very mature and state-of-the-art infrastructure, strong legal protection, no language barriers, and good tax incentives to set up offshore activities. However, its biggest drawback these days is in finding and retaining good software talent; in addition, the costs have increased substantially, making it very difficult to give a positive ROI in pure outsourcing. Companies still see value there in setting up their own offshore development centers, but ability to retain talent will still be a major issue.

Russia

Political: Democracy
Business: Despite tremendous efforts by the government still a relatively difficult place to do business. Laws protecting business interests are outdated if present at all, heavy reliance on local partners, and red tape.
Salary of Graduates U.S.$ p.a.: $1500
Total Number of Graduates p.a.: 200,000
Education System: Russian/English as secondary language
Software Exports: U.S.$650 million
Infrastructure: Pockets of good infrastructure, especially around St. Petersburg and Moscow.
Time Difference Based on EST: 8:00–9:00 hrs ahead based on DST/ST. (Based on the time zone in which St. Petersburg and Moscow are located)
Notes: The biggest problem with Russia is lack of good infrastructure beyond a few locations. Russia is plagued with economic problems, lack of protection for intellectual property, a bad tax system, and corruption. There has been a considerable amount of effort by the Russian government to promote itself as a software alternative to India, primarily on the grounds of exceptionally good engineering and pure science talent. However, until the business climate in Russia improves dramatically, it is by far one of the toughest places to outsource software.

Brazil

Political: Democracy
Business: Modern legal system, easy to do business and foreign investments.

Exhibit 4.2 (continued)   Country Comparison[a]

Salary of Graduates U.S.$ p.a.: $28,000
Total Number of Graduates p.a.: 150,000
Education System: Portuguese/English as secondary language
Software Exports: U.S.$700 million
Infrastructure: Good infrastructure, connectivity is not an issue due to a
  large domestic industry for both software and hardware.
Time Difference Based on EST: Same time zone as EST
Notes: Brazil, after Canada, is the best Nearshore outsourcing solution
  available to U.S. companies. It has time-zone proximity, which is so
  important in software development. In addition, Brazil has a very large
  local software market, and therefore has abundant talent in almost all
  levels of technology, and most of the technical resources are bilingual and
  understand western culture and values. The area in which Brazil loses is
  cost: the rates are higher and one cannot achieve the ROIs that India and
  the Philippines can deliver. The Brazilian government has taxes and invoice
  requirements structured to strongly encourage establishment of
  subsidiaries directly in Brazil.

Mexico

Political: Democracy
Business: Due to the close proximity to United States, relatively easy to do
  business and lack of barriers due to NAFTA for U.S.-based companies.
Salary of Graduates U.S.$ p.a.: $1400
Total Number of Graduates p.a.: 137,600
Education System: Mexican/Spanish/English as secondary language
Software Exports: U.S.$200 million
Infrastructure: Pockets of good infrastructure, telecomm facilities are good.
Time Difference Based on EST: 2 hours behind
Notes: Mexico brings some important advantages because of the NAFTA
  treaty, and low cost of labor. However, software firms in Mexico do not
  have enough maturity in doing high-end software development and are
  more focused on data entry and low-level services. Mexico may not have
  the technical talent base found in countries like India, Russia, Israel, and
  Brazil. Although this is changing, historically most of the technical talent
  coming out of local schools is not in the pure sciences and technology
  areas, creating a vacuum for high-end skills. In addition, Mexico also has
  language barriers and infrastructure issues (other than Mexico City and
  Monterrey). Mexico, however, is a good alternative to Nearshore as long
  as the development work is in basic technologies and is of DP (data
  processing) nature.

[a] Courtesy: Ted Podest, Citigroup Offshore Program Office.

Sources: Mckinsey, Carnegie Bosch Institute, Anderson, Giga, and Gartner.

India is the strong leader across the board, with a very sophisticated, technically educated, and English-speaking population, democratic government, and outstanding telecommunications infrastructure. Israel and Ireland are also known for their outstandingly skilled workforce, English-speaking skills, and excellent infrastructure, but are generally considered more expensive than India. Although not on the list, Canada is also a strong Nearshore presence — close to the United States in terms of physical proximity as well as time zone differences, Canada has of course very close legal and cultural ties to the United States and a wealth of sophisticated and English-speaking technical talent.

In general, Canadian resources can provide significant savings on an hourly basis (usually estimated at 70 to 80 percent of U.S. costs for a similar skill and experience set), and is located a short plane ride away. Many of the major India-based Offshore firms have a presence in Canada. Many of these firms are mixing Nearshore options, as the Citigroup Low Cost Alternative group discussed in Chapter One demonstrates, into their Offshore programs. This is a good way to coax reluctant IT managers to get on board, and enables them to move gradually into India-based Offshore without having to make the leap halfway around the world from the beginning. The strategy is to hire and enable the Offshore program with one of the India-based Offshore vendors that also has a Nearshore presence, and first implement Nearshore. Later, it is relatively transparent to the project effort to move the Offshore development team from Nearshore (e.g., Canada) to Offshore (e.g., Bangalore) once it has become a proven concept and the extra insurance of having the team a mere few hours away no longer seems necessary.

In general, of course, the closer the physical proximity is to the United States of the Nearshore location, the higher the price point is for the technical resource. Regarding the other countries actively vying for the Offshore investment, none have yet to create the overall experience of reassuring excellence that India has attained. Let's look at the phenomenon that has become Offshore in India. To close, we take another look at a comparison of country risk factors in Exhibit 4.3.

WHY OFFSHORE SERVICES LEADERSHIP IN INDIA, AND WHY NOW?

In many ways, the key to understanding Offshore is contained here in these next few pages — in the unique culture and history of India, and historical opportunities to apply these strengths at particular historical points in the United States. Offshore outsourcing was not invented in India, certainly, but has become a dramatically successful export of a

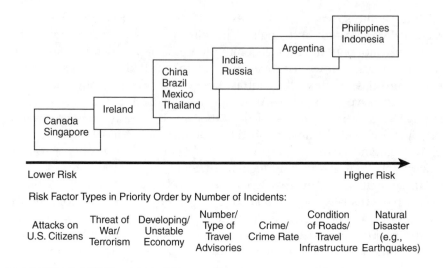

Lower Risk · Higher Risk

Risk Factor Types in Priority Order by Number of Incidents:

Attacks on U.S. Citizens	Threat of War/ Terrorism	Developing/ Unstable Economy	Number/ Type of Travel Advisories	Crime/ Crime Rate	Condition of Roads/ Travel Infrastructure	Natural Disaster (e.g., Earthquakes)

Exhibit 4.3 Country Risk Factors

highly specialized set of companies supported in turn by a unique convergence of broad societal factors and opportunities.

Although the history of India is not a topic we can reasonably attempt to cover here, there is a slice of it related to Offshore that illuminates. That slice relates to the India of the 1970s, 1980s, and 1990s. In the 1970s the first set of professionals from India, generally physicians, was welcomed into the United States to alleviate the war-related shortage of medical doctors. Within that first wave, a very small number of engineers joined in the movement to the United States from India. I spoke to one of the first, Sri Tanjore Swami Sridar.

One of the more interesting bits of information Sridar shared with me was that one of the legacies from 150 years of British rule is that the names of Indian nationals are in a different order than commonly understood in the United States. Indian names are structured in this order — prefix, location, surname, and individual name; for example, Sri Tanjore Swami Sridar.

This explains why many of the individuals from India are called familiarly by what we in the United States would consider their surname.

Sridar was involved in the very early efforts of General Electric, and came here to the United States soon after the first wave in the early 1980s. At that time, the INS (Immigration and Naturalization Services, a branch of the U.S. government) required a computer or electrical engineer to possess a postgraduate degree and ten years of experience to qualify for an initial six-month work visa.

Sridar recalled his experiences working in 1987 in downtown Manhattan. Sridar, to this day, feels greatly indebted to his first American supervisor.

"He drew a map for me," Sridar shared, "and gave me a week off to find my way around New York — to find vegetarian restaurants (Sridar, like many, is Hindu and is a practicing vegetarian) and otherwise get oriented." The success of Indian integration in the United States in the early days, Sridar believes, is the story of similar individual kindnesses, based upon the acceptance of those who were open-minded enough to welcome workers of a different color, speech accent, and culture. The deep gratitude, loyalty, and motivation he felt for this kind and supportive first manager still remains with Sridar to this day. *Many Indians share this sense of wonder at the acceptance of differences within American culture, and a similar deep thankfulness.*

Throughout most of the 1980s the technical infrastructure within India was almost nonexistent. IBM mainframe technology was directed towards Singapore for any meaningful support. *The first computer and telecommunications infrastructure truly established in India was workstation-based, upon mixes such as UNIX/Oracle/Powerbuilder and similar client/server software.*

Around this timeframe, several cultural shifts began to occur that would affect Offshore for years to come. The first shift was that the governments of India, which really function separately as a series of what we would conceptualize as city-states, began to fund colleges of engineering and computer science. The acceptance criteria of these colleges were structured to try to minimize the traditional caste system of India.

Prior to these government-sponsored engineering colleges, the Brahmin/Priest class dominated most slots in local colleges and universities due to their emphasis on learning within their caste. *The various governments of India used quotas to reduce the number of college and university seats available to these higher classes of citizenry in an attempt to level the opportunities across all castes.* Ultimately, within these new government-run colleges and universities, no individuals of the Brahmin/Priest class would be eligible for these highly prized educational slots unless they were in the top two to three percent of their class. This rather large class is not, as is typically assumed by those in the United States, an all elite ruling class. The Brahmin/Priest class has several layers, and is primarily made up of what would roughly be equivalent to upper-middle-class professionals within the United States.

The Brahmin/Priest class responded to this new competitive landscape by upping the emphasis on math and science skills for their children. If there were slots reserved for only the top two to three percent, it became a point of family pride to have raised a child that could meet those criteria. Starting at an age so early as to be inconceivable for Americans, Indian children are drilled in the basics of math and science for hours before and after school. The ultimate prize? Acceptance at IIT, a technical university so revered that the prospective applicants use America's top technical universities as "backup" schools. A recent edition of the television program *60 Minutes*, airing in the Spring of 2003, explored the significance and sophistication of this institution, arguably the best technical training institution in the world.

On an annual basis, the names of the individuals who passed the stringent entrance exam (in order of excellence, from high score to lowest admitted) are published via the Internet. This is the moment of truth and fruition for the years of math and science drilling. The lucky few who gain entrance into IIT are India's cultural heroes. IIT is open to women and men, and entrance is purely merit based. All college fees are paid. Some of the most successful companies of the world have been started and managed by IIT alumni.

Prior to the advent of what we refer to here as the cultural elevation of computers, math, and engineering skills within India, the best a working individual could aspire to was a job with the Indian government — essentially a steady paycheck closely comparable to a bank teller position here in the United States. Thus, the emphasis on these skills and the job opportunities they serve to fuel represents a huge cultural shift, an opportunity for the professional classes of India that has brought new meaning to their professional lives. Indian nationals tend to be very emotional when speaking about the opportunities of Offshore — at one meeting I attended, a young man was in tears — and it is not hard to understand why, given that these jobs present a new type of professional challenge for which these bright and ambitious individuals have been hungering over many generations.

Those individuals not lucky enough to win the technical knowledge sweepstakes of entrance to IIT began going instead to U.S. colleges and universities. It is hard for Americans to understand the sheer prestige associated with a successful technical career in India, apart from fame and money. Prestige is associated rather with intelligence and brainpower. *Nearly every parent in India dreams of raising a child smart enough to gain admittance to IIT.* As noted above, entrance to IIT is a complete meritocracy. Entrance is purely test-based, and all students who pass have all expenses paid in order to attend. Ironically, at least when it comes to technology education, India has achieved what we in the United States have not — a true democracy of education, where the best truly do earn opportunities through their own intelligence and hard work.

As a collection of independent city-states, India has several state governments, each with several official local languages. There are at least 25 separate state languages within India. The glue that holds them together, and the primary teaching language, is English.

Another strong cultural factor in Indian life is the Jesuits. This well-established school of thought served to teach values of respect for others and communication skills as the basis of problem resolution. The Jesuits were instrumental in teaching the value of personal discipline and of giving to the less fortunate. A deep cultural concept consists of paying back debts not to the giver, but to others less fortunate. These values meshed well with the Indian religion of Hinduism, which teaches that the road to spiritual fulfillment is through personal discipline. Playing the role that was assigned to the individual through the family and work system is one of the underlying themes of Hinduism. Individuals are expected to fulfill these roles selflessly, not looking "for the fruit" or the immediate personal gain. These values — giving back, communications, working as a source of spiritual fulfillment without emphasis on immediate gratification — are illustrated in the Infosys interview at the end of Chapter One. These beliefs stand in stark contrast to the U.S. leadership values embodied in a famous, rather shallow, and vacuous quote originating from same time period, the 1980s, asserting that "the one who dies with the most toys wins."

It is important not to create an artificial separation here, by putting Indian company leaders on a pedestal. One of the rumors going around in the Offshore community, for example, is that hiring of leading U.S. strategy executives hasn't been working well because the Indian owners of some privately held Offshore companies tended to treat their employees as servants, with their children running roughshod about their offices, and generally blurring the lines between business and family in a way totally foreign to U.S. business culture. But it is equally true that, perhaps because these workers have been so starved for challenging and interesting technology work, that a culture of awareness and giving back to the country of India seems to be emphasized much more strongly in Indian corporate leaders than in their U.S. counterparts. In the context of our earlier exploration of ethics, it is to be hoped that this emphasis is to be preserved, because it is also true that the country of India has many poor who desperately need to be helped. And too, the emphasis of unrealistically having to create greater and greater shareholder returns, year over year, is sadly and obviously taking its toll on the honesty and values of our U.S. company leaders.

To return to our historical overview, in the India of the 1980s there existed a culture elevating science and math, with a value system emphasizing long-term development of skills without emphasis on immediate gratification.

Into this cultural mix came the final catalyst — Y2K. Even though there was little to no exposure or understanding of mainframe technology or the COBOL programming language, the sons and daughters of India, trained as they were in technology practically from infancy, could learn these in a weekend. Y2K provided the catalyst of U.S. need that brought Offshore Outsourcing from the backwater province of a few large companies to the forefront of IT skills sourcing and execution for Fortune 100 firms.

This is the hardest and most subtle lesson for American IT managers relative to Offshore. When one is buying resources from India, this knowledge is not based (as in the U.S. market) upon a particular programming language, industry knowledge, or technology. One is not buying five years of COBOL mainframe experience, for example. One is buying highly sophisticated computer engineers who have been literally weaned on math, science, and computer technology. Now we can understand why some individuals in the United States find their Indian counterparts "frightening" in their ability to learn and create efficiencies. Resume review — the typical province of the IT manager — simply does not apply to Offshore, because these bright individuals have the educational background to learn anything related to technology, quickly and thoroughly, and apply it with ingenuity and understanding. *Despite the relative cost differential, the typical worker in India is closer to a master's-level engineering student in the United States in terms of skills, abilities, and background, with all the learning acumen that implies.*

Here too we see a window into the tunnel vision of many U.S. citizens when it comes to really focusing and understanding cultures outside the United States. A startling statistic is that only 20 percent of Americans have a passport. This means most of us — 80 percent — of U.S. citizens have not traveled outside Canada and Mexico. Within the large Fortune 100 firms who have a presence outside the United States, there usually remains a wide internal communications gap. It is important not to underestimate the not-invented-here vision of the typical U.S. manager, and the readiness of the U.S. worker to lump all Offshore country capabilities into a single, poorly understood category. Although Americans embrace individuals of many different backgrounds and cultures, to our credit, we may not necessarily dig deep to find the subtle truth about our nonnative worker counterparts. It is important to remember that every country has a cultural and historical context, and to become more educated in that context is a key way of understanding what an Offshore partnership can truly bring.

WHAT IS THE CURRENT STATE AND VIEW OF OFFSHORE?

Viewing the differences between countries in Offshore becomes more meaningful within the context of a firm's actual decisions. A recent body of research conducted by *Computerworld* and the InterUnity Group[1] outlines some interesting findings that can help us identify recent trends in utilization of Offshore via different countries. This study does not purport to be a comprehensive overview of all firms as they engage with Offshore — it is limited to firms who responded in detail to the *Computerworld* survey, with their unique demographic. However, the study does provide an interesting snapshot, especially as this particular slice of corporations views Offshore Outsourcing as compared to other types of outsourcing services.

The first view, of course, is a look at exactly how far ahead India is in terms of total Offshore market space. India has established a dramatic lead (again, despite the sometimes rather passionate debate on country advantages versus disadvantages that seems to dominate the press dialogue and the conferences). Even though this particular survey has a relatively low percentage allocated in India — 70 percent (estimates in most studies vary between 70 percent and slightly above 90 percent) — what is evident is the low percentage across many of the other countries. It takes a good handful of alternative countries to approximate the total business volume that India now hosts.

What types of IT applications do companies tend to move Offshore? Application development and maintenance make up the great majority of efforts, followed by technical administration (Web sites, PC support), and then data entry, and data center management. Call center management, although relatively small in numbers, is one of the most rapidly growing areas, and varies greatly by industry.

A comparison of the different types of applications being Offshored versus those being Outsourced to U.S.-based consulting resources shows again that application maintenance and application development are the clear leaders for Offshore versus U.S.-based Outsourcing; other areas that lead in Offshore but with less of a margin include help desk, Web site and PC administration and support, application integration, and data entry. *Applications where U.S.-based consulting support remains in the lead include database administration, network management, and for the time being at least (although this is rapidly changing), call center management.*

The survey showed that cost is an extremely important factor in choosing an Offshore partner for this, perhaps surprisingly so, even for this particular market space. Skillset and industry knowledge are slightly more important in Offshore — to the points above, perhaps not based upon real understanding of the abilities of Offshore personnel.

Flexibility of contract terms is a relatively less important selection criterion (perhaps because the norm for Offshore firms is generally pretty flexible in contract terms, because they have had to be in order to win customers). Reputation is somewhat less important in Offshore — perhaps because all India-based firms tend to be considered risky as a class by firms new to Offshore, so the relative reputation between them is not that important. CMM level, because it is one of the true advantages provided to Offshore customers, is not surprisingly a key selection criterion.

This study confirms that Offshore, as a volume savings strategy, tends to be utilized by companies much larger or somewhat larger than their industry average.

Perhaps the most significant single finding of the research is that Offshore, as discussed frequently throughout this book, is confirmed to be limited to 30 percent of the total IT budget — at the most.

Usually 70 percent or more of any corporate IT budget is comprised of salary, with software/hardware as a commodity, so this reflects the industry lore that Offshore IT outsourcing has a natural limit of 30 percent of the people budget/applications and maintenance/support work.

For most U.S. firms, the savings from Offshore and U.S.-based Outsourcing firms clusters at 30 percent, whereas the savings for Offshore varies widely. *What is interesting is that almost 10 percent have shown no savings for Offshore, and over 15 percent demonstrate over 70 percent savings — a rather wide range. Although the research does not delve into the reasons for this wide discrepancy in savings as a result of Offshore, we can venture an educated guess that these differences are due to the management of relatively large upfront costs related to infrastructure and knowledge management.* We discuss the pitfalls and management techniques relative to avoiding large unexpected costs in Chapters Five and Seven.

Concerning the criteria utilized in evaluating Offshore service partners' performance, areas of performance that are deemed "extremely important" include cost and perceived user satisfaction, the latter usually measured via questionnaires or interviews filled out by internal customers. "Very important" measures of vendor success include service availability, response time (measured by service-level agreements or other objective criteria), on-time and to-specification project delivery, and quality of personnel.

Regarding the internal workings of the Offshore reporting relationship, for this cross section of firms, *over 70 percent of the Offshore Service Providers reported to an Internal Project Manager located in the United States,* and 30 percent — note that more than one reporting relationship was allowed in the response — had the Offshore Provider report to another Outsourcing Service Provider (not recommended!).

The survey found that in the case of a disaster, the primary contingency plans of over 40 percent of the firms called for bringing the Offshore effort inhouse; just 20 percent plan to move it to another country. *Significantly, over 10 percent admitted to having had no plan* in place at all — it is easy to suspect that in reality, that number is much larger. Interestingly, there is little difference in the way firms treat Offshore and other Outsourcing contingency planning. Interestingly, there are few differences between the contingency plans for Offshore firms and those that are solely U.S. based.

On a closely related topic, the survey validated that the ongoing threat of war is no impediment to growth to the majority of large firms involved in utilization of Offshore services, a theme echoed strongly in both the continuing rapid market growth of these services and the Offshore Interest Group. Ironically, roughly 10 percent were concerned about the financial viability of the Offshore vendor, no doubt unaware that these firms are bounding head over heels in financial performance as compared to the U.S.-based competition.

What are the relative challenges that these firms face in going Offshore? Interestingly enough, most research does not touch upon the key barriers — the negative impact of press and views of employees, as well as the lack of enthusiasm of middle managers perceiving Offshore as a threat to their internal power base. It is unfortunate, perhaps, that it is not well understood that Offshore has a natural limit, and making the overall cost of the IT function lower most frequently strengthens the relative power of the IT organization and the individuals that comprise it. Language and security are the largest of the concerns, but again — if threat of war can be construed as the largest looming and most destructive threat, even within the same group, this ultimate threat is not enough to derail the growth and investment in Offshore.

How is Offshore used vis-à-vis inhouse IT resources? *The great majority of firms utilize Offshore as a supplement to the inhouse team,* slightly higher than the 32 percent of firms using U.S.-based Outsourcers in this category. Offshore is slightly more likely to be used as process Outsourcing, a trend that is likely to increase in coming years as call centers and other business process Outsourcing becomes more prevalent Offshore. Building a complete IT system is slightly less likely to be the province of Offshore service providers, whereas, significantly, *total IT Outsourcing is much less likely to be done via Offshore.*

How do the various industry vertical markets stack up relative to Offshore? The survey found that this sample is somewhat reflective of the firms widely believed to be in the forefront Offshore (based upon press coverage and similar research). These include, of course, insurance, financial services, telecomm, manufacturing, and banking.

The next set of research results compared these firms against other firms in their industries that are not utilizing Offshore services. In general, although no cause/effect is assumed, firms using Offshore services are more likely to show the following characteristics as compared to other firms in their industry:

- Demonstrate higher or much higher revenue growth
- Have a slightly higher level of IT automation
- Show slightly or much higher levels of profitability

These results are significant in that, even if there is not a cause and effect relationship among higher revenue, IT automation, and much higher profitability for Offshore, the firms that choose to do Offshore exhibit these positive industry standings vis-à-vis their peers. One can justifiably conclude that even if Offshore is not the only direct cause of these relative accomplishments, alignment with Offshore as a strategy implies an organizational structure with maturity, aggressiveness, and the all-important ability to leverage strategic IT initiatives (such as Offshore) on behalf of competitive standing.

Finally, our last set of data takes a look at why these firms decided to Offshore (vs. U.S.-based Outsource) in the first place, and how they heard about their chosen service provider or vendor. Offshore is much more cost-driven than U.S.-based Outsourcing; also Offshore firms are looking for access to world-class resources and process efficiencies (and we can interpret here, exposure to world-class methodologies and processes such as CMM).

CHAPTER SUMMARY

The emphasis on comparing countries is a relatively useless exercise for most firms going Offshore. It is much more pertinent to ensure that the vendor mix selected to implement Offshore offers a range of countries, in order to provide for a feasible risk mitigation strategy.

A deeper look at the cultural factors behind the tremendous Offshore market share lead in India shows that there are specific factors in place to support India's supremacy in Offshore for many years to come. These include an English-language-speaking educational system, based in a large democracy, with common values that in particular encourage young Indians to become cultural heroes if they excel in technology. Thus an incredibly intelligent and diligent labor pool is born. The typical worker in India is closer to a master's-level engineering student in the United States, with all the learning acumen that implies.

Research confirms that Offshore is generally limited to 30 percent of the IT budget, or headcount, or both. Firms that engage in Offshore tend to be larger, more profitable, and slightly more sophisticated in their use of the technology than their industry peers.

NOTES

1. *Emerging Trends: On-Shore and Off-Shore Outsourcing,* July 2003.
2. Richard Schneider: Web site, www.interunitygroup.com
   email: richardschneider@interunitygroup.com

5

THE OFFSHORE PROGRAM CHECKLIST: WHAT'S REALLY DIFFERENT?

The Offshore program checklist below outlines the steps required to successfully implement Offshore, for both IT application development as well as maintenance and support. Although no program checklist can claim to be complete and comprehensive in today's complex and tailored IT environments, the information below can serve as a useful basis and guideline for Offshore execution, in particular to help elucidate areas that may be overlooked completely because they are unique to Offshore. In addition, we take a look at the similarities and differences among Offshore and other large-scale, cross-geography technology implementation efforts.

As outlined in prior chapters, one fundamental difference between Offshore and other complex technology programs is the methodological sophistication and support available from the India-based Offshore firms. The leading firms have years of experience, are competing in a tough playing field that allows no public failure, and possess the ability and the motivation to ensure success through strong guidance. It is worth repeating the refrain of this book — the true challenge of Offshore is not in the tactical execution, but in the strategic management of IT personnel resources with a view to increasing the firm's competitive standing.

No book on Offshore IT, however, is complete without a detailed execution checklist. First, we recap some of the functions of the Program Manager in setting up a successful Offshore program. Once the program-level structures have been put in place we turn to the more detailed components of our program checklist, supporting Project Managers. Exhibit 5.1 summarizes the role of the Offshore Program Manager.

Exhibit 5.1   The Role of the Offshore Program Manager/PMO (Program Office)

- Serves as focal point for Offshore-related program information across the organization
- Establishes and ensures compliance with organizationwide Offshore vendor management policies and procedures, as they relate to...
  - Contract negotiation
  - Methodology and project approach
  - Network architecture
  - Risk management
- Communicates to management team via reports and meetings, including updates to the Steering Committee
- Establishes reporting standards for financial analysis, metrics, and SLAs
- Interfaces with, and keeps abreast of new requirements relating to industry and regulatory oversight
- Validates achievement of contractual obligations, including monitoring of performance and internal customer satisfaction metrics
- Tracks achievement of financial goals
- Focal point for employee fairness practices, including plans for reskilling and retooling for affected employees
- Ultimate point of authority and review for programwide risk management practices
- Coordinator of communications plan, including kick-off meetings with executive sponsors, Web sites, interface with corporate peers more mature in Offshore, and cross-cultural training
- Serves as central planning organization for trips overseas to evaluate vendors, conduct internal marketing with business partners, and ensure compliance with on-site security requirements
- Maintains central repository of documentation, both project-specific as well as templates and standards to be utilized programwide
- Tracks individual project managers' success via project plans to ensure that all groups are on target to meet their Offshore goals and target dates
- Works with executive team to increase understanding of the potential as well as impact of Offshore across different functional disciplines
  - Serves as a center of knowledge and excellence, tracking and disseminating best practices relating to industry norms for Offshore
- Drives impact to overall IT methodology, usually requiring extensions in level of detail as well as business process changes regarding program and project interface across geographically dispersed teams
- Owns vendor relationship management, including research, advice, and counsel on impact on vendor management practices across the organization

THE OFFSHORE PROGRAM CHECKLIST: LAYING THE GROUNDWORK FOR A SUCCESSFUL OFFSHORE PROGRAM

The primary tasks of the Offshore Program Manager are summarized in Exhibit 5.2 and then explored in detail.

Exhibit 5.2   Primary Tasks of the Offshore Program Manager

- Establish and communicate strategic objectives
  - Explain conceptual approach of program
  - Explain vendors selected, locations, type of applications, etc.
  - Outline program governance
    - Steering committee
      - Decision-making responsibilities
      - Success factors
    - Contact information of Offshore Program Office
- Establish vendor interface guidelines
  - Clear division of responsibility
- Create communications plan
  - Impact on employees
  - Outline core skills that will be focus for future onshore positions within IT
  - Establish sources of ongoing communications
  - Outline cross-cultural communications
- Initiate a systemwide review of vendor consents
  - Revamp legal process relating to contracts
- Establish programwide risk management program
  - Program office functions as governance
- Establish documentation guidelines
  - Utilize central storage repository tool accessible by Offshore team
  - Publish programwide standards for documentation, such as templates, timeliness, and content requirements
- Define precise methodology
  - Include roles and responsibilities of onshore vs. offshore team
    - All expectations to be explicit and in writing
    - Establish clear level of accountability
  - Production environment responsibility
    - Network support
    - Test
  - Define program-level logistics
    - Meeting schedule and expectations
    - Project reporting

Step 1. Program Manager: Establish Offshore Program Strategic Objectives

Step one is to define and communicate how the Offshore program aligns with the overall corporate strategic goals and objectives of firm. Although this is often assumed for other technology programs, and often deemed unnecessary, Offshore must be overtly aligned with these goals from the very start. Revisiting them annually for an update and refinement, as the organization learns more about Offshore, supports ongoing clarity and focus.

One question to be answered broadly and that publicly relates to how the cost savings generated by the program will ultimately be utilized, and how that will serve the organization. Will the organization increase the total number of IT projects for the same dollar investment, or keep the IT budget static and invest more in marketing or non-IT-related business costs, or a combination of both? Will the savings simply be a boost to shareholder value over time? Of course, the anticipated plan for how the savings will or will not be reinvested in the business becomes a value statement for the organization, and one that will inform all stakeholders of the overall business direction and strategy. Additional discussion points on strategy include:

- Impact on IT methodology, including supporting internal certification efforts such as CMM and Six Sigma
- Value statement regarding investment in IT core skills, what the organization is looking to grow in terms of IT skill capability versus those skills no longer anticipated to remain in demand Onshore
- Ethical strategic statement on corporate fairness to long-term employees
- How Offshore affects the organization's overall competitiveness/positioning in the marketplace

These strategic objectives help set the tone to broaden the view, and ultimately serve to validate the Offshore program. Most employees realize that the cost savings from Offshore is not optional over the long term — in these economic times, silent observance of company market share and other measures of viability are the norm. Even though most will realize Offshore is required in order to keep the business viable, it is also human nature to reject change. Many firms have strained relationships with rank-and-file employees around cost management — how cost savings are achieved amid perceptions of favoritism and cronyism. The only way to overcome the lack of understanding and fear fueled by the popular press is to keep the focus on the overall benefits at stake, and ideally to outline an objectively fair and reasonable plan. The typical Fortune 100 Program Manager will answer these questions in a variety of settings, some interactive. These include the kick-off meeting, various intermediary staff meetings, and ultimately the ubiquitous FAQs (Frequently Asked Questions) documents. If there is any program that only makes sense as part of the larger picture, it is Offshore.

On a more tactical level, of course, outlining how the overall program supports the strategic goals of the firm are simply good business practice. This is required information, to be used by individual Project Managers as a guide in their day-to-day decisions. Project Managers responsible for enabling Offshore in new application development as well as IT maintenance and support can utilize the strategic objectives as guidelines for establishing the working model for Offshore.

Step 2: Establish Vendor Interface Guidelines

Outlining the terms of the various contractual vendor relationships is an important function of the Offshore program office. If the organization is using the typical (and recommended) Co-Sourcing model, in which 70 to 80 percent of the team is Offshore and the remainder Onshore, it is important to clearly delineate the distinction between roles — generally at first, and more precisely at the application team level. Exactly how the division of work occurs is one of the tactical aspects of the Offshore model that can increase risk. Ask experienced program managers, and most of the challenges related to early implementation center on tasks that "fall between the cracks" across geographically dispersed teams. Clearly it is not an option for team members to meet face to face and negotiate the fine points of who is responsible for what task or deliverable.

Most of the India-based firms come to the table with a highly structured set of project plans and years of hard-built expertise in cross-cultural and geographic project practices. On a practical level, it is much more important to educate and support the organization's internal staff on the various roles and responsibilities — the Offshore firms are usually far in advance, and the methodologies much more flexible and well understood as part of years of training and investment across the organization.

Other baseline components of the Offshore program include not only introducing the Offshore vendors and clarifying their various roles and execution models, but also establishing clear reporting relationships and communications protocols. For example, most Offshore vendors provide at least one part-time dedicated organizational resource or company interface, or even a group fulfilling that function. Usually that group interfaces primarily with the internal dedicated Offshore program office, whereas the Onshore Project Manager only interfaces directly with his or her peer (dedicated to the project full- or part-time) in the overseas location.

Thus, a typical set of Co-Sourcing project team roles and responsibilities is structured as follows:

- An internal, Onshore Project Manager responsible for overall performance and delivery, responsible for managing Onshore team members. These Onshore teams are usually responsible for business relationship management, application architecture, business analysis, and overall project or application management.
- An external, Offshore Project Manager responsible for the Offshore team performance, and reporting up to the Onshore Project Manager. The Offshore team typically performs maintenance and support functions, or coding for new application development, and processes efficiency improvements for both functions.

The Program Manager typically runs a central meeting tracking all Offshore projects at a high level, documenting and tracking resolution of issues that pertain to programwide concerns, or that represent highest program priority and require visibility. The dedicated relationship managers from the various Offshore service providers usually attend that central Offshore program meeting (typically weekly, perhaps less often as the program matures), helping to deal with vendor relationship issues, fine tuning data for management reporting, and creating an atmosphere of crisp, accountable, cooperative, and positive program accountability for all players.

Each Offshore Project Manager represents his project(s) at these program office-level meetings, simultaneously conducting his own weekly project meetings as appropriate. Normally, a matrix-organizational structure is established, with the Project Manager heading the Offshore team (vendor) reporting to the Onshore Project Manager (employee). These two in turn are both responsible to the overall Offshore Program Manager (employee). Most large firms do not have direct reporting relationships reflecting these responsibilities — the Project Manager leading the Offshore team, of course, reports "directly" up to the vendor; the Onshore Project Manager usually reports into an IT "people manager." In these logistics and structure, of course, an Offshore program is not too different from any other complex, geographically diverse technology program.

If there is a general vendor strategy, it is important to communicate and build understanding through the extended team. For example, certain vendors may be aligned to focus on different internal customer groups, applications types, or to serve as backups for risk management geographic distribution.

Defining precise interface processes between the vendors and the extended team, such as the staffing process for an Offshore project, is one of the areas in which the Offshore PMO can step in to define, helping to ensure a smooth program launch. There is a natural reticence, almost a self-effacing quality, associated with many employees of the India-based Offshore vendors. Documenting processes in detail can serve to establish timetables and guidelines to avoid delays relating to uncertain or uncooperative internal managers, who are naturally suspicious at program inception (Exhibit 5.3).

Step 3: Create Communications Plan

The importance and focus of the Offshore communications plan are outlined in Chapter 2. One key function of the Offshore PMO is to keep the organization advised of the latest information and developments relating to Offshore, from both inside and outside the firm. These include ongoing updates on the employee impact and associated training programs, sources of factual (as opposed to popular press) data from research and other organizations involved in Offshore, and continuing updates on how Offshore is contributing to core skills development and methodology discipline within IT.

Cross-cultural education is a unique and interesting facet of the communications responsibility for the Offshore PMO. Keeping the exploration light, such meetings at lunchtime serving cuisine from different Offshore countries, can be surprisingly important and effective in creating a welcoming atmosphere for both visiting and permanent Offshore personnel. These cultures tend to be "high touch" and the importance of a personal acknowledgment, in the spirit of hospitality, cannot be overstated. At one of these lunches I personally hosted, there was a series of long tables serving Indian food, and the Onshore and Offshore teams took turns introducing themselves around the long table. These functions, although seemingly pro forma, acknowledge the existence of individuals from different backgrounds and validate their place in the organization within the context of welcoming and acknowledging cultural differences.

Step 4: Initiate a Systemwide Review of Vendor Consents

Vendor consents are best tracked and managed as one of the earliest efforts of the Offshore PMO. Third-party software contracts are frequently lengthy and most of these contracts were put in place long before Offshore was a consideration. Most third-party firms will be cooperative, but some will perceive Offshore as a "revenue opportunity" and may potentially

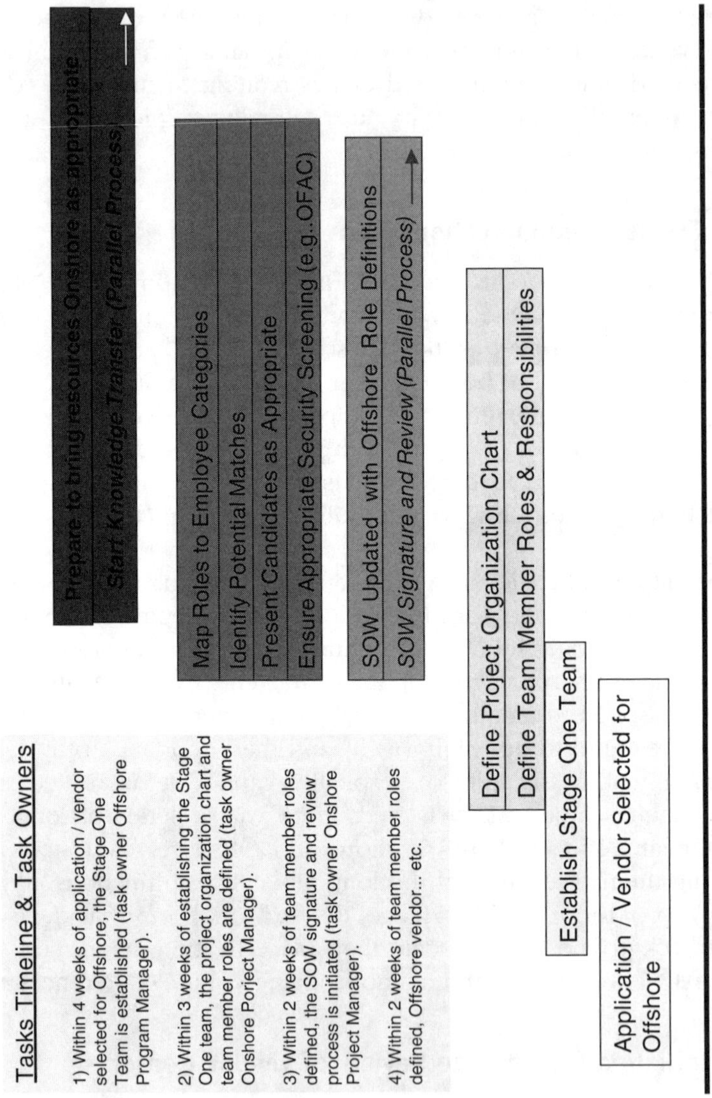

Prepare to bring resources Onshore as appropriate

Start *Knowledge Transfer (Parallel Process)*

Map Roles to Employee Categories

Identify Potential Matches

Present Candidates as Appropriate

Ensure Appropriate Security Screening (e.g., OFAC)

SOW Updated with Offshore Role Definitions

SOW Signature and Review *(Parallel Process)*

Define Project Organization Chart

Define Team Member Roles & Responsibilities

Establish Stage One Team

Application / Vendor Selected for Offshore

Tasks Timeline & Task Owners

1) Within 4 weeks of application / vendor selected for Offshore, the Stage One Team is established (task owner Offshore Program Manager).

2) Within 3 weeks of establishing the Stage One team, the project organization chart and team member roles are defined (task owner Onshore Project Manager).

3) Within 2 weeks of team member roles defined, the SOW signature and review process is initiated (task owner Onshore Project Manager).

4) Within 2 weeks of team member roles defined, Offshore vendor... etc.

Exhibit 5.3   Process Overview: Offshore Staffing

request relatively large sums to allow overseas consultants legal access to their licensed software. Although of course every Offshore program is unique, in general the rights of access traditionally rest with the firm granting the license, so if the software vendor decides to take this tack, there may be few alternatives.

As mentioned earlier, application software licenses that do not have provisions for Offshore resources under the current licensing agreements must be updated via negotiations with these software vendors. At times, these can be challenging to negotiate, and require additional unanticipated licensing fees. In particular, certain software firms become more concerned about specific Offshore partners such as the Big Four who may directly compete in their market space with their own software offerings. Coordinating, tracking, and establishing strategy and approach for vendor consents — working across the multiple internal management and legal teams responsible for the various software vendor relationships in large corporations — can be challenging and time consuming. Often, Offshore vendors can help with their particular contacts in various stages of the process, and need to be involved in the effort in an organized way. In particular, the application timetable for moving Offshore can be negatively affected by an unexpectedly difficult vendor consent negotiation. The Offshore PMO must remain in control and build in program flexibility, monitoring the progress of each contract and structuring the program so that a substitution of alternative applications is feasible.

Vendor consents require a new level of interdepartmental coordination, and it is recommended that this process be formalized in a written document that outlines the steps, the individuals responsible for each step, and the required formal signatures of organizational participants. The first step, of course, is to conduct a legal review of the licensing contracts for applications known to be in the first wave of Offshore. The legal department needs to establish standard clauses for all contracts so that Offshore is negotiated into all third-party software access rights moving forward. Some organizations undertake a comprehensive review of all application contracts, and proceed to negotiate Offshore rights for them even if they are not immediately planned to go Offshore — this can save a lot of time later on, when the success of Offshore becomes evident and subscribers to the program seem to expand exponentially.

Vendor consents, although a major focus of energy early on, soon become rote and manageable. The primary concern here is to ensure that unforeseen delays do not derail the program as a whole by eating into savings through lengthy and unanticipated delays.

Step 5: Establish a Programwide Risk Management Program

Establishing the initial steps of a programwide risk management program for Offshore is generally not as complex as it may appear. The Offshore PMO establishes the lead by choosing vendors supporting geographic diversity, and structuring knowledge transfer redundancy on a project-by-project basis. The Offshore PMO supervises and reviews the individual disaster recovery plans, one for each of the Offshore physical sites. The existing risk management review processes, such as the development and monitoring of application-specific risk documentation, can then be extended to include Offshore as appropriate. Usually, however, the great majority if not all of the additional risks of Offshore exist at the macro or program level (such as threat of overseas war). The difficult truth is, as we discuss more fully in Chapter Seven, there is no additional risk in allowing network access from India that doesn't exist from network access from the next city block.

The Offshore Co-Sourcing model usually means data and systems remain in the United States. As a result, the primary aspects of risk management relate to breach of network security, potential losses related to investment in knowledge management (loss of worker availability), and acts of deliberate sabotage by overseas workers. Network security is discussed more fully later in the book, but for now note that the primary initial effort is to manage the inhouse redesign to accommodate the new security requirements. Regarding sabotage, most Offshore firms have more extensive personnel screening requirements than in the United States, and geographic redundancy can cover loss of work, availability, and investment in knowledge management. Not to minimize these concerns, but a concerted effort by the PMO to break these into manageable executable tasks is an important prerequisite for success to this often guiltily ignored task.

Closely related to risk management is the requirement for the Offshore PMO to interface with the representatives from the various vertical industry regulatory agencies. The Offshore PMO generally does not need to restructure the current application risk management process itself — Offshore risk generally just becomes another component of the existing risk management program. The unique risks related to Offshore are added to existing risk document templates. Again, it is generally the Offshore PMO that is responsible for reviewing and updating the existing risk process as well as document content to include Offshore.

As part of the risk management function, Offshore is not infrequently the basis for an overdue, and very beneficial, overhaul and revamping of IT internal security practices. A good application security checklist is shown in Chapter Seven, relating to requirements as they pertain to password management, encryption, Web-enabled security, audit trail, and other brick-and-mortar components of an overall set of IT security procedures and standards. If these standards are in place, it is up to the Offshore Program Manager to ensure they are appropriately updated to meet the additional stringencies of Offshore. But if there are no documented corporate standards for IT security (rare these days), or if they exist but as in most organizations, are casually enforced (all but rare), it will be time to look at them more seriously.

Most large Fortune 100 firms have dual standards — the official security rulebook as published and IT application security as actually practiced. Many firms actually have written security requirements that are simply too hard to follow, such as severe strictures on the type of system access allowed to outside consultants. In most lifetimes of an application, there comes a time when it is vital to meet a deadline or revenue goal for an external consultant to step in and function in violation of those security strictures, such as when temporarily replacing an employee on leave. The importance of having realistic, enforceable, and balanced security standards and processes becomes much more important when Offshore is enabled, if for no other reason than IT security (usually in an inaccurate and misunderstood way) suddenly becomes highly visible as a concern across the organization.

New technology threats, and new ways of effectively mitigating those threats, are constantly created. It is not unusual for corporate security guidelines to be significantly out of date unless they are reviewed and updated frequently. The debate about Offshore may become the catalyst for all of the "secret" (as in well-known but not publicly acknowledged) security violations to be brought to light. The debate on Offshore frequently includes many security objections regarding supposed violations. In actual practice these so-called violations frequently align with the unwritten, accepted daily security practices within IT, especially regarding access of internal systems by remotely located consultants.

Step 6: Establish Program Documentation Guidelines

One way many firms choose to leverage the India-based Offshore firms, in particular, is for their knowledge relating to more mature methodology practices, such as CMM level. Most maintenance and support applications emerge from knowledge transfer with much more complete documentation and opportunity for streamlined processes. In addition, the overall IT organization often emerges from the startup phase in launching Offshore with improved and more disciplined methodology.

On a tactical level, the Offshore PMO serves as the focal point for creating a central software tool that can serve as a documentation repository for all intellectual capital generated by the Offshore program. In addition to passively collecting documentation, the PMO can actively establish standards of documentation excellence through templates related to technical specifications and other deliverables relating specifically to the Offshore program. In particular, a process (with review and formal signatures) is recommended to ensure that no application leaves knowledge transfer without a detailed outline of the following:

- Archive of application code
- Maintenance manual
- User manual
- Support process manual
- Additional related business process manuals as appropriate

Step 7: Define Offshore Methodology

Closely related to the documentation standard, it is also important that performance measures, process standards for SLAs (maintenance and support), project management, and methodology standards (new application development) are defined specifically for Offshore.

Defining precisely the methodology to be utilized by Offshore/Onshore joint teams, as outlined below in detail, is a key role of the Offshore PMO. There is little mystery regarding what comprises a complete and high-quality methodology — the goal is to establish complete clarity regarding who (roles) does what (deliverables definition), when (how deliverables relate to each other), and where (Onshore vs. Offshore functions). These questions need to be not only systematically answered, but also documented in the form of manuals and other user-friendly material. Clarification of cross-functional team member roles as they relate to the methodology includes setting explicit expectations in terms of accountability for the quality, timeliness, and level of effort.

Let's take a look at an example regarding accountability and process definition. For maintenance and support of a customer Web site, clearly documented SLAs are required to specifically spell out the type of actions expected of the individuals located Offshore, as well as the acceptable timeframe for those actions to occur. These descriptions typically delineate the different types of system bugs, which are in turn categorized in terms of severity and importance depending upon pre-set criteria. For example, critical-level system errors may have a required turnaround fix time of less than two hours due to potential business impact, whereas those less critical may allow a longer time period for resolution. Exhibits 5.4 and 5.5 outline Offshore SLAs in more detail.

If the error is not able to be resolved with the accepted timeframe, a well-structured escalation process, with accountability, contact information,

Exhibit 5.4   Sample SLA Definitions

Critical Priority

These are highest-severity errors resulting in an application that is down or completely unavailable to end users. For applications with different categories of users, this category includes application processes that cannot be completed for highest-priority end users. Includes problems of similar criticality for downstream dependent systems. Normally requires a response and resolution within hours or minutes.

Medium Priority

Medium-priority error resulting in a specific area of the application that is not functioning, but the overall application is still up and running. For applications with different categories of end users, may include application processes that cannot be completed for the typical (as opposed to high-priority) end user. Includes problems of similar criticality for downstream dependent systems. Normally requires a response and resolution within a portion of a day or a day.

Low Priority

Includes application errors with a technical workaround that represents inconvenience but not loss of functionality. For applications with different categories of end users, comprises an applications process that cannot be completed for the lowest-priority end users. Includes problems of similar criticality for downstream dependent systems. Requires response and resolution within a day or over several days.

---

and detailed task execution descriptions at every level, is required to avoid confusion and miscommunication. Eventually moving up to the Offshore Project Manager, a handbook specific to each Offshore application is required. The Application Handbook will delineate when and how the escalation and problem resolution responsibility are to be handed over to the Onshore Project Manager from the Project Manager residing Off-shore. If there is bad news to break to the internal customer, for example, regarding a serious and intractable system error that cannot be repaired within prior agreed contractual timeframes, it is up to the on-site, internal relationship manager to step in and broker those internal customer communications and monitor the situation.

The Project Manager heading up the Offshore portion of the application team is to notify the Onshore Project Manager well in advance (if possible) of negative exposure to the internal customer for system failure, so that everyone has an opportunity to be briefed and to bring their particular skills and additional resources in tackling the problem. Of course the overall Onshore application Project Manager, in this example, must work

Exhibit 5.5   Sample SLA Escalation Procedures Based upon Priority

Critical-Priority Process

1. Offshore team receives call from end user, and issues a problem ticket.
2. Offshore team attempts to resolve problem ticket within the SLA timeframe (usually in hours).
3. If problem is not resolved within 75% of designated time (if SLA requires one hour, then within 45 minutes), Offshore project manager is notified.
4. Upon lack of resolution within timeframe established in the SLA, Offshore project manager takes action outlined in escalation plan.
   a. Normally includes a phone call to the home of the Onshore project manager.
   b. The Offshore Project Manager follows up with an e-mail or other form of memo that provides a complete overview of the problem ticket, including originator, current understanding of technical cause, anticipated negative impact on downstream systems (in the case of a virus or other related issues), and anticipated time and type of problem resolution.
5. Onshore Project Manager notifies the affected end users with the full briefing. Onshore and Offshore team members work cooperatively until issue is resolved.
6. Management team is notified according to pre-established escalation procedures.
7. Post-mortem analysis includes all time added by additional personnel, and recommendations on avoiding similar issues in the future.

Medium- and Low-Priority Processes

For medium- and low-priority issues, usually the only difference in the escalation process above is how and when the escalation occurs, and how many resources are focused on resolving the problem outside of the normal team.

Note: The most successful escalation procedures have strict specifications and descriptions not only relating to the priority category of specific problems, but the exact timeframe and type of escalation (phone call or writing), backup contact numbers in case the designated individual is not reachable, and just as detailed follow-up requirements.

If there is a concern regarding lack of responsiveness or responsibility for the cause of the problem (e.g., there is a problem regarding the operations schedule not communicated to the appropriate person located overseas, close to project startup, that causes a series of systems errors), a clear escalation process should be established that allows the Onshore Project Manager to escalate these concerns within a well-defined process.

closely with the Offshore team to create a fix as soon as possible, and later on, conduct research to restructure the application to avoid the same problem in the future. The escalation process must be very precise, outlining exactly whom to call, when, and under what circumstances. The byword of successful IT management is avoidance of surprises. Achieving that communication level in Offshore depends upon a level of documentation detail and precision that is not the norm for most U.S. corporations, even those that are geographically dispersed.

Although most large U.S. corporations can legitimately claim experience in maintaining applications across many diverse countries or locations, few have experience in executing maintenance and support within a Co-Sourcing or shared responsibility where the same application has a split team, some in the United States, and some overseas, with a daily hand-off of responsibility and communication. However, most Offshore customers will pleasantly discover that the Offshore vendors are very aware of these critical success factors in terms of process, and take great pains to establish them. One Offshore Program Manager in the Offshore Interest Group was amazed to find, for example, not just a day-by-day project plan for Offshore launch as is typical of U.S.-based vendors, but a project plan detailing tasks on an hourly basis. This represented a completely new standard of detail and precision that the organization then could apply as appropriate across all applications.

Chapter 4 outlined research showing CMM certification support was one of the goals of bringing these vendors inhouse for more than a few customers. Although a detailed exploration of how CMM certifications can be implemented organizationwide is beyond the scope of this book, it is important to note that the culture of well-documented applications certainly doesn't hurt that effort. Moving up the CMM certification level means, among other disciplines, centralization of IT systems life-cycle functions that benefit from a single point of organizational control, such as regression testing. It is one of the functions of the Offshore Program Manager to work closely with the CMM program manager, or equivalent, to explore how the Offshore program can support the CMM certification process. It may make sense for some Offshore application development facilities to support their own centralized regression testing function, for example. Or, to continue the example, perhaps Offshore supports these improvements indirectly by freeing up former maintenance and support personnel to train and staff a dedicated centralized organizationwide test facility. Offshore can be a positive change agent and catalyst by providing the additional people resources and budget to further the IT organization's overall efficiency.

In the spirit of documenting clearly mutual responsibilities, another point to note is that the role of the PMO is defining the mutual production

Exhibit 5.6   Checklist for Operational Infrastructure Requirements[a]

- Corporate IDs
  - LAN ID
  - Intranet access
  - Mainframe ID
  - Remote access ID
  - Secure user ID
- Working infrastructure
  - Telephone/voicemail
  - E-mail ID
  - Laptop
  - Mobile phone or pager
  - Badge and applicable physical security access
  - Parking tag
  - Workstation and workspace
  - Analog line (for backup dialup)

[a] A process for distributing, updating, deleting (upon a resource leaving), and validating is required for all team members.

environment IT roles and responsibilities. In the Co-Sourcing model, usually the customer retains ownership of all hardware and software, and therefore maintains all operations responsibility. The Offshore vendor team also has rights relative to system access, and must learn not only how to work cooperatively across the distance with the Onshore development or leadership team, but to cope with the operations limitations of scheduled upgrades, downtime, and enhancements. The ongoing functions of the Offshore team require close partnership across the complex operations organizational environment, and again it is up to the Offshore PMO to help maintain objective and fair interactions and clear expectations on behalf of both parties. (See Exhibit 5.6 for an operations checklist.)

Network availability is also a critical shared responsibility. Most Offshore service providers have a U.S.-based network hub, and the responsibility for network availability is normally completely theirs from the point of that hub on through to all of the various overseas locations. It is up to the Offshore PMO to ensure, once again, that the mutual understanding is clear, and that there isn't an atmosphere of finger pointing if the handshaking between internal and external vendor networks isn't working.

Note that network technology reliability is generally not a serious barrier to the success of Offshore programs. Within the Offshore Interest Group, this challenge has never been mentioned as a serious ongoing concern over three years of meetings. Once set up successfully with clear mutual understanding of roles and responsibilities, the current state of network availability and technology is sophisticated enough to do the task, and most leading vendors have considerable investment and robust infrastructure.

THE OFFSHORE PROJECT MANAGER CHECKLIST

Having discussed the program-level preparation required for success, we are now ready to take a look at our second program checklist component, the checklist for project managers. Exhibit 5.7 shows the typical stages and steps in preparation for a project or maintenance and support application to go Offshore. It is upon the selection and allocation of a Project Manager responsible for a new application launch Offshore that the timeline truly begins.

Pre-Work: Validate Application Risk Level for Offshore

Upon selection of the application for Offshore, it is up to the Project Manager to validate in detail that, from a risk perspective, the application is indeed a good candidate for Offshore. Typically risks are listed, ranked, and assigned a value, and if the total risk goes over a certain threshold as represented by the sum of those values, that particular application might not be appropriate for Offshore.

Most risks are at the general organizational or enterprise level, and these are explored in Chapter Seven. From a program management perspective, it is helpful to Project Managers to have access to document templates prepopulated with potential risks related to Offshore. If a risk is legitimately identified that represents a showstopper, there need to be guidelines in place to help with the escalation and review of those risks prior to having that application move to the next stage in moving Offshore. Some organizations require the assessment team, as part of an overall risk assessment for Offshore, to undergo an application-specific review of the security architecture. The key here, of course, is early detection so that money and time are not wasted, and another more appropriate application goes Offshore instead.

The risk analysis specific to Offshore should be completed a maximum of four weeks after the assessment team indicates the application is selected for Offshore. It is recommended that these applications become part of the annual review or risk certification process.

Another strong recommendation is to have a formal business partner or business owner sign off for all risk areas identified, which will become less difficult and controversial as the Offshore program matures. It is

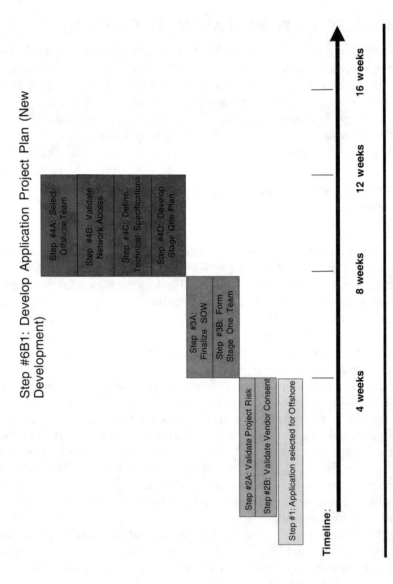

Exhibit 5.7   A Typical Offshore Program Timeline

important that all stakeholders agree to undertake the legitimate risks associated with Offshore. An Application Security Architecture checklist for the Project Manager is outlined in Exhibit 5.8.

Pre-Work: Validate Software License Vendor Consents

In parallel with the application risk assessment, the Offshore application project manager needs to validate that there are no software licensing impediments to going Offshore. Usually it is the responsibility of the Offshore Project Manager to obtain a signature on a standard form, signed by the legal department, and store that in the appropriate project repository.

As outlined above, it is normally the Offshore Program Manager who centrally tracks and manages this process programwide, but again it is helpful to have, as part of the checklist, a well-documented process that is required of the Offshore Project Manager to validate this step is indeed in place. The Offshore Project Manager should not be responsible for direct handling of vendor consents, because the potential legal delays must be identified far in advance of actually assigning a Project Manager.

Successful resolution of the third-party vendor consent is a prerequisite to assessing whether a project is appropriate for Offshore and, ideally, if there are impediments in that area, the project goes no further until they are resolved. Obtaining a formal signature from the legal department is the recommended limit of the responsibility for the Offshore Project Manager.

Now that the pre-work has been completed, let's look at the role of the Offshore Project Manager (Exhibit 5.9). Below are some of the tasks for which the Offshore Project Manager is responsible.

Month 1: Establish SOW for Offshore Application

As mentioned above, the Statement of Work (SOW) is typically the mechanism that bridges the gap between the more general vendor and centralized legal contract, and the individual IT application requirements. Normally, vendor contracts are negotiated at the organization level, but it is the SOW that defines precisely the work to be executed and the success criteria to be used to evaluate vendor performance.

The application-specific success criterion is applied to the Offshore application team in terms of objectively measurable performance metrics, which they are contractually obligated to fulfill. The SOW includes the specific skill-level requirements, roles, and structure of the vendor team members (a sample skillset requirement document can be found in Exhibit 5.10), a high-level outline of the tasks involved, and any other particular criteria specific to the application that would normally not be

Exhibit 5.8   Application Security Architecture Checklist

Confirm the confidentiality level of the application according to corporate standards.

Identify the ASPs (Application Service Providers) associated with the application.

Include the security certification (if any) associated with vendor.

List any independent security reviews/audits associated with the ASP.

Ensure a nondisclosure agreement, approved by the legal department, is on file for all ASPs and other related vendors.

Define security procedures specific to each type of potential security breach.

List all hardware and operating systems across all layers of the client/server architecture associated with the application.

List controls protecting operating system commands against tampering.

If application significantly different from standard software configuration (e.g., uses nonstandard software packages for security or communications), describe and give justification.

Identify physical location(s) of hardware platform, and whether it is in a formal computer room, etc.

Identify the location of exactly where within the corporate firewall the network access occurs.

Outline transport protocols, services, and ports for network access.

Identify the file transfer protocol, and describe the security level.

Describe the Web architecture, including supported wireless communications, including the parts of the application, if any, residing outside the corporate firewall.

Indicate if the application requires local administrator rights, and describe them and their security level.

Outline any security functions within the application itself, such as the ability to create user IDs.

Describe the different levels of security administrators with alternate privileges.

Document how access (an individual's or organization's) privileges are determined, and how those are updated and checked for accuracy over time.

Describe any self-diagnostic tools associated with the application.

If there is more than a typical security requirement due to highly confidential data, such as SecureID technology, document the need and whether it is sufficient to protect across the Offshore environment.

Document any security functionality within the technology of the application. For example, does it track if a user is logged on twice? Does it communicate with the operating system to ensure the user is using the same user ID as the operating system access?

Exhibit 5.9   Responsibilities of the Offshore Project Manager

Act as a primary point of contact for vendor project manager located Offshore. Supervise the knowledge transfer process. Participate in creation, execution, and evaluation of Offshore vendor performance criteria, including process definitions for SLA escalation procedures for maintenance and support application, and deliverable review processes for new application development. Interface to other organizations within the firm, such as operations, to support Offshore project team. Participate directly in evaluating performance of vendor according to criteria. Serve as focal point for compliance across many corporate areas, including methodology and process guidelines, security guidelines, etc. Ensure adherence to change control process to address issues in service or in new project development.

covered by a more general contract. It should include major milestones for the project, and key steps and timeframe for the Offshore launch. In addition, the SOW specifies the required resources in terms of steady-state performance criteria and consequences (if any) of not meeting those criteria, Offshore locations, resource costs (usually according to the centrally negotiated fees table), as well as SLAs for maintenance and support or the project timetable, acceptance criteria, and deliverables description for new application development.

All Project Managers should have access to several reference documents that are placed into an Offshore project documentation repository by the Offshore Program Manager. These help set the stage for successful execution of the application-specific SOWs. The recommended content of one of these documents, the vendor contract summary, is contained in Exhibit 5.11.

The specifics of the SOW are difficult to delve into, because they are usually very particular to a specific organization, suite of applications, vendor, and corporation. It is important that the SOW seamlessly take over where the more general legal vendor contract leaves off. Ideally, the Offshore Project Manager responsible for the overall application authors the associated SOW. This provides the Project Manager with an automatic authority relative to the vendor, and allows the Project Manager to actively participate in the final timetable, deliverables, and success criteria for which he or she is ultimately responsible.

The SOW is reviewed in turn by the legal department, the vendor, the Offshore Program Office, and the IT management team (and business

Exhibit 5.10 Sample Role Definition Requirements for Offshore Vendor Team Members[a]

Name	Location/ Status	Required Skills/Experience	Notes
Offshore delivery lead	U.S. location/ full time	Required: X years industry experience X years program/ project leadership Strong English language and communication skills Master's degree or equivalent experience Preferred: Application-specific experience (list technology)	At Knowledge Transfer/Transition: Supervise Offshore team during Onshore training Manage documentation of processes At steady-state: Lead Offshore team effort Responsible for Offshore team performance and goal achievement Responsible for problem escalation and resolution Develop and manage testing and release schedule for all regions Manage documentation of all phases of Offshore team effort Ensure methodology is followed Ensure compliance with all risk and security measures Status reporting

[a] This example is for the vendor overseas team lead.

management team as appropriate). The legal department and Offshore Program Manager can aid the Project Manager in ensuring that the SOW specifies suitable information, and relates to the umbrella contract appropriately. Clearly, the Project Manager must follow a strict set of approval signatures for every SOW.

Exhibit 5.11   Offshore Reference Document: Vendor Contract Summary (One per Vendor)

Vendor Contract Summary (One per Vendor), to include the following information:

- Length of contract (term in years).
- FTE volume commitments (if any).

  These are the minimum commitments that many Offshore vendors put into the customer agreements to provide incentives to use their resources. It is frequently one of the tasks of the Offshore Program Manager to track the level of utilization by vendors in order to ensure the minimum commitments are met.

- Vendor specialty or focus, if any.

  Some vendors may specialize in particular applications, business relationships, types of work (maintenance and support vs. new application of development), etc.

- Performance criteria (objective).

  Including measurement process and reporting requirements.

- Vendor service types.

  These may include:

  - Planning services such as Offshore application assessment, transition planning, and transition execution. (Frequently, the Tier Two India-based companies agree to provide these services for no fee to new customers or customers moving from another vendor.)
  - Maintenance and support services may include SLA response services according to pre-set criteria, documentation of ad hoc systems, fault repair, end-user support, preventive maintenance, and continuous improvement.
  - New development services may include services across the systems life cycle related to analysis, design, coding, and testing. These are usually contractual services that have specific criteria for acceptance, usually pertaining to measures of quality, timeliness, and efficiency.

One of the most important reasons that the Offshore Project Manager should be author of the SOW, and a strong participant in any further negotiations and refinement, is that it then empowers that individual to monitor the performance of the Offshore vendor in an application-specific way. This includes meeting all timetables relative to launch of the application to Offshore. It also includes ensuring the vendor meets expectations regarding the skill level of the Offshore staff, as well as any application-specific criteria needed to ensure application success.

The good news is that most Offshore vendors manage their primary asset — technology resources — with a precision and commitment to development and training generally unmatched in U.S. firms. Although key resources such as the application Project Manager physically located Offshore may be subject to interview approval, in general the majority of Offshore location team members are not subject to interview. In addition to the logistical difficulties, this is due to the simple fact that most vendor contracts are fixed price and have clear performance criteria attached to success, so that the risks associated with performance rest squarely on the vendors.

Month 1: Validate Operational Requirements

The additional support required of the operations team can be somewhat subtle. For example, many firms use the night shift to run batch reports, perform system backup, and other routine maintenance tasks. Of course, the timing for these tasks would now be during prime Offshore working hours, and run the risk of interfering with application performance. A restructuring of the operations schedule reallocating operations tasks and personnel according to a worldwide schedule, and the allocation of additional hardware disk space, may allow the Offshore staff to work in parallel when batch jobs are running. At times, the need for this type of organizational restructuring does not become evident until there is a cumulative load on the systems, and can add to delay when the performance threshold is crossed unexpectedly with the addition of a set of new Offshore applications.

Additional areas of operational impact are:

- User support, for example, support of password reset, which may need to be moved Offshore for the night shift or established as a 24-hour function.
- For new application development, confirmation of the availability of the appropriate separate staging hardware needed for different phases of the systems development life cycle, such as unit test.

Month 1: Application Risk and Compliance

It is hoped that Offshore risk and compliance programs exist within a well-structured overall IT application risk and compliance program. As part of the Project Manager's checklist, each application's existing risk management profile needs to be updated for Offshore. Normally this is a pro forma exercise, because the most indepth review occurs upon initial selection of the application for Offshore. The most important function of the Offshore Project Manager is to establish an initial discipline involving regular annual risk review. In addition, the Project Manager ensures that the appropriate team members validate that the network security architecture, as designed for general Offshore application, is still sufficient for the specific application.

Depending on the vertical industry, some application-specific risk plans may be subject to review by regulatory agencies. It is also anticipated that many regulatory agencies will become more and more involved in Offshore as it becomes part of the mainstream.

Some of the more typical application-specific risk areas for evaluation are:

■ Measures for vendor management and oversight
■ Controls for meeting operational requirements, such as response for and monitoring of high availability systems
■ Quality measures
■ Legal and regulatory compliance, such as those relating to healthcare reporting requirements
■ Process and technology in place to ensure privacy and customer confidentiality
■ Structure of overall information security architecture
■ Protection of intellectual capital and investment created in knowledge transfer
■ Alignment of Offshore with the corporate disaster recovery plan, supporting business resumption and crisis management
■ Due diligence in relation to secure hiring practices, including OFAC screening, security measures at the Offshore site such as badges and video surveillance, and so on

There may be some aspects of the application that represent inherent risk and that have escaped the prior notice of the initial assessment. These may be in the downstream interface of related systems, or the use of test data that is based upon real customer data, or other subtle risks.

Month 2: Support Redeployment of Affected Employees

Although the onus of responsibility for the overall management of affected employees certainly is not upon the individual Offshore Project Manager, de facto this indeed may be the case. The relative difficulty or ease of that role is reflective of the organization's overall ethical stance, as discussed in detail in Chapter 6.

Support and encouragement from the current project manager can be surprisingly important for employees in transition. Ideally project managers will have access to training and other sources of support in moving through these delicate and difficult situations.

Month 2: Form the Stage One Onshore and Offshore Team

For relatively complex applications, a stage one team will be formed to prepare for a successful Offshore transition. Simple applications may have just one experienced Offshore project manager comprising the entire team, whereas complex stage one teams may have several individuals representing a broad array of functional disciplines.

The stage one team will prepare the following:

- Project organization chart: validation of the roles and responsibilities outlined in the SOW
- Structure the regular project meeting schedule
- Establish the high-level project plan, confirming initial milestones in the SOW
- Define team communications norms
- Set up project tracking structure, documentation repository, and project reporting protocols such as status reporting and oversight of the Offshore team (metrics evaluation and tracking)
- Provide status updates to the PMO and management team

Depending upon the particular Offshore vendor, or application, identifying the appropriate potential candidates to fill out the team roster can require significant leadtime. Although most Project Managers do not interview the majority of Offshore team members, some sort of validation of skills is usually performed by the Project Manager — perhaps a review of a printed list of education and skills for each employee. Upon confirmation of the detailed staffing plan, which includes all-important timing for knowledge transfers, visas, and so on, it is time to define the launch schedule in detail. A sample go/no go responsibility matrix is provided in Exhibit 5.12.

Key processes to be addressed by the Stage one team:

- Describe the structure, membership, and responsibility of both Onshore and Offshore teams
- Locations of team members
- Workspace desktop requirements
- Structure knowledge transfer process
- Define technical infrastructure
- Outline business processes transfer/integration
- Operational application requirements

The staffing plan outlines the roles, base locations, required skills and strengths, and responsibilities for each team member, in enough detail to

Exhibit 5.12   Sample Offshore Go/No Go Approval Requirements Matrix[a]

Role	Vendor Consent	Risk Assessment	SOW	Operations Guide	Offshore Application Handbook	Go/No Go Approval for Launch
Project Manager		R		R, W	R, W	R, W
Offshore location lead				W	W	W
Offshore PMO	R		R, W	W	W	W
Legal	W		W			W
Compliance (risk, audit, etc.)		W		W	W	W
IT manager		W	W		W	W
Operations		W		W	W	W
Quality assurance		W		W	W	W
Offshore vendor				W	W	W
Business partner management		W				W
Senior management						W
Offshore service provider			W	W	W	W
Software vendor	W			W		W

[a] W = Written approval required; R = Responsible.

ensure that an objective assessment can be conducted to evaluate candidates for qualification. For example, if a particular role requires mainframe knowledge, the skills relating to COBOL, JCL, CICS, and MVS are outlined. If the application is third-party software, the number of years of experience is listed in both the SOW and this document.

Ultimately the staffing plan will used by the Offshore vendor as an aid to search for candidates. A sample structure of an Offshore team is illustrated in Exhibit 5.13.

Months 1 and 2: Create Detailed Project Plan

A good project plan is one of the basics of effective project management. It is the primary communication and tracking vehicle via which mutual expectations are communicated. The implications of progress (or lack of it) on project deliverables can be measured and understood. Ideally, one of the toolkits available to the Project Manager is a repository of sample Offshore project plans illustrating the methodology.

Offshore service providers normally provide a prototype project plan, often specific to a particular application package. In managing large application package, application support and development via Offshore, there are many complex decisions. Deciding how to structure the Offshore support, or how to approach a major system upgrade, are questions that can be answered with the help of the extensive experience of many Offshore vendors.

The project plan should be available to and tracked by the entire team in a regular meeting setting where the Project Manager calls for accountability — to deliverables or support functions and review, depending upon the type of application.

Month 2: Create Offshore Project Issues List

An issue is a problem or concern that has the potential to negatively derail a project by affecting quality, timeliness, or effort related to deliverables for new application development. For maintenance and support efforts, an issue is a problem or concern that may interfere with the project team meeting SLA and other measurements of success.

Although the Offshore PMO is responsible for tracking overall Offshore program issues, the Project Manager must oversee the tracking and resolution of application- or project-level issues. Components of the Offshore issues list include: date recorded, date due, issue description, severity (high, medium, low), issue reporter (person who discovered issue), issue owner (person responsible for resolving the issues by the date due), status relative to issue resolution, or brief interim notes.

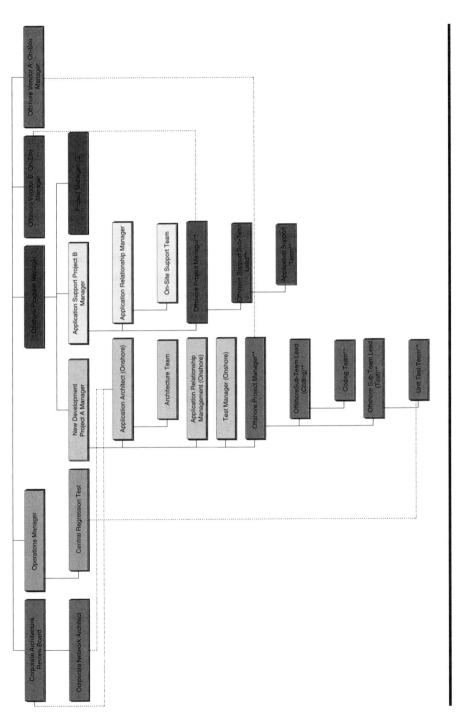

Exhibit 5.13   A Typical Offshore Project Team Structure

Highest-priority project issues, as well as issues that affect or involve several application teams, are reported up to the overall Offshore PMO. There they join the PMO-level issues list for higher-visibility tracking and accountability. Frequently these issues are included on management reports to the executive stakeholder team by the Offshore PMO on a regular basis.

Month 2: Create Offshore Functional Specifications

The infrastructure architecture for Offshore, including as it frequently does a network of firewalls and close handshaking with networks of various Offshore service providers, is a complex effort requiring a robust central architecture. One of the central tasks for the Onshore Project Manager is to identify the application-level infrastructure requirements for successful Offshore transition.

Most large organizations have a central body that validates changes to network architecture, sets standards, and ensures compliance with a centralized architecture. As mentioned above, it is up to the Offshore Project Manager, however, to make the distinction between the standard Offshore network architecture and the requirements of the application, to ensure these are a fit. Any differences with the standard architecture are outlined in the Functional Specifications.

The stage one team documents these and other application-specific infrastructure requirements. The level of additional security infrastructure is determined in large part by the foundation technology of the application. Mainframe technology is generally much easier to secure, technically speaking, than the complex interdependent parts of a client/server-based application. Many large software packages, running on both client/server as well as mainframe technology, may already include extensive network security functionality. The team members responsible for network security architecture need to review and approve all individual application technical specifications prior to Offshore application launch.

The Functional Specifications should include a complete list of components of the required architecture of the application, including hardware platforms, operating systems, client/server applications, network security requirements, servers, printers, network access, desktops, interfaces to enterprise software such as corporate e-mail, and so on.

A detailed list of the contents of the Functional Specifications is given in Exhibit 5.14.

Month 2 to 3: Complete Offshore Application Handbook

The Application Handbook is an amalgam of application-specific information from a variety of sources, and serves as the ultimate source and

Exhibit 5.14   Offshore Functional Specifications Document Contents

1. Project overview
   a. Business value of project, including relationship to overall strategic goals
   b. Description of what comprises overall project success
   c. Project stakeholders and executive sponsors (usually in the form of organizational roles, not individual names, although may be both)
2. Related business processes
   a. Business process diagrams and descriptions — for each
   b. Set of business users
   c. Objective performance metrics
   d. Reporting/statistics structure
3. Critical success factors
   a. Technical dependencies, e.g., Offshore vendor network performance, etc.
   b. Nontechnical dependencies, e.g., U.S. visa processing occurs within x timeframe
4. Training requirements
   a. Initial as well as long-term
   b. Include risk mitigation requirements for geographically dispersed personnel
5. Application architecture
   a. List hardware, operating systems, network, interface — all layers and components
   b. Diagrams
   c. Performance controls and measurements
6. Functional architecture
   a. Diagrams
7. Application interface requirements
   a. List of applications requiring access, e.g., access to automated defect tracking tool for maintenance and support
8. Repository requirements
   a. Disaster recovery plan reviewed, approved, signed off, and in project repository
   b. Risk assessment approved, signed off, and in project repository
   c. Project plan, including knowledge transfer schedule, approved, signed off, and in project repository
9. Sign off/acceptance
   a. Technical management team
   b. Operations management team
   c. Internal business stakeholders as appropriate

guide to successful launch of the Offshore project. These sources are listed below:

1. From the Functional Specifications document
   a. Application functional overview, including diagram
   b. Technical architecture and hardware infrastructure
   c. Software architecture, including operating systems, client/server architecture, associated programming languages and tools, databases
   d. Systems interdependencies
2. From risk documentation and matrices
   a. Application-specific Offshore risks
3. From SOW
   a. Application-specific vendor performance criteria and objectives
   b. Offshore location
   c. Financial run rate (Offshore personnel costs)
   d. Efficiency measures
      i. Provisions as to whether benefits are financially shared with Offshore vendor
   e. Offshore staffing model
   f. Project organization
   g. SLAs
      i. Escalation plans
   h. Change control processes
4. User population
   a. Descriptions of users: numbers, type, locations
   b. Subject matter experts and key business community members
   c. Training
5. Operations
   a. Description of the size, age, complexity, versions, planned upgrades of system, vendors
   b. Application-specific operational needs, if any
   c. Support hours and requirements
   d. Maintenance history
   e. Audit history of application and infrastructure problems
   f. Third-party relationships and support
   g. Current scheduled application enhancements
   h. Application freeze schedule (no enhancements allowed in preparation for Offshore)
6. Documentation logistics
   a. Location of application maintenance records
   b. Development, test, UAT, and production environment descriptions
   c. For maintenance and support applications

      i. Trouble tickets process
     ii. Statistical performance norms and history
    iii. SLAs
  d. For new development applications
      i. Methodology
     ii. Migration process among development, test, and production
7. Systems requirements by phase
  a. Major milestones and deliverables
  b. Application-specific acceptance criteria
  c. Application-specific change control processes and escalation procedures

Month 2 to 3: Proceed with Offshore Resource Hiring Process

First, the Offshore Project Manager must ensure that the OFAC screenings did indeed occur for all overseas resources. OFAC screening is a process designed to ensure that the wrong individuals do not enter the United States for security reasons, and is discussed more fully in Chapter Six.

In addition, working closely with the Offshore Vendor, it is up to the Onshore Project Manager to ensure that the application staffing process is followed within the specified timetable. In bringing together the Offshore vendor and the internal Project Managers for the first time, before trust is established, the best remedy for a smooth project initiation is precise clarity for all parties. Specifying a timeframe and deadline for every step in the staffing process may appear to be overkill, however, delays are costly and clear expectations in this initial joint task become a framework for problem solving within a positive team culture of cooperation. Each step in the staffing process should be elucidated with a timeline and person responsible, for example, the Offshore Project Manager has responsibility to ensure all potential Offshore team members are reviewed and approved/disapproved within three business days after a written qualifications review (or whatever the appropriate process for staffing).

Months 3 to 6: Proceed with Structuring of Knowledge Transfer

Synchronizing the arrival of Offshore resources for knowledge transfer with the remainder of the logistics for overall application readiness can be challenging. Delays relating to network infrastructure readiness, visa processing, air travel, and other challenges can easily cause havoc with tight schedules. Although the India-based Offshore firms have recently been able to minimize wait times for arrival of the Offshore team by establishing groups of ready-to-go resources here in the United States, this may not be true of a Big Four partner and their U.S.-based equivalents, which often still cling to a culture of offering consultants as individuals.

At any rate, it is safer to assume that the Offshore team member will require at least six to ten weeks for visa processing after the candidate has been officially accepted as a team member. Note that these timeframes may easily change as a result of shifts in international security requirements, here and abroad. Recent trends as this book is being written show that this leadtime is lengthening, not shrinking, due to lower availability of visas and the growing field of consultants who need them, as well as heightened security processes. Additional expenses accrue if the candidate arrives early (the individuals assigned for knowledge transfer may not have bandwidth for training), or late (missed savings from delays in implementation).

Generally, Offshore Project Managers report progress on staffing and completion of SOWs to the central Offshore PMO for management tracking and reporting, because these steps are direct hurdles to realization of savings for Offshore. Logistics relating to knowledge transfer, including airfare and other expense management, U.S. visa processing, hotel, transportation, and so on, are (contractually) usually the responsibility of the Offshore vendor.

It is important for the Offshore team members to have enough time to get oriented to the area, if they are the first group to arrive from that firm from India. Addressing the special dietary, cultural, and religious needs of the initial set of individuals from India sets the tone for welcome and of respect for the needs of others from different cultural backgrounds. Once the first group is acclimated, they can be instrumental in helping later arrivals find the necessary resources to feel comfortable in their new surroundings.

On a tactical level, workers from overseas participating in knowledge transfer, which can vary from 4 to 12 weeks, will need office space and a place to work, as well as the proper ID badges, user accounts, network IDs, and so on. In large corporations these processes can require some lead time, especially for a large group, so again it is important to plan so that the Offshore team can be productive throughout the planned knowledge transfer period.

Months 3 to 6: Proceed with Execution of Knowledge Transfer

The handshaking, or relative hand-off of responsibilities between on-site and overseas team members, must be clearly specified as part of the Offshore Application Handbook. First the division of labor can be defined at a high level, and later refined in more detail as the stage one team is established and the team populated with individuals. As is typical with all project organizations, the details of individuals' responsibilities are not fully defined until the specific skills and backgrounds of the individuals are present to help fine tune the specifics.

Exhibit 5.15 A Typical Offshore Project Team Division of Responsibilities

Task	Onshore	Primary Offshore Location	Backup Offshore Location (Risk)
Offshore application project A			
Requirements development	✓		
Architectural integration	✓		
Network security design and monitoring	✓	✓	✓
Application high-level design	✓		
Application detail design and build		✓	✓
Application testing	✓	✓	✓
Integration test	✓	✓	
Transition and implementation	✓	✓	
Post-implementation review and support	✓	✓	
Documentation	✓	✓	✓
Ongoing efficiencies analysis		✓	✓

Exhibit 5.15 outlines the role distinction among the typical team members — Onshore, primary Offshore, and backup Offshore. Backup Offshore team members are chiefly there to maintain knowledge transfer and other intangible investments, and generally devote roughly five percent of their time weekly to keep abreast of system changes, after the initial abbreviated period of application training.

The required knowledge to be collected, and formally documented, on behalf of the project is outlined in the knowledge transfer spreadsheet (Exhibit 5.16). The Offshore team member will populate the knowledge transfer spreadsheet by conducting functional and technical discussions with the Project Manager and Onshore application team members, including business subject matter experts. Although each application is unique, the spreadsheet provides a baseline for the categories of knowledge that are to be acquired by the Offshore staff member.

Each topic within the knowledge transfer spreadsheet is listed along with its meaning and importance to the overall application, and the recommendations regarding the process of transfer of this knowledge.

To be complete, the components of the knowledge transfer spreadsheet are as follows:

■ Expertise requirements, widely interpreted. These include transfer of all the skills, business processes, reporting, results interpretation, and functions now performed by the original team. Next to the skill itself, the level of expertise required should be listed. The topics to be learned are initially documented by the stage one

Exhibit 5.16   Knowledge Transfer Checklist for Subject Matter Experts

- Industry overview; where organization fits within overall industry picture
  - Includes organization charts, description of overall business environment, key business success factors, briefing on corporate history and culture
  - May be conducted by Offshore vendor for their own employees
- Application overview
  - Users
  - Importance to firm
  - Measures of success
- Application functionality
  - Navigation
  - Primary processes
- Application architecture
  - Layers including host and desktop, or middleware equivalent
- Application operations scheduling
  - Test regions
  - Communications processes and interface with Onshore operations team
- Onshore/Offshore network handshake and team expectations
  - For maintenance and support
    - Problem ticket management
    - Escalation procedures
    - Success measures
    - Continuous improvement processes
  - For new application development
    - Project plan
    - Methodology
    - Roles/responsibility of Onshore vs. Offshore team
    - Success measures
  - Change control
  - Documentation requirements
  - Testing procedures
  - Risk and security requirements

team, and validated later by the application Onshore and Offshore Project Managers and subject matter experts once the team has been assigned.

- ■ A list of the primary subject matter experts responsible for the training of the Offshore team members during knowledge transfer.
- ■ A description of the checkpoint process. This includes a description of the internal resource requirements, overall approach, estimates of required teaching time, and key milestones associated with

successful knowledge transfer. Passing these checkpoints is usually a requirement prior to the application going Offshore. Repeated failure of key resources to pass these checkpoints may mean substitution of that team member moving forward, and is usually one of the critical success factors in accepting Offshore personnel onto the application team.

- Initially, the checkpoints start as self-evaluations.
- The second checkpoint is performed by the subject matter expert training the Offshore team member.
- The final checkpoint is performed by a team, including the subject matter expert, Onshore Project Manager, and other stakeholders, usually in an interview setting.

■ A complete listing of application-related tasks and software modules, classified into different functional areas defined within the application. For example, Job A is the Review of Web Interfaces, and consists of software modules 1, 2, and 3.

Although the knowledge transfer spreadsheet begins at a high level, some time prior to the actual arrival of the Offshore team, a detailed knowledge transfer project plan is completed and tracked by the stage one team and Project Manager.

On a practical level, it is up to the Project Manager and stage one team to determine how, what, when, and where the required knowledge will be transferred. Some options include

■ Shadowing during regular work hours
- The de facto norm is this approach, usually part-time, with some self-study for the remainder of the work day
■ Special group meetings, such as half-day seminars or brown bag lunches
- Outside normal work hours
■ If resource is sophisticated, putting them to work doing more routine tasks for part of the time, and teaching more subtle or custom processes around essentially a working contributing role
■ Trouble-shooting the system, responding to SLAs, researching trouble tickets, or other maintenance tasks
■ Self-study of code

Parallel to the execution of knowledge transfer, the stage one team needs to define the next level of detail regarding hardware and network infrastructure and security for the application. If a test staging system is required, for example, the location, access, protocols, and system requirements, including interfaces to other applications, are defined. A detailed set of test plans, scripts, and success criteria, as well as an outline of organizational roles and responsibilities, is required. If there is a central regression testing process and set of resources Onshore, the interface to that organization must be specified in the Offshore Application Handbook as well as the project plan.

The impact on existing business processes must be evaluated and documented. Some of the factors affecting business processes when applications move Offshore include time zones, monetary rates of exchange, communication norms, infrastructure availability, risk management requirements, and off-shift support.

Month 2 to 3: Complete Offshore Operations Guide

The Offshore Operations Guide includes the following points of information:

1. An overview of the type of support required — production or maintenance.
   a. Standard support hours
   b. Holiday procedures (Onshore and Offshore)
2. Escalation criteria and procedures.
3. Problem ticket management, including processes on updating, routing, and closing problem tickets.
4. Change control — requires documentation of the reason for the change, a description of the change, and signatures of the appropriate approvers. These processes may differ slightly for change control process for a problem ticket or SLA versus a due date for system enhancements or new development.
5. Defect resolution — helpful pointers on common defects and their resolution.
6. Operations conflict scheduling — procedures to ensure development and production fixes are coordinated and do not interfere with each other in unexpected ways.
7. Transition procedures for moving support control between the Onshore and Offshore team. Detailed daily communications requirements/handshake are outlined in detail.
8. Documentation — includes standards, templates, version control, repository location and access, and review and approval processes.
9. Requirements gathering — will include some overview on requirements gathering for the line of business.
10. Operations schedule management/other administrative processes — software tools, time tracking and status reporting, weekly meeting schedule, and so on.

Exhibit 5.17 Offshore Launch Transition Success Criteria[a]

Knowledge transfer spreadsheet defined and in place for all application knowledge and roles (application IT manager, subject matter experts)
Knowledge transfer successfully completed (subject matter experts, overseas and Offshore project managers)
Systems documentation complete and up to specified standards (overseas and Offshore project managers)
Network and supporting communications infrastructure in place (Onshore and Offshore project managers, network security architects for vendor and inhouse)
Performance criteria and reporting well understood and ready to execute (overseas and Offshore project managers)
Operations scheduling and communications in place; for new application development, stable development or production systems environment is available (overseas and Offshore project managers, IT operations representatives)
All staffing in place for overseas and Offshore teams
Compliance, security, and risk management processes approved, signed off, and in place

[a] A typical list of success criteria for Offshore launch, followed by the team member responsible for completion.

At Offshore Launch

Project launch is the culmination of the entire Offshore preparation and stage one team effort. Knowledge transfer is completed, and the Offshore team is ready to return to the Offshore location they call home. Project launch occurs in three phases as outlined below.

Later in this chapter, additional information is provided to support effective Offshore launch. Exhibit 5.17 lists sample Offshore launch transition criteria for the stage one team. Exhibit 5.18 provides a sample Offshore launch internal announcement.

Phase 1: Validation via Go/No Go

The first phase validates readiness via a thorough review process culminating in a go/no go decision meeting. At times, especially at first, these are really a series of meetings that identify roadblocks and action plans to eliminate them, it is hoped of short duration, before the next go/no go can be scheduled.

All functional disciplines, as well as the Offshore and Onshore project managers, must be present to confirm application readiness. Prerequisites

Exhibit 5.18   Sample Offshore Launch Notification

To: Business users and management team   Date: xxx
cc: Stakeholders

Greetings:
The [application a] team will be transitioning to [offshore location] on mm/dd/yyyy. Keep a copy of this memo, which will help you answer questions regarding contacting the new team members responsible for application functions.

What is the time difference between [Offshore location] and [Onshore end-user location(s)]?
[Offshore location] is y hours ahead of the [end user location(s)]. This means that when it is noon in the United States, it is (time) on the same day in [Offshore location].

What are the Offshore team's core hours?
[Offshore team] core hours are x a.m. - y p.m. local time, with pager support during (time).

What is the Offshore team structure?
The team will be composed of [vendor name, offshore location] personnel who have been certified through a recent testing process as successfully completing knowledge transfer on application a.

The lead for the entire [Offshore location one] team is xxx. The rest of the team is composed of:

Role	Name
Xxx	xxx

How do I contact the [vendor, offshore location, application a] team?
For nonemergency contacts, e-mail is the preferred method of contact. Please find a list of team members and e-mail addresses at the end of this memo.

For direct phone contact, dial 9, 011 for international direct dial, xx for the country code, x for the city code, and the number.

The local vendor office has a trunk line: xxx-xxxx. During [offshore vendor] core hours, dial this number and give the extension or name of the person you would like to contact. The lead has a direct line. To contact them, dial 9, 011 [xxx] and the number instead.

Exhibit 5.18 (continued)   Sample Offshore Launch Notification

All contact information (e-mail, pagers, mobiles, etc.) is listed below. Office numbers —

Role	Phone Number	Voicemail Number	Page Number	E-Mail Address
xxx	xxx	xxx	xxx	xxx
Primary Support	xxx	xxx	xxx	xxx
Secondary Support	xxx	xxx	xxx	xxx

Fax:
The overall project fax number is **xxx**

Who will provide support for the team from the United States?
The IT manager of application a _____, as well as the onshore project manager _____, remains the same.

Will the problem ticket queue processes change due to the transition?
No. The movement to Offshore should be completely transparent.

For any ongoing issues or concerns, please feel free to contact the Offshore project manager [name] at [contact information] or the Offshore PMO at [contact information], at any time.

Sincerely,

[name]
Offshore Project Manager

include successful completion of all knowledge transfer activities, including assessments of the subject matter experts, review and approval of the Operations Guide, and the successful preparation of the Offshore infrastructure. Go/no go meetings may occur on a weekly basis for a few weeks until all issues are resolved.

The functional disciplines represented in the go/no go team are:

■ Driver: overall Offshore Project Manager
■ Risk management
■ Network security architecture
■ Subject matter experts responsible for training Offshore personnel
■ Operations
■ IT management

- Business owners (depending upon corporate culture)
- Disaster recovery/security
- Offshore program management
- Vendor Onshore and Offshore leads
- Compliance arms: Legal, Risk, Audit, etc.

All of these representatives must be willing to personally represent their discipline in validating that the application is ready to move Offshore.

Phase 2: Offshore Team Returns

Under close watch of Onshore team members and leadership, the Offshore team members return to their homes overseas. This phase includes monitoring of activities. Monitoring is dropped after a preset period of time representing acceptance testing of Offshore processes and personnel.

Phase 3: Final Acceptance

After successful execution of application tasks within a predefined time period, a final acceptance meeting is conducted by the Offshore Project Manager. This meeting results in a formal agreement that steady-state has been achieved, and that the normal processes evaluating performance and success as outlined in the SOW now take precedence in the vendor relationship.

Steady-state may be achieved in a staggered fashion, as Offshore team members return from knowledge transfer one at a time, or it may occur on a set start date with all team members starting at once. Each approach has implications in terms of cost of transition, and these decisions frequently vary from application to application to accommodate different timing requirements and dependencies.

Upon reaching steady-state, the application is subject to the ongoing review and performance measurement processes established by the SOW and the Offshore Program Office.

Post-Launch: Monitor SLAs

As outlined in prior chapters, a service-level agreement is one type of individual metric associated with maintenance and support application performance, and agreed upon by the Offshore Services vendor. SLAs usually have several parts: definition of action taken, and acceptable timeframe for that action to occur. Well-defined escalation procedures define the steps Offshore personnel and managers must take if the specified service cannot be achieved within the agreed-upon timeframe.

Frequently, an automated software application is used to track SLAs for high-profile applications. When application users experience system errors the next step is to call the application help desk and receive a problem ticket generated by the automated system. The problem ticket serves as a common reference number for tracking the problem. The automated system prompts the help desk personnel to describe the user problem. Based upon the description of the problem, the appropriate SLA is invoked. It is the SLA that determines the actions and time requirements of the response to each individual problem ticket. For example, high-profile problems/SLAs may require that the Offshore personnel repair the problem and report back to the user within a few hours.

Infrastructure readiness, in terms of access of Offshore personnel to the online SLA management tool, is obviously one of many prerequisites to successful Offshore launch. Offshore application support personnel monitor the tool to ensure that they can immediately respond to high-priority user problems with the determined SLA time period. For highest-priority problems, the help desk may directly call the Offshore application support group, and will reach the manager in charge of that SLA if necessary.

Upon resolution of the ticket, it is up to the support person to close it by reporting the time it was closed and the resolution.

One of the more critical vendor performance metrics reported by the Offshore PMO is the percentage of late responses to SLAs. Ongoing violation of these performance criteria is usually written into the vendor contract as cause for cancellation, or is understood as reason for non-renewal of the contract when the term has expired. Fortunately, to date vendor-related performance problems are extremely rare.

For new application development, the same methodology utilized to monitor the quality, timeliness, and budget of Onshore application development generally applies to the Offshore model. In discussions in the Offshore Interest Group, most Program Managers recommend more frequent and earlier checkpoints than is typical for project execution. These are because, despite careful planning, cross-cultural and geographical difficulties do create misunderstandings. With new application development, there is a general sense that the Offshore team will undoubtedly build a new system efficiently and inexpensively — the primary concern is that they will build the system that is requested rather than a misinterpretation of those requests. Frequent communications and formal checkpoints are the key.

Post-Launch: Monitor Offshore Application Performance

There are several primary tasks for post-launch in the project management checklist:

- Ensure scope and change control processes are well defined and followed, with the appropriate notifications, approvals, and signatures.
- Documentation is updated and stored in the central repository as appropriate.
- Implement project-level performance reporting and tracking.

One frequently utilized management reporting tool is the Balanced Scorecard. Usually divided into quadrants, these may vary but usually include logistic/tracking quadrants in these areas:

- Financial — budgeted versus actual costs
- Quality measures — staffing turnover, results from end-user surveys, other metrics
- Performance measures — SLAs, timeline
- Schedule adherence/issues

A sample status biweekly report for an Offshore new development project in the process of moving Offshore is shown in Exhibit 5.19.

These project scorecards are summarized or rolled up to a variety of reporting views, including vendor view, offshore location view, and the overall Offshore program view.

A word of caution in terms of vendor evaluation — although the balanced scorecard is a useful and mercifully brief (one- to two-page) reporting mechanism, it may not be the most effective vendor performance tool within the context of a legal contract or even a specific application. This is because the overall performance "score" is balanced among the four quadrants. Low scores in one area may be nullified in the summary by very high scores in the other three areas. It is important to evaluate the minimum acceptable performance for each area of Offshore service provider or vendor contribution, and ensure that these minimums are indeed reflected in the contractual terms of the individual SOW.

Exhibit 5.20 shows some typical performance measures that are included in application-level performance reporting for Offshore.

PROGRAM AND PROJECT CHECKLIST — FINAL THOUGHTS

In summary, the lack of high visibility failures over at least a fifteen-year history for Offshore — in a press environment eager to find them — speaks for itself on general feasibility. What is affected by the sloppy or politically killed Offshore project or program is the savings accrued. These program and project checklists can serve as reminders to ensure that critical topics that can have an impact on delays in Offshore are at least

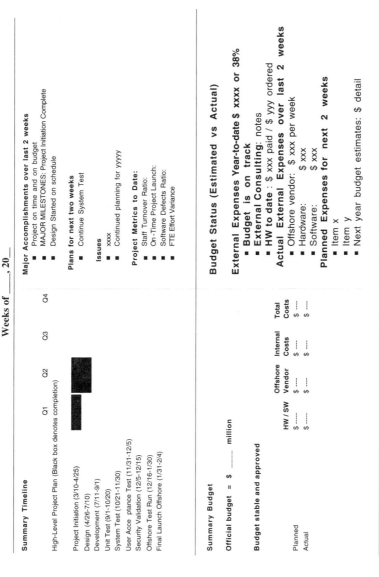

OFFSHORE PROJECT X
Bi-Monthly STATUS REPORT
Weeks of ____, 20__

Summary Timeline

	Q1	Q2	Q3	Q4

High-Level Project Plan (Black box denotes completion)

Project Initiation (3/10-4/25)
Design (4/26-7/10)
Development (7/11-9/1)
Unit Test (9/1-10/20)
System Test (10/21-11/30)
User Acceptance Test (11/31-12/5)
Security Validation (12/5-12/15)
Offshore Test Run (12/16-1/30)
Final Launch Offshore (1/31-2/4)

Major Accomplishments over last 2 weeks
- Project on time and on budget
- MAJOR MILESTONES: Project Initiation Complete
- Design Started on schedule

Plans for next two weeks
- Continue System Test

Issues
- xxxx
- Continued planning for yyyy

Project Metrics to Date:
- Staff Turnover Ratio:
- On-Time Project Launch:
- Software Defects Ratio:
- FTE Effort Variance

Summary Budget

Official budget = $ ____ million

Budget stable and approved

	HW / SW	Offshore Vendor	Internal Costs	Total Costs
Planned	$ ----	$ ----	$ ----	$ ----
Actual	$ ----	$ ----	$ ----	$ ----

Budget Status (Estimated vs Actual)

External Expenses Year-to-date $ xxxx or 38%
- **Budget is on track**
- **External Consulting**: notes
- **HW to date** : $ xxx paid / $ yyy ordered
Actual External Expenses over last 2 weeks
- Offshore vendor: $ xxx per week
- Hardware: $ xxx
- Software: $ xxx
Planned Expenses for next 2 weeks
- Item x
- Item y
- Next year budget estimates: $ detail

Exhibit 5.19   A Sample Project-Level Balanced Scorecard

Exhibit 5.20   Typical Performance Measures that Are Included in Application-Level Performance Reporting

Performance Measure	Meaning	Report Frequency
Success rate problem ticket resolution	Percentage problem tickets meeting priority timeframe specification for successful resolution	Monthly
On-time Offshore project launch	Planned versus actual launch dates	Monthly
Rework rate	Percentage of items/problems that are repeats of earlier problem reports	Monthly
Defect ratio	Defects/output for new project development (by software module)	Monthly
FTE effort variance	Planned FTE (full-time equivalent) labor effort versus actual FTE effort for new project development	Monthly
Staff turnover ratio	Percentage of team leaving vendor — measured separately for offshore and onshore teams	Monthly

part of the initial discussion and awareness, in this complex yet ultimately very achievable broad technical effort.

The next set of tactical documents provides additional reminders, in that spirit, to ensure completeness of the Offshore planning process.

- Exhibit 5.6 provides a baseline for Offshore IT operational requirements.
- Exhibits 5.3 and 5.4 outline additional information on Offshore SLAs.
    - Exhibit 5.4 provides sample SLA definitions as a useful model.
    - Exhibit 5.5 outlines a typical SLA escalation procedure.
- Exhibit 5.10 provides a sample role definition and skillset requirement document for one Offshore team member (overseas team lead).
- Exhibit 5.21 provides a short summary of the operations functions usually performed by the overseas maintenance and support team.
- Exhibits 5.16 and 5.17 provide additional support on the Offshore launch process.
    - Exhibit 5.17 lists sample Offshore launch transition criteria for the stage one team.
    - Exhibit 5.18 provides a sample Offshore launch internal announcement.

Exhibit 5.21   Typical Operations Functions of Overseas Team for Maintenance and Support Applications

---

Ongoing Testing Daily Application Processes

Application functional test, including daily production test and monitoring
Test scheduling and release management
Coordination of Offshore (multiple geographies) and test regions
Management of test script execution
Participation or management of regression test, depending upon organizational structure
Defect tracking, management, and documentation

Production Support

Problem ticket management and reporting according to SLAs
Escalation management

Documentation

Create/maintain/update application test scripts
Create/maintain/update all systems-related documentation, including related business process flows, background, architectural flows, training materials, functionality description, user manuals, etc.
Maintain documentation repository structure according to guidelines

Reporting

Time reporting
Status and other performance metrics as outlined in SOW

- Exhibit 5.22 contains tactical recommendations for the creation of an Offshore project-level meeting schedule/communications.
- Finally, Exhibit 5.12 provides sample Offshore go/no go approval requirements.

Exhibit 5.22 Sample Offshore/Onshore Project Team Meeting Schedule/Communications Guidelines[a]

Ongoing Communications
Weekly Meetings
• Overseas and onshore application team weekly meeting.
– Ensure existing communications processes are working; make changes as needed.
• Only team leaders (Offshore project manager, overseas team leader) attend weekly Offshore PMO meeting.
– Appropriate escalations and tracking of program-level issues that either are high priority or also affect other application teams.
• Focus is application status, issues, risks, or concerns.
Day-to-Day Communications
• VPN-enabled (or similar technology) enterprisewide mail system used to exchange routine communications/handoff.
• Backup communications via secondary secure network mail system.
• Both overseas and Offshore project team managers will carry pagers during their daily responsibility.
• Conference calls and phone are used for escalation and resolution of other communication difficulties as needed.
• Typical corporate mechanisms are to be used for file transfer and voicemail where appropriate.

[a] This information is a component of the Offshore Application Handbook.

SECTION 3

THE OFFSHORE PROGRAM CHALLENGE

Now that we have looked, in Section One, at the overall growth of Offshore, and established the history and tactical execution requirements in Section Two, we turn to the challenges of Offshore. First, in Chapter Six, we explore the most difficult challenge of all — the ethical and financial implications of the displaced worker. Chapter Seven looks at the risk factors related to Offshore, and how to mitigate them. Finally, Chapter Eight sums up with a quick and handy list of our top "do's and don'ts" of Offshore.

6

MANAGING EMPLOYEE IMPACT: VILLAIN OR SAVIOR?

THE CASE FOR ETHICS AS GOOD BUSINESS: STRATEGIC RESOURCE MANAGEMENT FOR OFFSHORE

Employee impact is the pink elephant in the middle of the room for Offshore. This chapter brings that elephant to the forefront of discussion, and explores the difficult questions and challenges relating to the ethical question of the displaced worker.

Sorting through the hype and legitimate concerns relating to Offshore-related worker impact can be overwhelming. The reality is, even the largest and most innovative firm is not a sure bet for economic security year over year. We need look no further to observe the ephemeral nature of large corporate job security than the story of Digital Equipment Corporation. In the late 1980s Digital boasted over 200,000 employees, and held a triumphant DECworld on the QEII docked in Boston Harbor. DEC was founded in the mid-1950s, had always been conservatively managed, with plenty of cash on hand, blue-chip clients, outstanding infrastructure such as its own internal telephone system, and valuable northeast land holdings. A handful of years later, Digital underwent a systematic disman-tling by its own president and board of directors in the deep recession of the early 1990s, culminating in the sale to Compaq, a competitor that was not even in the same ranking five years prior. Fortune 100 ranking, technical excellence, and even employee loyalty (Digital had, at least in reputation, excelled at all three) were not sufficient to provide corporate longevity. A year-over-year study of the Dow Jones and similar benchmarks shows a surprising turnover in the membership of the Fortune 100.

The assumption of corporate profitability/shareholder value as reason-ably increasing or even doubling on a consistent basis, in the sober light of the post-millennium economy, is in question. Increasingly U.S. corporate leadership is bowing to these unrealistic pressures through measures ranging from mergers and acquisitions to out-and-out fraud — everything except the old-fashioned approach of slowly building the business through adding unique value to the customer. It is fair to say that the debate regarding negative employee impact of Offshore is occurring within an overall crisis of ethics in large corporate America, and most employees look at job security, and corporate fairness as it relates to their jobs, with suspicion at best.

There is nothing quite so disheartening as belonging to an organization under unethical leadership. Most individual contributors correctly understand that it is only a matter of time before they are treated as the worst victims under the corporate hierarchy.

It is part of the complexity of our times that earning a living often means making compromises in what is acceptable in the most personal of realms — personal accountability and ethical conduct. The best intentioned of compromises can mean a slide down the very slippery slope. If all around you are bending the rules, is it ethical or rigidity to resist? These are murky waters, in shades of gray, not black and white. Yet we all can recognize, in hindsight or under public scrutiny, when the line crosses to the clearly unethical. The challenge is also to recognize when we are on the way there.

LOOKING BEYOND THE POPULAR PRESS SOUND BITE: WHAT IS THE THREAT OF OFFSHORE TO TODAY'S IT WORKERS?

Here's a summary of our exploration on this topic in previous chapters:

■ Most companies have a natural limit to the overall amount of and type of IT work they are able to move Offshore. A case in point is GE, the corporate poster child of Offshore, with the famous "70/70/70" rule (Exhibit 6.1) that is often quoted across the Offshore

Exhibit 6.1   70:70:70 Rule of GE

The world's most revered chief executive Jack Welch introduced a new rule. It was called the 70:70:70 rule. Welch decided that 70% of GE's work would be outsourced. Out of this, 70% would be done from offshore development centers. And out of this, about 70% would have to be done in India. This ultimately boiled down to about 30% of GE's work being outsourced to India.

Source: Business World Magazine, March 2000.

community. Even with their long history and outspoken commitment, *the sum total of 30 percent of GE's IT applications are Offshored. Most organizations Offshore only 15 to 20 percent of their IT applications,* due to concerns relating to (1) regulations limiting network access to sensitive customer data and (2) preservation of intellectual capital.

■ Discriminating further, not all IT skillsets are equally likely to be Offshored. The further down the IT skills pyramid, the more likely a job is to go Offshore, and the more likely the individual holding that job will be affected. To date, most of the roles held by Offshore consultants are for maintenance and support, programming, and some beginning analysis roles. Higher-level core skills, such as program and project management, IT architecture, specialist roles such as network security design, and of course business relationship management, remain Onshore even within the Offshore model.

■ The great majority of organizations that have undertaken Offshore to date have been large corporations, because Offshore is a volume-driven cost savings program. Generally, Offshore vendors request at least the potential for 50 individuals to go Offshore in order to engage, and many of the larger Offshore service firms want to see a minimum of 100 FTE for the best savings. This means, using the general rule of thumb of 10 to 15 percent maximum Offshore, that the organization needs to employ overall a minimum of roughly 1000 IT workers to be a viable candidate for Offshore. Even at 1000 IT workers/100 Offshore workers, the savings is not fully realizable, because most firms want to spread across more than one vendor to minimize risk. Offshore is really tailored towards the large corporation with a minimum of 1500 workers, with a minimum of 200 FTE Offshore. Clearly, as the market matures, this trend may shift.

■ Finally, most firms fitting this picture employ many highly priced consultants. Replacing individual consultants with Offshore resources is a double win, from a savings perspective, because the hourly rates for consultants are usually far higher than hourly employee rates. The premium pay for consultants has generally been thought of as the price needed to bring on specialized skills, or to have a flexible workforce that can be downsized without the overhead and negative press associated with employee layoffs. Today, however, these specialized skills are often found Offshore, and the availability of consultants is much greater due to the economic downturn.

Putting in place a handful of Offshore firms instead of hundreds of individual or smaller boutique firm consultants has many benefits, not the least of which is ensuring that the firm is not overpaying its consultants in the new economy. If there are hundreds of individual contracts, most of them stay in place just due to inertia or the logistical complexity of reviewing them, even if market forces have forced prices lower in the interim. Most large firms do not put formal incentives or review processes in place to catch outdated contracts, and the IT or project managers who oversee the individual consultants have little to no motivation to rock the boat by asking for contractual reviews.

Even if they are caught annually, the logistics of managing multiple contracts and ensuring they truly reflect market conditions is expensive in terms of overhead, lack of standardized methodology and quality assurance, and of course, high prices between annual checkpoints. Press reports to the contrary, most large firms achieve Offshore savings without any employee layoffs, focusing instead on elimination of consultants. Many participants in the Offshore Interest Group have confirmed no negative employee impact for their programs due to this strategy.

If it is true that

- 30 percent FTE of the only largest firms (IT organization over 1500 FTE) go Offshore and
- Of those 30 percent, only specific functions (programming, maintenance, and support) go Offshore and
- Within those 30 percent that are coding, maintenance, and support roles, most firms have eliminated consultants then…
- …*Who is* at risk for Offshore?

There *is* one group clearly at risk. These are the employees affected by Offshore that cannot or will not be retrained to participate in the organization on a higher IT skill level. There may be a variety of logistical reasons that an organization cannot (or will not) eliminate consultants. Some consultants are not replaceable by affected employees, no matter how extensive the training, because they represent highly specialized and scarce skills.

Most large corporations have plenty of external consultants doing lower-level coding or even maintenance and support, so with some careful planning and perhaps some shifting around, employee impact may not be an issue. But there will be those large firms who don't have the option to eliminate consultants, or decide to eliminate employees for a variety of reasons. What is clear is that employees affected by Offshore who are unable or unwilling to move to higher IT skill pyramid roles are the ones who are most likely to be out of a job.

Unfortunately, these are often the most vulnerable of workers, in terms of age and financial commitments. They are most likely to be workers in the middle of life, rather than younger workers who can more easily move into new careers, and have many community and family financial responsibilities. It is in the treatment of these, often at once the most loyal (in terms of work ethic and years of valued service) and most vulnerable of workers, that the true ethical test of management resides. It is certain that the rest of the organization will be watching very carefully to see how these individuals, in particular, are treated.

It is the strong recommendation here that part of the savings for Offshore be utilized to create new career alternatives (not just "training") for these workers, and that the investment for achieving this be considered part of the upfront cost of the Offshore program. The savings associated with Offshore should allow for generous and complete solutions for workers caught in the middle.

Factoring in the cost of retraining and supporting loyal workers to find new careers, and thereby providing them more than a casual handshake, is an ethical imperative for executing Offshore, and requires guts and leadership, and does not occur by accident and without commitment, savvy, and planning.

Let's step back to take a look at the overall impact of Offshore on the economy as a whole. Will the economic impact of Offshore be an ever-increasing negative drag, day after day, year after year?

McKinsey Global Institute, in an interesting study entitled "Offshoring: Is It a Win–Win Game?"[1] addresses these questions. In it, McKinsey asked, "Does India benefit at America's expense or are the benefits shared more widely?" To underscore the importance of the debate, the document cites again the study by Forrester, in which 3.3 million jobs are expected to move Offshore, representing $136 billion in wages. Forrester predicts roughly 8 percent, or 473,000, of all IT jobs will ultimately move overseas.

McKinsey concluded that much of the negative press related to IT job losses due to Offshore was overstated. The job losses Forrester references translate into a loss of about 200,000 jobs a year over the next decade. Even in good times, mass layoff numbers are much higher, McKinsey notes. "In 1999, for instance, 1.15 million workers lost their jobs through mass layoffs. In 1996, the number was 1.18 million. The recent changes driving Offshoring are not that different or radical from the changes that dynamic, competitive, technologically evolving economies have experienced for the last few decades."[2] In other words, the overall relative number of job losses makes Offshore a small micro trend within the larger realities involving IT job availability and growth, despite press coverage to the contrary.

In response to questions on the overall impact on the economy, McKinsey concludes:

> *Offshoring creates wealth for U.S. companies and consumer and therefore for the United States as a whole: that is why companies choose to follow this course. Offshoring is just one more example of the innovation that keeps U.S. companies at the leading edge....Moreover, while still receiving services that employees were previously engaged in, the economy could now generate additional input (and thus income) when these workers take new jobs. Thus, Offshoring...creates a net additional value for the U.S. economy that did not exist before...through....reduced costs, increased revenues, repatriated earnings, and the redeployment of additional labor.*[3]

Finally, the U.S. economy is expected to have a "de-boom" as former baby boomers retire, with a five percent decrease in the workforce by 2015 as compared to 2001. *McKinsey closes the research article by recommending the government as well as businesses use a portion of the large surplus from Offshore to support displaced workers in obtaining new jobs, creating a win–win for all parties.*

Looking at the implications of Offshoring, we can take a hint from other industries that have undergone a similar cycle Offshore, such as shoe manufacturers in the 1950s. It is true that factories, companies, and even whole cities, and the minieconomies that depend upon those core jobs, may never be the same. It also seems clear from the vantage point of over 50 years that the individuals and their families were able to move on across the decades and changes they brought with them. The key is to be supportive and fiscally compassionate to the workers caught unawares in the middle of the cycle, unable or unwilling to shift to new jobs, and with financial commitments to young children, aging parents, and communities.

STRATEGIC RESOURCE MANAGEMENT: CHALLENGE OF THE DECADE?

In the recent dot-com boom that turned bust, catching most of us completely unawares, talk of the IT professionals in Silicon Valley went from who was getting the next private wine cellar to smiling thinly through the thirtieth consecutive, fruitless job interview. If most large companies are riding a series of tidal economic waves, dropping and adding percentages of their workforce as ballast, the challenge becomes harnessing and motivating these workers to create a unique value proposition. IT had been protected from these waves due to the unusual skills that were for the first 30 years relatively rare — and now, to varying degrees, have become commodities through Offshore. Strategic resource management is the art of marrying the many facets of the workforce — temporary versus permanent, core versus secondary skills, remote versus local — to the unpredictable forces of the competitive marketplace, and somehow come up a winner.

Within the world of the large corporation, where expenses are often hidden by complex allocation formulas and managing the complex internal corporate culture can in itself be a full-time job, it can be easy to lose sight of the winds of market change until it is too late. For many IT workers and management, "too late" can translate into the overall firing of the internal IT function as it is completely Outsourced to a third party (as opposed to Co-Sourced within the Offshore model, which preserves a minimum of 70 percent of the internal IT organization). For workers waking up one day to find the entire organization gone, it may be well to wonder how this could occur, and what the signposts were along the way.

One way Traditional (replacing the entire IT organization and function) Outsourcers are able to take hold is through the lack of accountability of real costs, and dissociation with the value proposition provided by the IT, associated with large corporations. The traditional gaps between internal IT leaders and their business counterparts — of communications, understanding, alignment, and power base — can serve to create a valid case that the outside party can provide the same IT services at much less cost than the inhouse organization. It is no accident that keeping the focus on these macro issues in the large, insular IT organization is the key to successfully communicating the imperative for Offshore. Most organizations mature in Offshore understand that it is necessary for the viability of the whole to keep a focus on the cost structure as if the wolf is at the door — which it certainly ·always is in these days.

Leveraging Offshore for strategic IT resource management — strategic as in creating competitive edge — is usually required to be achieved in several phases for most large corporations. First and most obviously is the elimination of the total chaos of hundreds of individual contractors. Companies such as Merrill Lynch share with Offshore conference audiences how their management of contractor resources has shifted dramatically as a result of Offshore. The many dozens, sometimes hundreds of individual consultants or boutiques that most IT firms use in decentralized silos have a large hidden cost — they are essentially unmanageable. Replacing these by fewer Offshore firms — minimizing overhead, enabling visibility, and tracking of costs — essentially enables the management and quality assurance of IT resources for the first time. These firms provide IT resources across all time zones — Onshore, Offshore, and even on site — under broad centrally managed agreements.

Simplifying and cleaning up the vendor management structure and process of the firm is easier said than done. At stake of course is shifting the decision making from the individual IT manager, used to ultimately driving the hiring decision for the individual application, to a centrally managed and empowered Offshore PMO. Most organizations simply cannot achieve power shifts in decision making without top-down mandates, and centralization of authority may appear to conflict with the matrix management culture of project management across large firms. Even the firms that do centralize the vendor management function often hesitate to tie formal real incentives to their use in programs. Companies that directly tie bonuses to create incentives for the use of low-cost consulting resources are far and few between.

Having established the initial hurdle — mandated low-cost IT vendor management, and all of the organizational upheaval that implies — the second phase of strategic resource management is bringing the function of resource management visibility and importance to the executive decision-making process within IT, as reflected by the role of CRO or Chief Resource Officer.

For vertical industries where IT plays a pivotal role in driving competitive edge, strategic resource management means actively creating the optimal mix of core IT skills to support the most creative of organizational cultures. Interestingly, this reflects the current challenges of many large firms in utilizing IT to the fullest. That challenge rests upon establishing the right balance of central authority and matrix management, where certain key decisions are centrally driven, yet others are very much the province of cross-functional, hands-on business and technology specialists who must work closely together to understand and implement the best joint solutions.

How are these two concepts related? Traditionally, the challenge between IT and the internal business partners they support is establishing more of a dialogue of equals. Even though "business" (as a shorthand) is ultimately responsible for the bottom line, increasingly the ability for everyone to meet those goals is dependent upon a level of authority in which IT must have the ability to drive certain decisions. Most large companies are still harboring sideline IT organizations — small caches of technical consulting resources that bypass reporting to the formal IT structure because the business partners just can't seem to get all their project needs met. Unfortunately, in many large corporations it is only through the charismatic leadership of a few individuals in IT that creativity flourishes and project-based cross-organizational excellence is achieved.

These are signs of an IT organization that does not have enough clout, and will have a weakened business impact as well.

Most of the CMM and other certification processes recognize the importance of centralization of key functions within the IT organization. Business intelligence and data warehouse technology reflect this necessity in relation to corporate data standards; a similar lesson is to be learned in leveraging centralized hardware, software, and network architectures.

A negative cycle is established for the disenfranchised IT organization. The less IT is empowered, the harder it is to enforce corporatewide standards as they apply to data, systems, architecture, and now resource management. The harder it is to enforce these standards, the more difficult it is to meet business partner needs quickly, efficiently, and proactively. The lack of data standards means there are no meaningful reports available for competitive analysis. Poor systems standards mean long and expensive project costs to restructure technology to respond to market changes. Ineffectual resource standards, as explored here, mean less methodology and cost discipline, with all that implies in terms of competitive impact.

Of course, the less IT is able to meet the needs of business partners, the more rogue IT organizations pop up. The more these pop up, the less empowered IT becomes. And the negative circle continues. In essence, strategic resource management cannot be separated from the overall efficacy of IT as a strong and equal partner at the executive planning table.

A surprising number of large firms don't have a true CIO (technology still reports up to the finance function, as first established in the 1950s, for example). These are the firms where the internal culture and organizational structure will make it very hard, if not impossible, to fully leverage not only Offshore, but future strategic technology initiatives.

And in truth, most of the discussion in the Offshore Interest Group, made up primarily of hands-on Program Managers responsible for the execution of large Fortune 100 organizations, centers on the frustrations of disempowerment. Offshore clearly works as a model — if there is any technology trend that has received more negative press, it is difficult to name. The notable lack of high-visibility failures publicly distributed as a warning is a kind of negative testimony to Offshore's efficacy. Yet most Offshore Program Managers, and Offshore PMOs, are structured as voluntary programs. Offshore Program Managers must "sell'" the concept internally to their business partners, whose primary knowledge of Offshore is what they read in the papers, and who are of course risk averse and protective of their technology end users. Although it is tempting to believe this is a result of the unpopularity specific to Offshore, it is also the truth that all strategic IT initiatives are not often won without vision and empowerment.

Putting strategic advantage decisions in the hands of business partners who are (rightly) measured by short-term profitability is a good way to ensure a long, drawn-out, and painful adoption process. In the meantime, a smarter and more disciplined competitor, with a true understanding of the savings at stake, may be moving more quickly. Banking and reinvesting the consequent savings in myriad ways may create a formidable new level of industry competition, similar to the way Wal-Mart, for example, was famously able to leverage the strategic technologies of knowledge management, data warehousing, and data mining (clearly along with other business strategies) to grow exponentially while larger and temporarily stronger competitors went by the wayside.

Strategic resource management is, then, similar to many strategic technology initiatives in that it is in the art, rather than the science, that the winners are established. The stakes are high, perhaps survival itself. Run the IT organization too tightly in terms of centralized authority, and the delicate and mission-critical project-focused culture of teaming may be adversely affected. Run the IT organization too loosely, and the savings potential of Offshore, along with the competitive opportunities they represent, fall short. Most strategic technologies today require teams of specialists, all with their own expertise, to be able to combine and create. Strategic resource planning is about the conscious creation of those corporate synergies of culture and expertise that support brilliance.

For the relatively rare large company that is organizationally prepared to move forward rapidly, aligned with an executive team that understands Offshore's potential and ability to strike that balance, even then the task is formidable. For most large firms, strategic planning, despite the fancy name, means the next 12-month IT budget allocation based upon and revised within a 6-month rolling business forecast. IT resource management is traditionally the realm of hidden hallway negotiations followed by the ubiquitous, officially published and updated org chart. Bringing the decision process out into the open by driving it from the top down and formally aligning it with the competitive strategy of the company is not an easy shift.

Although Offshore is not rocket science as it relates to project execution, synching up industry and economic trends with Offshore may be just that. The challenge to leveraging the potential that is represented by the incredibly high-quality and low-cost labor pool of India is the very long leadtime associated with execution. Not only is there need for a crystal ball, it also must be able to predict these conditions for a relative eternity within the business world (more than six months). Of late, many firms simply will not undertake any large initiative that requires more than a year or two. Here we are looking at strategic impact for a minimum of three years, probably five. Here, of course, we are not referencing the typical Offshore initiative, but that rare firm that brings Offshore into the control tower, consciously using it as one of several chess pieces within the overall competitive game. The business world is still awaiting the "Wal-Mart" of the Offshore world, but we can be assured it is out there somewhere.

Before we turn to the ethics of good business, let's summarize the major points here.

- *Leveraging Offshore is not substantially different from the challenge of other strategic IT technology initiatives.* As such, an organizational structure supporting an empowered IT function and the appropriate focus on long-term IT investments is a critical success factor.
- *Understanding the challenges and potential of Offshore as it affects specific industry and economic trends is the most difficult to accomplish, but of course has the highest payback.* The length of time to plan and execute Offshore makes these predictions all the trickier.
- *Ultimately, bringing IT resource management into the macro competitive planning executive function is what is required* — creation of a comprehensive view of core IT skills management, their locations, their cost impact, and their potential. For most large firms, the IT function occurs within a matrix-management execution model. Overcoming the culture of silos of IT resource management to bring a strong central focus may be extremely difficult.
- *Nonetheless, the rewards are equally as great.* Other strategic technologies such as knowledge management/data warehousing show us the likelihood of a new handful of industry leaders who will emerge based upon their ability to harness the potential of Offshore.

AFFECTED WORKERS: RECOMMENDATIONS AND LOGISTICS FOR OFFSHORE

We have defined more precisely the profile of those most vulnerable of workers — usually older workers with the most long-term financial burdens and the least ability and likelihood of an easy shift to a new line of work. These former employees have usually provided years of loyal service in critical roles, and are being displaced through no fault of their own. It is a reasonable, ethical, necessary, and even pragmatic move to include the cost of retraining these workers as part of the upfront cost of Offshore. There have been examples of outstanding successes, and all hinge upon providing loyal long-term workers a viable option to create a new ongoing source of job-related income that does not represent significant personal economic loss. If these are achieved, Offshore truly does become a win–win for all parties.

Do not nurse the delusion that unfairly treated affected IT workers do not leave a trail of destruction behind them, far more insidious than the occasional IT system sabotage. That is the fear and resentment of the individuals working side by side with them, remaining on as employees. Arbitrary and politically motivated cuts, ruining lives, leave behind a workforce afraid to take risks. Employee cuts, handled poorly, contribute to creating a company culture of bandits, encouraging business decisions to be overtly based not upon the interests of the customer, the business, or the project, but solely upon whether it would benefit that individual and his position within the firm.

Of course these occur anyway, perhaps frequently, throughout the business world, but an aggressive and openly acknowledged negative trend — communicating that it didn't matter what was the best decision for the business, only the individual representing the business — may be dramatic. Disaffected employees, perceiving their focus on personal gain as necessary in a large firm so dismissive to loyal and caring employees, ultimately create the next Enron. Sometimes ethical and fair actions can be the best business decision of all.

Let's look at the logistics of a fair and equitable placement program for affected employees. Prior to Offshore, the typical Fortune 50 firm is an amalgam of individual consultants, boutique firms, and U.S.-based large consulting firms providing a wide variety of IT services from coding, maintenance, and support to analysis, architecture, and strategy. Employees are usually mixed in, often wearing several hats and filling a combination of roles — leading a project part of the time, for example, and maintaining perhaps an old legacy system the rest of the time.

Step one is to shuffle employee responsibilities to focus purely on higher IT skills pyramid functions such as project management, architecture, and relationship development with business partners. Thus, a worker doing some coding and some project management would refocused to be totally dedicated to project management.

The next step is to evaluate whether some employees can be trained to replace internal consultants. These measures are frequently very unpopular with IT managers, who don't like to put additional risk into their already challenging daily work lives, but are necessary for fair and ethical treatment of the workforce. This type of program only works if the employee to be trained truly has the capacity to fill the shoes of the consultant, and stretching the possibilities here does a disservice to the employee and the IT manager responsible for the success of the application. Of course, setting up an employee to fail as a result of training for a new role is to be avoided through careful assessment and support. As long as these opportunities aren't stretched too thin in terms of matching skills and abilities, this is not only a wonderful way to reward long-term employees with a new set of skills and potential career, it also keeps valuable knowledge within the firm.

Upon exhausting these options, it is time to look at creating opportunities for external retraining. Within the 40-plus Fortune 50 members of the Offshore Interest Group, only a small percentage of companies actually reached the point where they needed to dismiss employees as a result of Offshore, and even fewer on a large scale. Because of the negative focus of the press, however, many layoffs that are occurring due to general business downturn are often associated with Offshore by employees. Communications to the contrary may be simply dismissed as false. Over time, the realities become clear, however, and unfounded fears begin to lessen. Putting out a clear value statement that there is an organized funded program to help support individuals in creating new careers, however, is a tangible way to show clarity of ethics and the will to follow through on those values. IT workers are a notoriously jaded bunch, as we have observed before, and tend to believe only what they see.

Creative problem solving with a strong force of leadership to watch out for vulnerable employees is what is required for success. Former employees need help and support in being redirected to a new way of making a living over the long term (not a short-term, lump sum handout — although always appreciated, these aren't sufficient to solve the problem). One example, discussed earlier in the book, is a northeast energy utility, which created a win–win by providing two options for displaced workers. One option was for a training program, the other was to join the U.S.-based Offshore consulting firm and essentially keep their old jobs (and have chances for new jobs) at the same salary with higher benefits and greater professional opportunity.

The shift to the new employer was structured so that the affected employee had exactly one year of guaranteed work at the new Offshore firm. After that year, employees were subject to the same review process as all employees within the Offshore firm, and were subject to dismissal for poor performance. When I interviewed the CIO seven years later, only one former employee had left his new Offshore company (voluntarily), and many employees stopped by to thank him personally for the improvement in their lives. With care, foresight, and creativity, it is possible to execute Offshore in a way that no one is treated unfairly. Let's turn now to tactical recommendations regarding retraining and supporting individuals who are affected by Offshore, looking at the above process in greater detail.

THE EMPLOYEE PLACEMENT PROGRAM: RECOMMENDATIONS AND LOGISTICS

The logistical challenges of ensuring fairness to displaced vulnerable work-ers can make or break the Offshore program. It is usually up to the Offshore Program Manager to become the conscience of the organization and to make the goals achievable by ensuring that the right communications and message are put forth, and that key functional areas are represented appropriately. One of the (perhaps dubious) benefits of Offshore, the flip side of the overdramatization of the feared impact and focus from the organization, is that there is an expectation of extensive change upon the launch of the program. In other words, there exists an opportunity for leadership and a window of opportunity when corporate leaders will want to be involved. Moving quickly to establish a working understanding and programmatic structure across the organization is important — later on, when the experience has become more rote and attention has shifted to the next new initiative, there may not be the same opportunity.

The following is a checklist to a truly workable program for displaced employees, listing major tasks and the functional roles responsible.

1. Prior to formally working on any placement program, the Offshore Program Manager works with senior executives to agree to set aside a budget to support displaced employees, as part of the upfront cost of program implementation. Five percent of the annual savings related to the program may a good rule of thumb.

2. The Offshore Program Manager creates a broad cross-functional team with representatives from human resources, legal, IT manage-ment, application managers, and other roles. One key factor for determining participation is a personal commitment to the principle of fairness to the affected employees, so that the individual can serve as a champion within the department. In addition, it is important that the individuals have the knowledge, communication ability, and internal connections so that they can successfully func-tion as champion. It is vital to have at least one relatively powerful IT manager as an active participant in this group.

3. Various tactical preparations occur in preparation for the orderly rollout of what we call here the "Employee Placement Program."

4. A database or similar collection of data details the skills, hourly rates, length of service, reporting relationship, and roles of all existing external consultants. IT managers, human resource repre-sentatives, the Offshore PMO, and other functional team members identify the employees affected by the Offshore program.

5. Based upon the above analysis, the estimated budget set aside for employee re-skill effort is confirmed, and appropriate training and job placement services are engaged for those employees.

6. The team establishes an orderly process to support notification and placement of displaced workers. If possible, outline the process in detail, publish it on a centralized Web page, and give it an identifiable name. An example process is pictured in Exhibit 6.2.

7. IT managers engage in resource planning for their groups, shifting personnel that are splitting their time between maintenance and support, or coding, and other functions such as architecture design or project management. These employees are no longer to split their attention and time, and are to be full-time in their other role (e.g., project management).

8. For those individuals with the skills to replace a full-time external consultant, with or without training, the road ends there with a new position inside the firm. For those individuals unable to do so because of a skills gap or reduced need for workers due to increased efficiencies or other factors, a comprehensive, individualized skills assessment and training program enables the worker to become established in a new career.

9. The processes associated with the Employee Placement Program are formalized. It is usually, but not always, IT managers working closely with Human Resources to ensure successful execution of the employee transition process.

10. HR and the management team communicate the goals and processes of the Placement Program across the organization, including support for front-line managers in understanding and communicating the program to their direct reports.

11. HR working with the IT management team creates, supervises, and ensures success of individual employee training plans; creates a comprehensive mapping of how individual employees' skills map to existing consultants' roles, new job openings, and other job opportunities; and coaches employees through self-assessment and matching to existing roles.

It is not usual for employees to be required to interview with that application's team lead and the new IT manager in the new role replacing a consultant. This is where the structure of the overall and original team behind the Placement program is so important. Application managers and IT managers may be loath to give up a consultant that is functioning well in his or her job for an unknown internal employee. Some will understand the importance of the principle at stake and work to bring on the employee

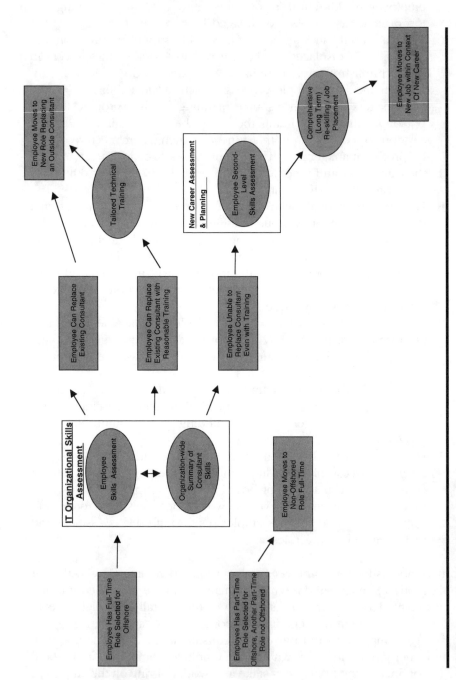

Exhibit 6.2 Sample Employee Placement Process

in the new role and make him or her successful. For those who do not take that view, it is important that they understand that great organizational pressure will be brought to bear if consultants are favored over employees when the latter can do the job.

If one of the choices is to offer employees an opportunity to make the transition to a job at one of the Offshore firms, the legal department and the Offshore Program Office will need to outline the terms and structure of that agreement. This is a creative and interesting option that should always be explored with Offshore service providers. India-based firms have needs for Onshore representatives for a growing customer base, and of course U.S.-based firms may also have needs for these particular skills. If a mutual agreement is in order, some of the questions that need to be outlined for transitioning employees are:

- *Is the job with the Offshore provider guaranteed, and if so, for what length of time?* This varies — a standard time period for guaranteed employee is one year.
- *How do the benefits compare?* Usually the employee takes the new company's benefit structure without additional compensation.
- *Does the salary stay the same?* Typically the answer is yes.
- *How are my retirement/pension plans to be handled?* This varies — usually vacation time is transferred over; retirement and pension are handled on a case-by-case basis.

The Offshore PMO tracks the results and costs of the Employee Placement Program in regular, usually monthly, reports to the executive team, similar to the reporting on other program investment expenses such as knowledge management or network infrastructure work efforts.

Most important, it is up to the Offshore Program Manager to make the most of the early days, when the organization is focused on Offshore and there is an ability to shape the initiative and to lay the foundation for a commitment to fairness for employees. This may take the form of an Offshore Program Standards of Business Conduct published on the Web page; a commitment by critical IT managers to participate and support the process (very important when replacing consultants with employees); and last but not least, ensuring that the external consulting firms who also provide IT levels, do not by default drive employee retention decisions by virtue of their usually long-term relationship with the IT executive suite.

OFFSHORE: IMPACT ON THE FUTURE OF IT

Offshore, then, is arguably not necessarily bad news for the economy as a whole, and corporations moving Offshore can make the good business decision to build in the costs of retraining and supporting the transition of the most vulnerable of workers as part of the cost of Offshore. What is the impact on the IT profession as whole?

Offshore, when part of the mainstream, will make it more difficult to come up through the technology ranks. It will be harder to find a way to learn from the bottom up, always an advantage in technology where there is no substitution for hands-on experience. New entrants will need to start in the middle.

The typical career path of today's IT worker usually begins with some hands-on programming.

Although the type of programming depends upon the generation to which that individual belongs — some notable generational milestones are COBOL/FORTRAN to fourth generation languages (4GL) to the more recent Web-based Java applet programming — this initiation serves as a solid foundation for the other roles that follow. It is much easier to be an effective project lead or indepth architect specialist with several solid years of programming under one's belt. These entry-level opportunities are going to be harder to find, and the new generation will probably need to lead without first having the opportunity to learn how to follow. This trend is not absolute, however, because 70 percent of most organization applications will remain Onshore, and the programmers with them.

Other implications for the IT profession as a whole are the increasing importance of communications and other so-called soft skills. Rather like the final closing of the Western frontier, the days of the curmudgeon senior technical specialist, left alone in the corner to work technical magic despite blustering his way through the touchy corporate hierarchy, are coming to a close. IT workers will need to be able to work effectively and closely with team members they are never, ever going to meet in person. The ability to build bridges across cultural, geographic, and other communication barriers will be prized as much as technical acumen, and perhaps more.

Technology that supports seamless communication across large global distances will be prized. As more and more companies decide to move into Offshore for themselves — what is today called Build, Operate, Transfer — it is likely that overseas divisions in large corporations will integrate even more into the mainstream of corporate life. Working side by side through the virtual network will become commonplace, and one hopes that the highly striated, geographically based power structures of today's Fortune 100 firms will be more equalized. Although most large U.S.-based corporations have large overseas divisions, they are far more likely to be perceived as backwaters with diminished political clout, even for their size and revenue or support contribution, than the U.S. resident divisions.

Finally, the question remains whether technology will continue to be the career of choice for the best and brightest new college students and workers in the United States. The bloom is off the rose in terms of a technology career's guarantee of relatively high pay, job security, and the opportunity to freely move between jobs and companies to explore and express one's creativity. Yet it is hard to come up with an alternative facet of the business world that is so consistently able to shift the rules of the game, making the carpet ride an interesting one, if not predictable and secure.

To close this chapter, we take another look at ethics in the workplace, citing some of the new voices in what is fast becoming not only a required course at business schools, but also a new body of literature, and a very bottom-line-oriented focus of the investment community.

APPENDIX: THE INHERENT VALUE OF JOBS

An Article from *Business Respect*[4]

In the last few days, HSBC has announced that it is to move 4,000 jobs from the UK to a more competitive location — i.e. in the developing world. The move has caused outrage amongst the trade unions, who have been quoted as saying that the company's claims to corporate social responsibility could effectively now be discarded. Is that right?

I suppose that if we were to say that the inherent value of a human life was the same in the developing countries as in the industrialised countries, few would argue with that. Notwithstanding the cash value of someone's expected earning power, the value placed on their life should be the same.

Is there something similar here about the inherent — as opposed to the cash — value of a job? Does the creation of 4,000 jobs in a developing country equate to the creation of 4,000 jobs in an industrialised country? And if not, what would be the factors that would be relevant in making a distinction?

On the one hand, one could argue that the social value of jobs is higher if they are created where the need is greatest. Good jobs in areas where potentially skilled and loyal workers would otherwise have no access to such jobs are surely a good thing. And although one shouldn't be too black and white about this, such a criteria [sic] would tend to favour the value being highest for jobs in developing countries.

The company will also plead the need to be profitable. This, of course, is the argument that creates the most disgust from the opponents of such moves, but the inability of a long-term unprofitable company to preserve jobs and livelihoods is rather well documented. If your biggest potential positive impact on society comes from the goods and services you provide, and the jobs you create, then going bust is the most socially irresponsible thing you can do.

Often companies are responding to pressure from new entrants to their respective marketplace who don't carry the same sort of overheads that they carry. So, in banking for instance, the UK marketplace has been transformed by the entrance of the dotcom banks — which have no branch network to bear the cost of. Those who have existing infrastructures to support have been losing customers hand over fist to the newcomers. Nobody hammers the newcomers for the impact they have had, however.

When BT recently announced a similar move, the outcome was slightly different. The company came to an amicable agreement with the unions. This was partly based on the company's commitment that the UK job reductions would not be achieved through compulsory redundancy — not a great hardship in the call center industry, where turnover is extremely high anyway. But it also agreed measures to show that it would manage responsibly the conditions of the Indian workers it proposed to take on. This was a first — and an encouraging sign of how unions can act as a progressive force, working co-operatively with companies that have shown their intent to do the right thing.

Of course, 4,000 are a lot of people. And HSBC has said that — although it will achieve as many of these as possible from natural wastage — it expects that there will also be compulsory redundancies. The unions in this case have not really seemed interested in what may happen with the new workers — it is a case of defending British jobs for British workers. And that's that. No interest in how the company will undertake the exercise — what sort of severance packages, how much support provided, etc.

I don't mind the union taking this position — there is a logic for them as representatives of said British workers. I do mind their equation of corporate social responsibility with their line, however. I can't identify the CSR principle that says you should retain activities in unprofitable places, regardless of the consequences. The danger must surely be that the CSR label becomes co-opted by every interest group to mean just what their special interest decides they would most like it to mean.

That being said, there is no doubting the seriousness of the situation for the 4,000 that will be affected. If you lose your job, it is a painful experience, and you won't be much inclined to be understanding or supportive towards the company that has cast you aside.

I do wonder if companies always think through the consequences of such actions as well as they might. I am mindful of the fact that companies that resist to the end the pressures to let people go often turn out to be highly successful. Take Southwest Airlines, for instance. The only U.S.

airline to not lay people off in the wake of September 11th. The only U.S. airline to remain profitable during same period. Coincidence?

It may well not be a case of corporate irresponsibility to decide to relocate key staff in the face of economic hard times — but given the impact such moves have on the morale and loyalty of the thousands of staff that remain behind, it is just possible that the real impossible-to-measure costs of the move come close to outweighing the short term benefits.

It's hard to persuade your people that they are your greatest assets — the oft-repeated claim — if at the same time you are telling them that they are dispensable at short notice. Whilst not condemning those who make that tough choice, the CSR movement should celebrate the companies who show that putting the mantra of 'our people first' into practice in difficult times can pay off in terms of successful business practice. This is an area where the development of best practice in terms of corporate social responsibility is only just emerging.

NOTES

1. McKinsey & Company, "Offshoring: Is it a Win–Win Game?" August, 2003.
2. Ibid.
3. Ibid.
4. Mallen Baker, *Business Respect,* 64: October 19, 2003.

7

MANAGING RISK THROUGH AN OFFSHORE NETWORK SECURITY ARCHITECTURE

Risk management is a focus of a great deal of discussion and energy in Offshore. As in many other aspects, it is not always easy to find the middle ground. Views of risk management run the gamut from being ignored, to becoming a reason for not engaging in Offshore in the first place.

One effective way to cut through the uncertainty, particularly in this arena, is to look at firms who have extensive experience, and how they have approached their risk management process. Below is a summary of our discussion on risk management we've touched upon in prior chapters, in order to explore these more fully.

- There are two categories of risk:
  - Macro-level risks, applying to the Offshore effort as a whole, and
  - Application-level risks, specific to the particular IT application.
- Macro-level risks (Exhibit 7.1), such as threat of war in Offshore countries, are monitored and where possible mitigated. An example of risk mitigation is geographic diversity of intellectual capital related to knowledge transfer. These threats are not considered a reason to avoid Offshoring altogether. This view is confirmed in the research cited in depth in the last chapter, as well confirmed in the growing numbers of companies moving IT Offshore despite escalation of terrorism and other safety concerns across the globe.
  - Sad to say, it is not a reasonable assumption in today's world that Offshore locations are inherently more dangerous than Nearshore, or even U.S., locations.

Exhibit 7.1 Typical Program: Wide Risks and Mitigation Strategies

i. Risk: Lack of clear communications handoff between Offshore and Onshore team.

Mitigation: Clear responsibilities, hour by hour if necessary, with equally clearly defined escalation procedures.

Controls: Statement of Work; Offshore Application Launch Plan; Ongoing Application Metrics.

Responsibility: Project Manager.

ii. Risk: Offshore and Onshore team turnover negatively affects performance or return on investment due to additional knowledge transfer and other training costs.

Mitigation: Clear documentation; additional resources in place from beginning to support promotions/training/minimized impact of staff turnover.

Controls: Offshore Application Launch Plan; Vendor Contract Avoiding "Learn as You Burn."

Responsibility: Regarding overall program structure — Legal Department and Offshore Program Manager; for Offshore Application — Project Manager.

iii. Risk: Regulatory, privacy or legal compliance violation(s).

Mitigation: Yearly legal/regulatory audit and review across Offshore program.

Controls: PMO Offshore Compliance Program; Application specific risk management process updated for Offshore; contractual vendor notification process for trigger events.

Responsibility: Regarding overall program structure — Legal Department and Offshore Program Manager; for Offshore Application — Project Manager.

iv. Risk: Negative employee perception of Offshore program due to perceptions of job instability.

Mitigation: Clear communications on core skills needs in IT, and impact to employees displaced by program.

Controls: Offshore Communications Plan; Media/Public Relations Script; Set aside funds to support training as part of costs of program.

Responsibility: Offshore Program Manager; Media Relations.

v. Risk: Operations schedules could affect Offshore program requirements.

Mitigation: Coordinate schedules; regular weekly review meetings to address changes and updates.

Controls: Network Security Infrastructure Guidelines; Operations Schedule; Operations Guide; Offshore Application Launch Plan.

Responsibility: Offshore Program Manager; Operations Manager; Project Manager.

Exhibit 7.1 (continued)   Typical Program: Wide Risks and Mitigation Strategies

vi. Risk: Security breach of Offshore facilities.

Mitigation: Offshore vendors contractually required to follow secure facility guidelines, including picture badges, video cameras, etc. Regular on-site audits conducted to validate compliance.

Controls: PMO Offshore Compliance Program; Application specific risk management process updated for Offshore; contractual vendor notification process for trigger events.

Responsibility: Regarding overall program structure — Legal Department and Offshore Program Manager; for Offshore Application — Project Manager.

vii. Risk: Offshore vendor financially insolvent.

Mitigation: Multiple vendor strategy; initial financial review updated annually.

Controls: Multiple vendor strategy; Contingency Plan; Vendor Exit Plan.

Responsibility: Legal Department; Offshore Program Manager.

viii. Risk: Threat of war; geopolitical concerns.

Mitigation: Diversity of Offshore locations; proactive management of knowledge transfer and systems documentations across multiple locations.

Controls: PMO Offshore Compliance Program; Application specific risk management process updated for Offshore; contractual vendor notification process for trigger events.

Responsibility: Regarding overall program structure — Legal Department and Offshore Program Manager; for Offshore Application — Project Manager.

ix. Risk: Vendor does not meet performance criteria.

Mitigation: Multiple vendor strategy; consistent performance reviews with clear and objective strategy.

Controls: Multiple vendor strategy; Contingency Plan; Vendor Exit Plan.

Responsibility: Legal Department; Offshore Program Manager.

x. Risk: Regulatory changes in Offshore country that negatively affect ability of vendor to fulfill contract.

Mitigation: Diversity of Offshore locations; proactive management of knowledge transfer and systems documentations across multiple locations.

Controls: Multiple geographic location strategy; Contingency Plan; Vendor Exit Plan.

Responsibility: Legal Department; Offshore Program Manager.

Exhibit 7.1 (continued)   Typical Program: Wide Risks and Mitigation Strategies

xi. Risk: Negative customer perception due to bad press related to Offshore.
Mitigation: Ethical and fair treatment of employees impacted by Offshore.
Controls: Offshore Communications Plan; Media/Public Relations Script; Set aside funds to support training as part of costs of program.
Responsibility: Offshore Program Manager; Media Relations.

xii. Risk: Network failures make Offshore personnel hard to reach for critical communications.
Mitigation: Backup communications protocols established.
Controls: PMO Offshore Compliance Program; Application specific risk management process updated for Offshore; contractual vendor notification process for trigger events.
Responsibility: Regarding overall program structure — Legal Department and Offshore Program Manager; for Offshore Application — Project Manager.

xiii. Risk: Ineffective disaster or application recovery planning.
Mitigation: Offshore vendors contractually required to meet specific criteria in disaster and application recovery practices; regular audits to ensure compliance.
Controls: Vendor specific disaster recovery requirements based upon firm specifications and industry regulations; Application specific risk management process updated for Offshore; contractual vendor notification process for trigger events.
Responsibility: Regarding overall program structure — Legal Department and Offshore Program Manager; for Offshore Application — Project Manager.

- These macro-level threats have not changed substantially during the last 17 years or so that many companies have established Offshore programs. It is hard to view the threat of war, for example, as a "crisis" for the length of 17 years, and in reality, not much has actually changed during that time period. So these macro-level risks are best viewed as ongoing concerns to be constantly watched and addressed with strategy, with the understanding that the situation indeed may move into crisis at any time.
- The Offshore program can easily get bogged down in an endless debate if there isn't an attitude across the team that truly enables creative problem solving, and supports working around problems and issues. *Key to assessing Offshore risk is realizing that there is no qualitative risk difference between the consultant*

accessing the network from across the street, and the consultant accessing the network from India. We explore the implications of this in detail below.

- Finally, it is a reasonable assumption that the Offshore industry itself, increasingly the mainstay of foreign economies such as in India, represents a powerful force for discouragement of global conflict. It is not unusual for articles on the potential conflicts of Offshore countries to cite the major firms invested in Offshore as having not only a large stake in the outcome, but also a collective voice in the debate relative to the conflict at hand. The growing economic force that Offshore represents is clearly worth preserving, and acts as a powerful deterrent to conflict.

■ Application-level risks (Exhibit 7.2) clearly differ not only for each application, but also for the particular Offshore program execution model chosen by the firm.

- Co-Sourcing is an Offshore model utilized most frequently due to the many benefits it affords. In the Co-Sourcing model, roughly 80 percent of the team is usually overseas in tactical roles, and more strategic roles such as project management and relationship management for the application remain Onshore. In this model, data and systems remain Onshore. As a result, many risk management aspects, such as network integrity management and disaster recovery, remain Onshore. What does need to be managed by the Offshore program are risks relative to loss of breach of network, loss of worker-invested time relative to knowledge management, time and service losses related to the compromise of the physical facility itself, and employee sabotage. We explore and make recommendations on each of these risks, one by one, below.

- For a different model, for example, new application development where the systems physically reside Offshore, the more standard risk model (e.g., Onshore risk management) applies. It is often simplest here to have Offshore vendors provide the equivalent risk management contingencies and action plans to the Onshore divisions and properties of the hiring firm, with modifications as appropriate.

■ The primary focus for application-level risk usually has to do with sensitivity related to customer data. Customer data can be in a continuum — clearly, access to customer data is not acceptable, but how about access to invalid test data that is based upon real customer data (as many large firms are)? These are some of the more subtle questions that must be reviewed and answered, program by program and organization by organization.

Exhibit 7.2   Typical Application-Specific Risks and Mitigation Strategies

i. Risk: Lack of clear definition, documentation, and communication of Onshore and Offshore application system roles, expectations, and responsibilities.

Mitigation: Clearly delineated test periods, with contingency staff on standby if necessary, until all processes are shown to be working. For application development, very early and thorough code walkthroughs or similar quality assurance checks.

Controls: Statement of Work; Offshore Application Launch Plan with specific exit criteria before steady state; ongoing Application Metrics.

Responsibility: Project Manager.

ii. Risk: Ensure Offshore service firms' hiring practices meet all Human Resource policies and guidelines (e.g., qualifications, background checks (OFAC), required government paperwork (visas), discrimination and harassment policies, etc.).

Mitigation: Vendor contract hiring provisions; Statement of Work application specific requirements; appropriate screening and review of key project resources such as Offshore application leads.

Controls: Strong personal project management interface with Offshore leadership; specification for hiring practices in SOW.

Responsibility: Project Manager; Program Manager.

iii. Risk: Application-specific success criteria are not met, such as SLA/QA standards for maintenance and support, or project deliverables do not meet time/quality/cost specifications for new project development.

Mitigation: Vendor contract hiring provisions; Statement of Work application-specific requirements; clear contractual exit criteria for failed obligations.

Controls: Clear metrics measurement and reporting responsibilities outlined in SOW; signature and other formal requirements for all project transitions; early checkpoints.

Responsibility: Project Manager.

iv. Risk: Key application resources, such as Offshore lead, leave Offshore firm.

Mitigation: Critical roles have backup in waiting at all times; Statement of Work is fixed price.

Controls: Clear notification and hiring process spelled out in SOW.

Responsibility: Project Manager and Program Manager.

v. Risk: Identification, accountability, dispute escalation and resolution, tracking, aging, and reporting processes for issues resolution and customer complaints are not followed, effective, or understood correctly.

Mitigation: Clearly delineated test periods, with contingency staff on standby if necessary, until all processes are shown to be working. For application development, very early and thorough code walkthroughs or similar quality assurance checks.

Exhibit 7.2 (continued) Typical Application-Specific Risks and Mitigation Strategies

Controls: Statement of Work; Offshore Application Launch Plan with specific exit criteria before steady-state; ongoing Application Metrics. Responsibility: Project Manager.

Above and beyond the actual management of risk, there is also the task of successful interface to regulatory agencies. These agencies are new to the Offshore model and have been relatively quiescent, but all indications are they will be updating their requirements and engaging in oversight at a new level. Although the emphasis and structure of these agencies vary by industry, they generally will want some sort of validation that the following risk areas have been considered, and an execution plan in place where appropriate, for the following.

- *Overall security* — May include safety requirements for physical facility such as video surveillance, picture badges, security patrols off-hours, and other measures to provide a secure physical environment as well as validate identity of all participants as harmless.
- *Vendor longevity as it relates to financial stability* — As related in the research in the last chapter, this is one of the largest concerns. We discuss the underlying costs and risks related to switching vendors below — mature Offshore programs (companies that have engaged in Offshore for more than three years) are often much less dependent upon the individual vendors, and able to put this particular risk in perspective. As a result, a case can be made that this particular risk is greatly minimized over time, as the customer becomes more independent in vendor management and oversight, and other key program processes.
- *Offshore program office vendor management and oversight* — Although the functions of the Offshore PMO were discussed in Chapter Five, an empowered PMO is key to effective risk mitigation, and is ultimately responsible for ensuring compliance and for conducting the reviews required for reporting and monitoring the program. This includes minimum standards for vendor review and due diligence relative to hiring of resources. Hiring practices are specified by the firm, and include OFAC screening to meet U.S. visa requirements. OFAC is outlined further in Exhibit 7.3.
- *Quality metrics, including daily, weekly, and monthly operational measures* — Application-specific requirements as outlined in the SOW still need to meet overall specifications as set by the PMO for consistency of measurement across the organization, as well as to meet regulatory specifications as appropriate.

Exhibit 7.3   OFAC Outline

What Is OFAC?

An OFAC screening is generally required for every Offshore team member. OFAC stands for the Office of Foreign Assets Control, a set of laws administered by the Department of Treasury Laws/Regulations. These laws are designed to block prohibited transactions with designated foreign countries (e.g., Libya, North Korea) that the federal government has declared "a threat to the U.S." OFAC regulations impose economic sanctions against governmental entities, officials, businesses, and citizens of those countries, or with persons or businesses regardless of location controlled by those countries. These parties are referred to as specially designated Nationals, special designated terrorists, specially designated narcotics traffickers, blocked persons, or blocked vessels and are collectively referred to as "SDNs".

   The regulations prohibit U.S. firms from establishing or maintaining relationships or employing and contracting with SDNs. Violators will be subject to penalties administered and enforced by OFAC.

- *Legal and regulatory compliance, including privacy and confidentiality* — Establishing appropriate baseline vendor contracts that meet regulatory requirements; following through on regular reviews so that these are updated as needed.
- *Security of information/knowledge transfer/intellectual capital* — Security focus for the Co-Sourcing model, as outlined above, generally relates to network security architecture because the data and systems reside Onshore. Intellectual capital and knowledge transfer risk mitigation is established primarily through geographic diversity. This remains one of the most frequently overlooked and ignored aspects of risk mitigation for new Offshore participants.
- *Disaster recovery/crisis management* — Creating minimum specifications for vendors; establishing a regular review schedule to ensure compliance in even the most remote of locations.

MACRO-LEVEL PROGRAM RISKS: A BASELINE

Below is a list of the primary macro-level risks to serve as a baseline, and a typical mitigation approach for each one. This information can be utilized to support the risk analysis process in several ways.

- It can serve as a risk template to be placed upon the program repository, to be used by project managers to validate the appropriateness of the application for Offshore prior to final Offshore launch. Project managers can also use this list to create an application-specific set of risk action items to monitor and review.

Typically, Offshore is added to the existing risk analysis documents and annual review process.

■ As a basis for discussion with the executive-level risk management team, the list is particularly useful as the initial Offshore assessment for the organization gets underway. The executive risk team will usually want to obtain validations and signatures from all major risk stakeholders. This usually includes the legal department, compliance, IT audit, network security, IT management, and the business management team. A regular meeting of these disciplines is a useful venue to work through any concerns regarding how Offshore would affect a particular discipline.

■ Finally, the macro risk list below is useful in creating standard vendor contracts, to ensure that as the firm enters into the vendor relationship for the first time (and with the most leverage), the costs and effort of managing risk are also part of the cost negotiation.

Let's turn our attention to exploring the macro-level risks in detail. As a whole, we rank the severity of program-level risk as Low, Medium, and High, based upon the general experience of the Offshore Interest Group.

Macro Risk I: Lack of Clear Communications Handoff between Offshore and Onshore Team (Low)

Mitigating the risk regarding communications between Offshore and Onshore project team members is the primary reason behind the years of methodology discipline associated with Offshore service providers. To put it into a larger perspective — most of the risk, contractually, is usually taken upon the Offshore vendors; the lack of high visibility failures in the press related to Offshore, as pointed out in an earlier chapter, is a sort of negative testament to the care and skill in execution of the India-based Offshore service providers. This is not to say a passive stance is recommended; however, India-based firms are process experts, and it is generally safe to assume a watchful level of closely supervised trust. Most U.S.-based firms emerge from the initial implementation of Offshore with a cleaned-out "closet" of IT applications — inventories, documented and benefiting from the additional focus with greater overall efficiencies.

Macro Risk II: Offshore and Onshore Team Turnover Negatively Affects Performance or Program Costs Due to Additional Knowledge Transfer, Visa, and Other Training Delays or Costs (Medium)

Although the majority of India-based Offshore service firms generally assign additional team members at no charge to ensure seamless execution in the face of promotions, training requirements, and other forms of staff attrition, there are larger risk aspects at play here. One of the more lively topics of recent debate for experienced firms in Offshore is whether the market for individual contributors will require active poaching of the other companies' employees to maintain adequate staffing. Although this type of active staff raiding, at the time of the writing of this book, appears to be limited to the brand new and rapidly burgeoning BPO space, unseen market forces may make significant changes. High staff turnover can add to the delays and costs of Offshore.

In addition, recent trends show that visa processing and access have become more difficult to manage, not less. Although many of the India-based Offshore services firms have created special government relationships, as Offshore grows, finding shortcuts around local bureaucracy becomes more challenging. The threats of the post-9/11 world suggest only greater delays in U.S. visa processing as caution is formalized; the increasing furor over negative press for Offshore may also limit the flow of allowable temporary and permanent U.S. visas in the future. Visa limitations are subject to the ups and downs of governmental sanctions, and it may become more difficult to bring individuals Onshore temporarily for knowledge transfer. Two related articles on visa processing are found later in this chapter, in Appendix C.

Although vendor management is the subject of another chapter, it is important to note within the context of risk management that the primary risk relates to runaway costs, and how to avoid them. Avoiding "learn while you burn" during knowledge transfer is primarily a function of a well-negotiated vendor contract. It is helpful in this regard to structure knowledge transfer so that it is fixed price, to be held despite delays in staffing, visa processing, and other risks. This encourages vendors to manage their staffing to ensure success. One caution here, strangely enough, is driving too hard a bargain for hungry Tier Two and Tier Three firms — large customer corporations may find they need to modify how much prices are driven down even for the sake of fairness and company longevity, just as they may have to modify how the modest India-based firms present their outstanding qualifications whereas U.S.-based firms may exaggerate lesser capabilities. Larger India-based firms and the U.S.-based consulting firms will generally be less flexible on pricing.

Macro Risk III: Regulatory, Privacy, or Legal Compliance Violation(s) (Medium)

Key to successful risk management at the macro or program level is the establishment of solid program-level processes, understanding each particular risk and ensuring that it is monitored appropriately and has the right level of detailed action specified in writing to ensure clear actionable response, and the appropriate accountability.

An Offshore compliance program identifies, monitors, and performs operational and system impact analysis of both U.S. and Offshore country laws and regulations. The analysis should include legal and statutory conflicts between the United States and the Offshore country. Although the specific regulations vary by industry, they include these regulations:

- U.S. Patriot Act
- Office of Foreign Asset Control (OFAC)
- U.S. Export Laws
- Privacy, such as the healthcare industry's HIPAA regulations
- Money management, such as the banking industry's Security Act

Although discussing in detail the components of an overall risk management program is beyond the scope of this book, these programs usually involve a set of application-specific documentation that details the risk for each application. These documents must meet specified criteria for the type of information and the requisite actions. These risk programs include the following.

- *Business policies and procedures* — These include policies relating to review of business content relating to the application. For example, business end users enter data with built-in automated error checks (limits to the type of fields such as numbers only for dates, etc.). A related policy would be a manual that would detail what the end user would do in the eventuality that data was missing for a particular entry, or other operational instructions.
- *Application of self-monitoring mechanisms (internal test and monitoring procedures)* — Many large databases, new Web-enabled applications, and other application packages have the capability to internally monitor and report upon potential security breaches. These procedures detail the frequency and level of review of these reports, and other actions related to ensuring security.
- *Training for IT and business team members in compliance* — This includes orientation of the steps required for project managers and team members to participate in the ongoing compliance rules as well as biannual or annual detailed review process.
- *Early warning monitoring technology* — Network security and other applications have graduated levels of warnings for monitoring personnel.
- *Escalation and corrective action processes, call lists, and decision-making processes for application issues and exceptions* — Trial runs

are suggested to test out the clarity of the Offshore–Onshore escalation and exception management process as a component of the trial period prior to final Offshore application acceptance.

■ *Overall acceptability guidelines for new, strategic business initiatives* — These include company-specific requirements for interpreting industry regulations, such as fine points for evaluating security concerns related to exposure of customer data. Although most companies, to continue our example, have wisely drawn the line in terms of allowing access to customer data, test data that is based upon real customer data is usually allowable Offshore, as long as it is not directly traceable to the customer.

■ *Network safety and security guidelines* — Establishes requirements for placement of firewalls, usually according to security classification of data and applications from low to high.

■ *Reporting and knowledge management validations of steady-state* — These include risk management of downstream applications, and summary reports comprised of enterprisewide systems.

Macro Risk IV: Negative Employee Perception of Offshore Program Due to Perceptions of Job Instability (High)

Losing top performers is always a concern, and frequently one that receives much less emphasis than recruitment of new employees. Although communications may be helpful, it is difficult to overcome the inherently jaded view of many employees regarding official management messages. Ultimately, fair treatment of workers is the most effective means of quieting concerns.

Macro Risk V: Operations Schedules Could Affect Offshore Program Requirements (Low)

Offshore is not much different from other complex technology initiatives that need to be integrated into the overall operations schedule. The primary challenge will be ensuring clear communications between the Offshore project team leads in the daily operational tasks and handshake. The operations team will have a learning curve relating to understanding the the unique impact on system resources relating to differences in time zone, filtering through the network, remote support needs, and other challenges relating to geographically dispersed users. However, time has certainly shown that the technology is present to meet these challenges in the long successful history of Offshore.

Macro Risk VI: Security Breach of Offshore Facilities (Low)

Certain measures can serve to minimize the chances of a security breach. Although they affect different aspects of risk management, they are listed in one place below for convenience.

- Limit Offshore file access to quarantined servers when possible.
- Limit Internet access for internal development environments on internal network where feasible. Physical access to all servers and systems is strictly limited and monitored. Log files for access of systems are reviewed regularly.
- For test environment access, plan to ensure minimal security breach potential across types of access, systems, and firewalls, for both unit and systems testing processes.
- Establish clear categories of user access for production environments, and review and update these regularly.
- Do not allow Offshore users to be granted access to unspecified applications and servers, and are commensurate with job responsibilities.
- Establish a clear policy for Offshore consultant's exposure to customer, employee, and other sensitive data.
- For new application development, clearly define responsibility regarding how moves code across test functions into production, including approval processes.
- Create clear contingency plans in case of network outages, in particular ensuring no negative impact on critical SLAs. Network design is high availability, eliminating a single point of failure, is protected by an adequate firewall solution, and possesses sufficient bandwidth.
- Robust authentication protocols are enabled to present unauthorized access, including network infrastructure components equipped with adequate tools for both prevention and detection.
- Security policies and directives are communicated Offshore on a regular basis, including signature authorization and review.
- Offshore physical facilities are subject to random independent audit for both physical and process procedural compliance. Internal Offshore processes are audited independently at least annually, perhaps more frequently under certain trigger conditions, including financial, internal control, and security reviews.
- Disaster recovery responsibilities and test plans are developed, documented, and approved prior to implementation according to specified industry and company requirements.

Macro Risk VII: Offshore Vendor Financially Insolvent (Low for Large Vendors)

For firms new to Offshore, most choose leading India-based firms to avoid this eventuality; Big 5 firms are also very safe. Market conditions for Tier Two and Three Offshore firms point to likely consolidations and continued intense competition, however, to date there have been no high-profile bankruptcies or difficult mergers that have left customers complaining.

As customers mature in Offshore (over three years experience), the familiarity and institutionalization of Offshore program processes support a much greater degree of vendor independence. Financial insolvency is likely to become a well-understood and highly tolerated risk for firms wanting the lower prices offered by the lower-tiered vendors.

Macro Risk VIII: Threat of War; Geopolitical Concerns (Medium)

There's not much any individual customer firm can do other than monitor and create a mitigation strategy. The main point here is to not miss the overall Offshore boat due to these concerns, and to choose Offshore service vendors that allow geographic distribution. As a new Offshore customer, it is not practical or desirable to establish new country relationships independent of the vendor, yet distribution is the only way to create a workable contingency.

Ensuring system documentation and procedures reside in more than one country, and that multiple-location personnel are cross-trained, is generally sufficient for most firms. The Offshore Program Office should also actively monitor and report on any germane geopolitical events, in particular relative to travel.

Macro Risk IX: Vendor Does Not Meet Performance Criteria (Low)

Vendor contracts are of course the primary venue that defines the parameters of these events. Given the general track record of execution excellence of Offshore firms, this is probably the least likely risk of the list. Rather than elaborate formulas resulting in financial fines, and so on, most Offshore service vendors understand that the real threat of an unhappy customer is the difficulty it means in winning new business, or in getting that contract renewed over the long term. In the small and closed club that is the Fortune 100, word gets around fast. Most Offshore firms have myriad resources to throw at a problem, and do so, before the customer even has a chance to have cause for complaint.

Macro Risk X: Regulatory Changes in the Offshore Country That Negatively Affect Ability of Vendor to Fulfill Contract (Low)

Most Offshore countries are competing hard for the business U.S. Offshore services represent, and are highly unlikely to put roadblocks between these revenue sources. One interesting area to watch is countries with policies that provide significant tax advantages to U.S. firms that create direct jobs with the Offshore workforce, such as Brazil's grants to manufacturing firms.

The top foreign employers in Brazil are exempt from certain customary and generally worldwide import and export taxes of raw material, but must host local physical facilities that directly employ Brazilian workers in order to qualify. A certain amount of corporate taxes from all foreign employers in Brazil are reinvested in educating the workforce, so a circle of benefit is established, wherein that employer has access to an increasingly better educated workforce. Variations on these kinds of creative country policies seem likely for other countries vying for these investment revenues from the United States.

Macro Risk XI: Negative Customer Perception Due to Bad Press Related to Offshore (Low)

For many firms, this is the unspoken fear that prevents a foray into the unknown. Although financial services companies, banks especially, are particularly known as "sticky" (customers avoid rather than look to switch banks), some industries have been very concerned. A well-publicized incident regarding the state of New Jersey, receiving negative press and public feedback when a support line for unemployed individuals was discovered to be Offshored, actually resulted in the cancellation of that Offshore contract. Health care is likely a good candidate for Offshore, with the emphasis on cost management, but again is likely to be concerned about privacy regulations and negative press.

Emphasizing the relatively small percentage of IT applications moving Offshore can help, as can directly making ties to lower customer costs as a result of Offshore. This is an arena where proactive and intelligently managed communications can literally make the difference between acceptance and a potential PR nightmare.

Macro Risk XII: Network Failures Make Offshore Personnel Hard to Reach for Critical Communications (Low)

Generally network management is one of the areas of expertise where Offshore service firms excel. With sufficient testing and preparation, it not rote, then not a focus of challenge and difficulty.

Macro Risk XIII: Ineffective Disaster or Application Recovery Planning (Low)

Disaster recovery programs are focused on temporary physical replacement of computer centers in the event of sudden unexpected interruptions. Backup computers and applications are waiting in remote locations in the eventuality of earthquake or other physical disaster. For Offshore, disaster recovery means a different type of planning.

- Disaster recovery for the vendor-owned physical facilities, according to well-defined similar programs of the customer firm, is usually based upon a combination of internal customer and industry standards.
- Disaster recovery for knowledge transfer and intellectual capital, meaning cross-training of teams in diverse geographic facilities.

Although these are never casual, both of these are well-understood competencies and are within the comfort zone of most large IT organizations.

As a further example, one large and very experienced financial institution has many applications maintained Offshore that cannot be offline for more than a few hours. This firm has a strategy in which all systems components, including knowledge transfer and associated intellectual capital, are sent around the world several times during the day to be stored in multiple locations across Europe, India, and other locations.

APPLICATION-SPECIFIC PROGRAM RISKS

Most application-specific program risks are related to methodology execution, and essentially represent the strength of the Offshore vendors. It is true that the challenges of Offshore due to geographically and culturally diverse teams add a need for added precision. It is also true that the commitment and excellence of methodology exhibited by Offshore firms, who understand this discipline is their bread and butter, more than cover the additional challenges.

In summary, risk management is a discipline addressed via review and mitigation strategies. As in most large IT programs, these program and application-level risks are managed via a corporate risk process.

Most important, assessing risk for Offshore requires unemotional and objective judgment. Despite our feelings to the contrary, there is absolutely no qualitative difference in risk between a consultant accessing the network in the next building or town, and one accessing the network from an Offshore location.

Application-level risks are generally mitigated by good methodology and project management practices, and include

- Project scope
- Metrics relating to performance of SLA and benchmarks
- MIS requirements
- Audit processes
- Cost and compensation
- Ownership and licensing
- Confidentiality and security (including privacy guidelines)

Program-level risks are mitigated by well-documented and clear processes, expectations, legal contracts, escalation procedures, and approvals regarding

- Business resumption and contingency plans
- Legal structures relating to indemnification and jurisdictional covenants
- Insurance
- Dispute resolution
- Limits of liability
- Vendor default and termination
- Customer and end-user complaint management

APPENDIX A

A Veteran's View of Network Design for Offshore Outsourcing

In this addendum, we look closely at not only the technology, but also the individual profile of a successful lead network architect. The ability to walk the delicate line between compromise and orthodoxy is nowhere more important. The willingness of the lead network architect to create a workaround business process where a straightforward technology solution is not feasible is a critical success factor in Offshore. A network architect secure in the art of compromise, but also knowing where to draw the line and refuse to bend, is an irreplaceable asset. Thus, we look here as much at the character of an individual in this leadership role as we do the role itself.

Introduction: Profile of a Successful Network Architect

The network security architecture is often one of the critical components of success and failure for Offshore. The key of the conundrum is one we've noted before — although many organizations have a significant number of employees and consultants logging in remotely to perform work, it is easy to keep this under the radar screen and ignore the implications and potential problems. When Offshore comes on the horizon, low visibility is usually not part of the picture. Network security challenges relating to remote system access of key systems come to the forefront. Challenges that have been swept under the rug as too complex and expensive to put into this year's budget suddenly become a focal point of the discussion for assessing the costs and risks of the Offshore program.

And indeed, addressing network security is both potentially expensive and complex, and frequently figures as one of the highest initial startup costs. Key to the success of resolving this challenge is the ability of the individual in charge to design and offer solutions. These solutions must balance the need for ultimate network security with the reasonable compromises that enable the legitimate business goals of the organization. Fortunately for me in the Offshore program I managed, Erik Hacker (his real name) is such an individual, and our collaboration was a very successful one.

Erik demonstrates the intent stillness that is characteristic of the good listener. He has a way of contributing to group conversations in a low-key way that nonetheless is very effective. Erik's comments were often pivotal to decision making in the largest of groups, where his quiet intensity had a calming effect on the often-heated discussions.

He graduated with a double major in math and philosophy (an early sign of his unique combination of skills). He started as a network administrator shortly after graduating, and became a self-taught network guru within a few years by simply demonstrating he could get the job done. It wasn't long before his role felt limiting and he wanted more challenge. He joined a small consulting firm and started working with a large hospital with deep security challenges. As a consultant, Erik learned valuable customer interface skills as well as broadened his network skills. He perfected his skills in learning about architecting and managing cutting-edge network technology before they were well documented and understood, and learned how to effectively communicate and problem solve with customers who were not technically literate. Interacting with Erik as a "client" is to experience a very gentle listening, with firmness when it is needed.

As is typical of many of the profiles here of successful contributors, Erik is not only a good listener, but genuinely likes other people's ideas. He wants the best idea even if it does not necessarily start with him. His background in philosophy leads him to embrace questioning everything (à la Socrates), so although he is pragmatic and certainly no pushover, he also does not exhibit any of that rigid orthodoxy that can be so negative to collaborative partnership. More important, his openness has led to an objectivity that lends him great respect in group settings, as team members feel they can trust his leadership is not based upon petty considerations but the good of the whole.

Successful Network Security Architecture Design Principles for Offshore Outsourcing

As is implied in Erik's experience and profile, his view of Network Security Architecture is a subtle one. He starts by explaining that many security people still focus on security as a "state" rather than a "process." Approaching the question of network security as a continuum rather than an absolute brings a sense of business realism into this most technically esoteric of design disciplines.

Thus, the statement "We are now secure" is essentially impossible. Unless a computer is literally unplugged from the network in standalone mode, eternal vigilance is necessary, because there is no such thing as an absolutely secure network. So, then the focus becomes on the degree of compromise — with the understanding that everything is a compromise.

Although it is tempting to say, "Now we are secure," for example, upon the installation of a firewall, Erik points out that the firewall itself is insufficient. A solid and consistent security review and change control process as well as a good testing process are also required. A firewall without these is only as good as an unused seatbelt in preventing network security "accidents."

Understanding that security is always a journey, and not a steady state, and one that is dependent upon human vigilance in adhering to good security processes and procedures sets the stage for a solid Offshore network security foundation. The second component is a set of security policies that provide guidelines for the individual architects on specific Offshore subprograms and projects. These are usually high-level, akin to an overall methodology, and are then interpreted by security experts as they are tailored to the task at hand.

For example, a security policy may state that there must be network audits conducted on a regular basis for each project. The network architect would then determine the specific scope and frequency of those audits as part of the design process for that project's security architecture.

A second component Erik recommends as a key is the attainment of the appropriate security certifications, such as the Certified Information Systems Security Professional (CISSP). These certifications validate that the practitioner has a minimum body of knowledge established as an industry standard for the role of security network architect. They are certified through a series of exams and mandated refresher courses for credits every three years, and generally require a minimum number of years of experience as a prerequisite to sitting for the exam.

There are several outcomes from the concept of security as a process rather than a state. One outcome is that a successful network architect design effort is a joint collaboration between the business drivers and goals and the security they require for their particular needs. A second corollary is that the mitigation of risk is not necessarily technology-driven, but also business process-driven. The network security architect as a well-rounded and multitool consultant becomes a key to success.

Executing a Successful Network Security Architecture for Offshore Outsourcing

Now that we have established the groundwork, we can define the steps required for successful network security architecture design for Offshore.

It is rare, but a blessing, that an architect has the opportunity to design a network from scratch for the task at hand. In the typical Fortune 100 firm, he or she is inheriting a hodgepodge of tactical solutions, each representing the height of security of its time, but outmoded and rather patched together in the present.

Erik describes the typical corporate environment of today as a "hard shell surrounding a soft inner core." In other words, it's relatively hard to get inside the network, but once inside, it's easy to go anywhere — even places where one shouldn't.

Modern security architecture for Offshore Outsourcing, then, is primarily about controlling access within this "soft inner core" so that once inside, the Offshore consultants will stay where they belong. This is usually achieved by a combination of intrusion detection, security monitoring, and access controls. The individual solutions in these areas are arrived at through a series of educational and iterative discussions among the network technology architects and their business partners. They are weighing three factors — business needs, cost, and security tools and processes, to come to a final solution (Exhibit 7.4).

To address the issues relative to the soft inner core, the first step is to build the toolbox. Erik advises "building the tool box before you build your house." As in home architecture, you need to finish the blueprint before you construct any of the individual rooms, as tempting as it may be to start with one room and add from there.

Erik recommends starting by defining precisely the kind of access, by whom, in what location, to drive the definition of the building blocks of the network security. Usually the soft inner core requires some sort of

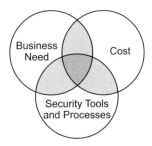

Exhibit 7.4   The Three Balancing Factors to Network Security Architecture for Offshore Outsourcing

creative and intelligent segregation of the current network relying on a combination of technology and security business processes.

Erik's experience as the Network Architect started with the realization that this was so new, the team didn't know what they didn't know. Offshore was so far outside of the way the firm was operating, and outside of current policies and procedures, that the program required a willingness to embrace a completely new view.

What was more, the infrastructure organization at the firm was not organized in such a way as to support this broad a network security program. Prior to the Offshore initiative, the focus was on individual projects. Most of the work prior to Offshore involved either responding to the tactical requests of the business partners for the appropriate network access or creating an environment specific to an individual project. The Offshore Program encompassed over 125 team members and 26 projects, and as such was much broader and deeper in scope than most.

Initially, just understanding that the typical roles fulfilled by team members under the typical processes would no longer work was a big adjustment. There were several weeks when tasks did not complete because well-meaning individuals were convinced it was the responsibility of others. A series of phone calls was required to define the respective roles vis-à-vis the Offshore Program because there was no precedent and therefore no clarity. When embarking on new endeavors it is part of the risk profile that work tasks fall between individuals like a poorly played game of badminton.

The infrastructure team was required to look at the entire work cycle and associated processes, from strategy, project planning, cost management, high-level execution, risk management, and even the companywide technology review and approval process — and update them for the Offshore Program.

Once the team completed the intellectual and emotional process of coming to grips with the scope of the Offshore program, the primary challenges were to ensure safe outer third-party (nonemployee) access, to deal effectively with remote locations not under the firm's physical control, and to ensure risk management processes were updated.

To deal with the risk management process, for example, a brand new process and group (referenced earlier), called the Risk Leadership Team, was formed. This team was comprised of the heads of the Legal Department, Compliance, Audit, and Network Security. At these team meetings, the entire team reviewed all network security architecture options in detail. Erik was generally very effective at explaining the security options and costs to our legal and other representatives. But you can imagine how disastrous a less interpersonally skilled network architect would have been in this scenario. Having the signatures of all leads in these key areas, not to mention the indepth discussions regarding the various security options and trade-offs (relating to level of security, cost, level of effort, etc.) that Erik put together, was an important learning experience for the organization as a whole.

Erik couches the Co-Sourcing model (some team members Offshore, others Onshore) as one of the most difficult network security problems to resolve. If the work were completely outsourced, this is simpler, because the network security issues would be outsourced as well. If inhouse, then the hard outer shell with the soft inner core would be fine. It is trying to do both — keep the outer shell hard and inner shell soft for everyone but legitimate Offshore consultants — that is tricky.

After consideration of all of the options, Erik recommended a VPN rather than a more expensive leased line for connectivity to the locations in India and the Philippines, for this particular firm. He and his management team also insisted upon a neutral security audit performed by a firm not affiliated with the Offshore providers to review the remote locations and ensure compliance with the firm's security standards (such as allowing entry only to employees with appropriate badges, etc.). Erik feels strongly that compliance reviews should never be conducted by the same company providing the Offshore services.

Upon stepping back to review the project-related processes to ensure they are updated for a program of the size and scope of Offshore, the next step is to review the regulatory requirements for Offshore. Regulatory controls vary by industry, of course, but most regulatory bodies have not kept up with the Offshore revolution. When Erik did his research in the financial services arena, there was little to go by as it related specifically to the Co-Sourcing model of Offshore services. He then looked at other, smaller projects within the firm as prototypes for a norm for establishing security. The model the firm used in the past seemed to be moving existing systems into new segregated areas called sandboxes or shells, protected by a series of firewalls, rather than build new systems.

Having scoped out the high-level components of the solution, Erik worked to put in the details. A significant challenge was that it was impossible to move all of the systems into their shells or sandboxes because of the way they were originally created or implanted. Erik likened the problem to trying to haul a couch by a VW Beetle — great car, but not quite the right size equipment for the task at hand.

Erik solved the problem within acceptable cost limits by combining intrusion detection technology and processes along with a stronger user access control authentication process.

Erik was able to creatively use the same technology tools in new ways, due to his unique skills and abilities in communicating viable options along a spectrum of cost/risk for business partners to debate, evaluate, and select. Even with the careful structuring of the solution, as is typical of new and complex technology endeavors, some of the technology did not perform as expected and needed to be tweaked. The team ultimately ended up with a Citrix server solution over the VPN for file access from remote locations into the systems in the United States.

APPENDIX B

For Geeks Only: More Detail on Offshore Network Architecture — A Step-by-Step Guide

Step (1) Define Remote Access Needs

Review of access by remote personnel is reviewed at two levels. The first level is the protocol level (how communication is going to take place). The second level is the authorization within the host or operating system. Looking more closely at the protocols, it is important as a security architect to understand how that communication is going to take place and what risks take place in the communication. For example, HTTP is used for Web browsers, and is relatively secure as a protocol. There have been problems with people being able to attack Web servers through HTTP but a strong Web server management program can effectively mitigate that risk. Another full protocol is MSRPC, which can provide access to the complete system, including Microsoft registry, any file on the system, and authorization to start and stop processes. Having a requirement to use the MSRPC communication protocol can clearly raise the overall risk. Much of this depends upon the existing protocols within the network and what choices the network architect has in terms of introducing new protocols.

Regarding the authorization level, the challenge was to explain the risk to the business partners and ensure their full understanding of the options and the risks associated with those options. Erik tried where possible to eliminate authorizations through business processes, for example, by requiring that an inhouse team member perform functions that required administrator system privileges, instead of an Offshore resource.

Step (2) Evaluate Policy and Regulatory Compliance

The next step is to evaluate how required permissions, and the like, differ from current security policies, and work through discrepancies. Many organizations may not have to segregate the network as much because the regulatory requirements are not that strict.

Step (3) Document and Assign Costs to Each Solution Level

Once the above needs have been evaluated, and your high-level solution investigated, it's time to put down the options and assign costs to each one. Erik tries to put as many options on the table as possible, especially those that are process-oriented and therefore are less expensive to implement than those relying solely on technology solutions. The ideal in terms of security is to have the remote locations only working with sanitized test data. See whether this is possible in some rather than all of the solutions.

Step (4) Evaluate

There are three options to help you evaluate the efficacy of the chosen solution. (a) Pick up the entire system and stick it behind a firewall with the communications protocol you've selected, and then "see what breaks." (b) Pick it up and move it behind a firewall but use liberal firewall rules to watch for things you may have missed earlier. Or (c) add another network interface to the host, then migrate communication flows via the new interface. The biggest advantage of the latter is there is very little risk of application downtime. The disadvantage is that you still need to finish before you allow Offshore workers access to the system.

In conclusion, as in many complex technology initiatives, both decision making, and the leadership qualities that inform those decisions, must be at the ground level. Offshore is complex enough that management team members are unlikely to be able to maintain the technology skills to effectively achieve the objectives, and must delegate decision-making authority to the direct network security architects. These individuals must in turn step up to the leadership challenge, like Erik, and possess the skills and capabilities of leadership, in terms of appropriate compromise, persuasion, creativity, and communication, and yet still hold firm to ensuring network safety requirements are indeed met. Offshore may indeed breed a whole new generation of network "techies" able to defend, persuade, visualize, and create.

APPENDIX C

H-1B Visa Overview

"1B Bill 2000 Passes!"[1]

The House shocked us all by passing S.2045 on Tuesday, October 4. The bill raises the H-1B cap, provides special provisions for students, changes per-country quota rules, gives extensions for those with pending adjustments who have reached the six month/one year limit, and more. Following are the details.

After a short debate, the House took a voice vote yesterday in favor of the bill. The Senate passed the bill by a margin of 96 to 1, leaving Lamar Smith and the other H-1B opponents in the lurch, and the President is expected to sign this week.

The new H-1B bill can be summarized as follows:

1. Verifies that the Act is entitled the "American Competitiveness in the Twenty-First Century Act of 2000."
2. Increases the existing visa quotas as follows:
   a. FY 2000 — increase from 115,000 to 195,000
   b. FY 2001 — increase from 107,500 to 195,000
   c. FY 2002 — increase from 65,000 to 195,000
3. Establishes new rules involving universities, recent advanced degree graduates and research institutions:
   a. For starters, the H-1B cap will no longer impact any foreigner who is employed — or has a written offer of employment — by a university, college or related nonprofit organization. Neither will nonprofit or government research organizations are [sic] subject to the quota. Once a person under these categories leaves the related position, however, they do become subject to the H-1B cap once again, unless the subsequent employer is likewise exempt.
   b. Second, for those with a petition filed no more than 90 days prior and no more than 180 days following the completion of a graduate degree, the cap will not be applicable.
4. Revises the rules on per-country quotas for those adjusting status based on employment:

a. The goal here is that no immigrant visas shall go unused if there are pending applications which would be accepted, if not for the per-country cap.

b. If the aggregate number of visas (green cards) available in the five employment-based green card categories exceeds the number of submitted applications, then the percentile limitations (stipulating that no given country may represent more than 7% of the applicant pool for employment-based green cards), shall be suspended.

c. An additional provision states that any H-1B visa holder who has a pending employment-based immigrant visa petition and would otherwise be subject to the per-country limit, may apply for an extension of their current H-1B status, to keep them in status until the green card is approved or denied.

5. Makes it easier to begin working sooner, and to transfer an H-1B visa without work interruption:

a. Effective the moment President Clinton signs this bill, an H-1B visa holder may begin to work for a new employer when a non-frivolous, legally viable H-1B petition is submitted, and no longer must wait for approval before doing so. If denied, the authorization will be terminated, but it relinquishes the difficult waiting-period that leaves so many foreign workers in precarious limbo.

b. At the day of the bill's signing, anyone awaiting approval of an H-1B transfer may legally begin to work for his or her new employer.

6. Allows for an extension of stay when application delays are the fault of the INS:

a. For H-1B visa holders with a pending employment-based green card, and who filed a labor certification or I-140 at least one year prior, the six year time limit it waived, with extensions granted in one year increments until the green card petition is either approved or denied.

7. Extends portions of the 1998 H-1B legislation:

a. An extension has been granted from October 1, 2001 to October 1, 2002 for the attestation requirements governing for H-1B dependent employers. Also extended is implementation of the new $500 retraining fee for H-1B visa petitions, from October 1, 2001 to October 1, 2002.

b. Additionally, Department of Labor investigation provisions in the 1998 law have been extended by one year to September 30, 2002.

8. Recovers fraudulently used visas:

a. If an H-1B visa holder — whose visa was subject to the cap — has the visa revoked due to fraud or willful misrepresentation, that visa will be returned to the visa pool as unused, and available to another applicant, regardless of the year of original issue.

9. Requires that a National Science Foundation study be conducted:
   a. The NSF is now compelled to conduct a "digital divide" study to make determinations on how technology access impacts those in society who have it, versus those who don't. The study must be complete within 18 months from the passing of the bill.

H-1B Visas Drop, L-1 Abuses Come to Light

At first glance, the 75 percent drop in H-1B visas seems a reflection of the ailing economy. But a closer look reveals that companies have found a loophole with the L-1 program, making it faster and easier to get foreign workers into the country. According to John W. Steadman, president-elect of the Institute of Electrical & Electronics Engineers-USA, the unemployment rate for engineers reached a record 7 percent in the first quarter of 2003.

Steadman testified in front of a Senate panel that the H-1B program was a major contributor to this staggering level of joblessness. Even when the economy was booming, there were Americans who claimed they had the education and background for these jobs, but had to compete against foreigners to get them. Still, the booming economy and a huge need for the technical workers seemed to justify the visas, as American companies aimed to remain productive and competitive. H1-B visas allow foreigners to work in the United States for up to six years. They were established to do away with a shortage of skilled workers such as medical professionals, technical experts, and even fashion models.

Three years ago, when technology companies — mostly in the Internet and other computer-related fields — were booming, the H-1B program was expanded under pressure from the big players. Congress passed a temporary increase on the annual cap, which went from 65,000 to 195,000. That temporary cap is about to expire, and unless Congress acts by October 1, the previous cap will go back into effect. To many, this would seem all well and good because the number of H-1B visas has dropped 75 percent in one year, according to a report by the American Electronics Association, a trade group representing 3000 tech firms.

The number of H1-B petitions went down to 26,659 in 2002, compared with 105,692 in 2001. According to Charity Wilson, lead analyst of equity issues at the AFL-CIO, which represents 65 unions with 13 million members, 250,000 workers were laid off in 2002, including 100,000 programmers, but companies were still filing petitions for thousands upon thousands of H1-B visas. Wilson and many others want to know why. Technical industry representatives claim that they still need the technical skills foreigners can provide. Industry bigwigs say that not enough Americans are undertaking studies in advanced sciences and math, forcing their country to hire foreign-born workers.

American technical workers are crying foul, and hope to get support from their representatives. Senator Dianne Feinstein (D-Calif.) recounted complaints by unemployed technical workers who tell her point blank they were replaced by foreign-born workers willing to accept one-third the pay they had been receiving. "It's not easy to hear someone say, 'This is a program that you helped create, and I'm losing my job because of it,'" Feinstein admitted. Stephen Yale-Loehr, an attorney who represents the American Immigration Lawyers Association, asked that lawmakers consider a new cap of 115,000 H-1B visas, and opponents are asking senators to allow the visa program to fall to the previous 65,000 annual level.

But changes in the H-1B visa program alone may not solve the problem at all. The tech industry has turned to the L-1 visa, taking advantage of a loophole that allows them to get foreign workers in faster, and with fewer hoops to jump through. Senator Saxby Chambliss (R-Ga.) announced his plans to introduce legislation that would restrict the visa program and limit abuses. "American workers have been displaced, and this must stop," he told the Senate. The purpose of the L-1 visa is to allow international companies to import to America, on a temporary basis, specially skilled employees from abroad. But foreign companies have been setting up U.S. offices with the specific goal of bringing in thousands of low-cost tech workers, who they then contract out to U.S. companies, pulling the employment rug right out from under American contractors. Both foreign and U.S. companies have realized that there is an even easier way to bring people into the United States than the H-1B visa. With L-1 visas there are no caps, no explanations required about qualifications, and no proof is necessary to show that they are not displacing a U.S. worker.

In August of 2003, U.S. Representative Rosa DeLauro (D-Conn.) introduced a bill for an L-1 cap, and a prevailing wage requirement so that companies would not be able to abuse foreigners or displace American workers so easily. Lawmakers may be closing in on the abusers, but many are hesitant to restrict business and industry in any way: they are the pulse of the economy and everyone worries about strangling them financially by forcing them to do things a certain way. What the Senate plans to do remains to be seen.

Note from U.S. Department of State Web Site[2]

Recent changes in U.S. visa policy and procedures have increased the amount of time it can take to obtain a visa. Apply early!

Changes introduced shortly after September 11, 2001 caused long processing times, which varied from country to country. Backlogs accumulated and delays became indefinite in some cases.

Improved interagency and automated procedures have reduced delays and speeded up visa processing. The State Department's goal is visa delivery no more than 30 days from the time of application in most cases. Sometimes it can take less than that, and sometimes longer. If your name or a close variation is matched in a database indicating law enforcement concerns, the process will take several weeks longer to resolve.

NOTES

1. Jennifer and Peter Wipf, *Immigration Issues,* http://immigration.about.com, 2002.
2. U.S. Department of State Web Site, Visa processing time, Introduction, November, 2003.

8

PULLING IT ALL TOGETHER:
TOP 10 DO'S AND DON'TS
OF OFFSHORE

This chapter completes our tour on moving IT Offshore. It is hoped the journey is just beginning. Offshore offers myriad benefits to the organization. The benefits most usually anticipated with Offshore include, of course, dramatic overall cost savings, with all of the competitive opportunities that implies. Many companies also experience the positive results from the required higher level of methodology discipline, including improved documentation, and greater overall efficiency.

As is typical of most return on investment analyses, however, the real benefits of Offshore are those that are subtler and harder to quantify. An IT organization capable of complex execution across geographies, countries, and cultures engenders both maturity and creativity. Sometime after the dust has cleared, the IT organization has not only an opportunity to broaden horizons in a literal sense, but establishes a new baseline of sophisticated skills upon which to build.

There is a generation of companies that are building unique value propositions upon this new sophistication. Some are venturing into creating directly owned Offshore facilities through Build, Operate, and Transfer. Others are reinvesting Offshore savings to raise the cost of entry into existing or newly created markets. Like many rites of passage, it may be that the ultimate benefit of Offshore is the ability to simply stay in the game.

THE TOP 10 "DO'S AND DON'TS" OF OFFSHORE

1. Timing

DO: Embark upon Offshore Sooner Rather Than Later

Although time consuming and a bit of a puzzle to unravel, Offshore is now a well-proven capability. Delays may mean a loss of competitive standing as other firms reinvest savings in new capabilities.

DON'T: Underestimate the Leadtime Required to Enable Offshore

Offshore is a long-term play, and has a lengthy incubation period. Offshore usually means coming to completely new terms with key corporate processes such as network security design and deployment, third-party software vendor licensing practices, corporate vendor management organizational structure and processes, the vagaries of U.S. visa processing, and (ideally) strategic resource management as a key component of the firm's competitive positioning. The good news is, the benefits are long-term too, and far outweigh the costs.

2. Intelligent Consumption

DO: Discover the Unique Advantages of Offshore and Apply Them to Rewrite the Rules of the Game

Too often, when something new comes along, it is tempting to think about it within the old framework. Recognize the unique historical factors behind the Offshore leadership of India, and the value of the particular strengths of the Offshore model as they apply to the firm. The challenge is to look beyond the all-encompassing, inward-looking complex culture of Fortune 100 companies. One leading organization, calling itself truly global, objected to the very term "Offshore" as too U.S.-centric. The very terminology of Offshore betrays the collective bias. An opportunity awaits for the leadership of a handful of firms to leverage the unique opportunity that is Offshore — the future will tell.

DON'T: Overlook the Need for Equal IT Partnership

Offshore enables firms to invest in new core skills that emphasize IT leadership — in relationship management, technical projects and program management, and technical architecture, to name a few. Building communications bridges between IT and their internal business partners is, within most industries, one if not the key driver of overall competitive positioning. Intentional empowerment of the IT function by such means as organizational restructuring, or reinvesting savings accrued from Offshore, may be the catalyst to finally achieve that partnership. Empowerment of IT within the corporate structure — or at least something approximating equality — is necessary to leverage Offshore (as is true of any strategic IT initiative).

3. Program Authority

DO: Drive the Program from the Top Down, Empowering IT to Enforce Organizationwide Technology and Process Standards

As in many efforts where IT is utilized to provide competitive advantage, Offshore works best within an empowered IT organization that has the authority to enforce process standards. Requiring Offshore to win the popular vote of either internal business partners focusing (as they are paid to) on immediate revenue, or already stressed IT managers appropriately seeking the familiar and proven path of least resistance, can result in a weak effort with severely watered down benefits and savings.

The more experienced a firm is in Offshore, the more likely participation is via executive management directives that define minimum participation. There is an increasing recognition that the old paradigm of decentralized IT vendor management — *for the particular type of tactical IT resources (maintenance and support, coding) best provided by Offshore* — compromises not only cost, but quality and efficiency.

DON'T: Grant Program Authority without Reference to the Real Challenge of Offshore

To the typical large, busy, highly distracted organization viewing Offshore as just one in a series of complex technical IT initiatives, it often comes as a surprise that the true challenge is not in technology program deployment, but in the much more difficult task of proactively planning IT resource management across the organization. Not only in the narrow sense as it affects displaced employees, but also in the sense of aligning IT resources with the needs of the firm over the long term to create competitive advantage. Ultimately, intelligent management of Offshore is about intelligent management of IT people resources in the broadest sense.

Although it is typical for most large firms to utilize strategic IT partners to help launch new and unfamiliar technology initiatives, doing so on automatic pilot without reference to the underlying resource implications that Offshore ultimately requires is unwise. Placing any outside party in charge of what ultimately becomes, decision by decision, the IT sourcing strategy of the firm, abdicates the critical responsibility of the executive team. It can also leave the most vulnerable employees unprotected and without an advocate when they need it most. Be aware of whom and how you empower in decision making for Offshore.

4. Expert Support for Program Initiation

DO: Consider Bringing in Expert Help in Key Areas

Shoring up the internal and external communications function, so very prone to misunderstanding and mistrust, may be helpful for Offshore. External legal counsel, often combined with vendor negotiation support, may be useful as well.

DON'T: Spend Large Amounts on a Lengthy, Upfront Execution Analysis Consulting Effort

Many large firms will start the Offshore initiative by hiring expert help to make sweeping recommendations, application by application, putting them in categories that determine suitability for Offshore. This is based upon the assumption that major initial challenges are related to tactical execution, deployment, and risk mitigation. It is also an approach that is usually valid — many large technical programs are launched in this way, avoiding waste and expense from misdirection.

This exercise, however, does not often provide long-term value for Offshore unless the focus is primarily a much-postponed organization of the messy IT application closet that needs to happen anyway in preparation for program deployment. Most large firms are the product of multiple mergers and acquisitions, and the IT application mix is a true mish-mash. It is very helpful to finally know what is out there via a comprehensive IT catalogue.

The view of application suitability for Offshore, however, is very organization-specific, almost unique. What constitutes risk relative to Offshore, the typical driver for early decisions on application suitability, inevitably undergoes a radical revision — both pro and con — once Offshore becomes well understood and part of the regular IT toolkit. Building a strategy based upon early assumptions generally means the planning process must be repeated after a year or two.

Tortuous and expensive comparisons of vendors and countries are also not worth a large cash outlay. Of course the firm will need to perform the analysis and due diligence relating to vendor selection. However, vendor quality is not a large risk factor in the overall picture for the top 20 or so India-based firms — the options tend to range between safe, safer, and safest — and don't warrant exhaustive expense. Organizations experienced in Offshore frequently include at least one, and probably more, Tier Two vendors due to their even more competitive pricing, and their overall comfort with the Offshore process. Also recommended is making the trip to India to visit the vendor sites. These are truly inspirational experiences, and are often the catalyst to swing the nonbelievers, especially nervous internal business partners.

5. Choosing Vendors

DO: Create a Vendor Strategy Incorporating Geographic or Country Diversification for Risk Mitigation

Although it is difficult to go wrong with any of the leading India-based vendors due to the overall quality of services they represent (and the level of competition among them), it is important that the final vendors choices are based in — offer Offshore services in — more than one country. This provides the basic tools for risk mitigation. No company wants to be forced into a position to deal with complex international legal, visa processing, and hiring practices. Geographic diversity provides the requisite multiple locations for knowledge transfer and intellectual capital, the primary investments within a Co-Sourcing model. Why not just add another country later? Unless it is part of the original vendor strategy, additional vendors raise the overall price point (Offshore service providers offer volume pricing of resources across the board). Most India-based firms also have Nearshore facilities in locations such as Canada and Mexico, at a higher price point than India, but worthwhile for the risk mitigation. U.S.-based Offshore service providers often have bases in several countries. This is one of those areas where foresight pays off handsomely.

DON'T: Invest Large Amounts in Lengthy External Consultant Efforts Involving Upfront Vendor or Country Comparisons

Most large corporations, which make up the vast majority of Offshore customers, have a very decentralized means of managing their external consultants beyond the centrally negotiated contract. The recent economic downturn highlighted the disadvantages of this approach — although independent consultants' rates easily keep pace with hourly rate increases, unless they are centrally managed they rarely keep pace with economically driven rate decreases. Add to this the cost of administrative overhead, the chaos of merging methodologies, and the negative culture of building silos of individual spheres where information rarely goes beyond the consultant's immediate internal manager, and centralized external IT resource decision making becomes very attractive indeed.

Some leading firms contract with Offshore service providers for all phases of work — traditional on-site consulting, Nearshore (e.g., Canada,

Mexico) as well as Offshore. Shifting from hundreds and perhaps even thousands of individual consultants to several dozen centrally managed Offshore service providers has advantages beyond lower hourly rate costs, in reduced administrative overhead and higher overall efficiency and quality. A surprising number, but not all, of the requisite skills are available through Offshore service providers, but usually there is enough of a critical mass to make significant improvements in the overall manageability of the vendor management function.

6. Vendor Management

DO: Leverage Offshore as a Broad Initiative to Help Streamline the Way All External IT Resources Are Managed

Most large corporations, which make up the vast majority of Offshore customers, have a very decentralized means of managing their external consultants beyond the centralized contract negotiation for large firms. The recent economic downturn highlighted the disadvantages of this approach — although independent consultants' rates easily keep pace with hourly rate increases, unless they are centrally managed they rarely keep pace with economically driven rate decreases. Add to this the costs of administrative overhead, the chaos of merging methodologies, and the negative culture of building silos of individual spheres where information rarely goes beyond the consultant's immediate internal manager. Centralized external IT resource decision making becomes very attractive indeed.

Some leading firms contract with Offshore service providers for all phases of work — traditional on-site consulting, Nearshore, as well as Offshore. Shifting from hundreds and perhaps even thousands of individual consultants to several dozen centrally managed Offshore service providers lowers hourly rate costs, reduces administrative overhead, and enables higher efficiency and quality. A surprising number, but not all, of the requisite skills are available through Offshore service providers, but usually there is enough of a critical mass to make significant improvements in the overall manageability of the vendor management function.

DON'T: Apply Yesterday's Vendor Management Model to Offshore

Offshore is frequently an exercise in letting go. For example, the Offshore fixed-priced contracts, combined with the superiority of methodological execution, make it no longer practical or helpful for the individual IT or project manager to interview every team member providing services overseas. Offshore requires much discipline from the internal IT department, and not only in the obvious areas such as system documentation, procedural integrity, and clarity of communications, but also in acceptance of delegation of authority. In order to fully realize the benefits of Offshore, the overseas team must be given the trust and authority to do their part. Then and only then can the internal IT department really take advantage of Offshore.

Focusing on developing greater capability relative to non-Offshore roles such as program and project management, architecture, and relationship management provides high value to the organization. It is important to set these philosophical differences and expectations from the beginning, and structure the Offshore program to kindly, gently, but inexorably shift the work responsibilities appropriately.

7. Contract Negotiation

DO: Understand the Complex Relationship among Risk Management, Vendor Selection, and Contract Negotiation

Contract negotiation is very closely aligned with vendor strategy and the overall perceptions of risk relative to Offshore. The key to vendor strategy is to balance several opposing interests. These include geopolitical risk mitigation (choosing vendors with multiple geographic/country options), volume discounts (fewer vendors), leveraging vendor strengths while minimizing dependency (more vendors), and finally, creating competition between vendors to keep prices down (more vendors).

The relative differences related to cost for India-based service providers, however, even at a 10 percent difference, are incremental. A large difference, such as 10 percent, is only $2.50 an hour for an hourly rate of $25.00. Although this is subject to market forces and therefore change, most large Offshore customer firms find that pricing and related costs between the India-based vendors is not the driving factor because they are frequently so close (for the initial set of Offshore vendors — later, many firms focus much effort on driving down Offshore pricing).

Looking at the big picture, to date most customers of Offshore service vendors are large Fortune 100 firms. Most of these firms will be evaluating the top 20 or so India-based Offshore service firms, as well as their pick of the Big Four or other large U.S.-based firms that offer Offshore services. U.S.-based firms may play upon the generally exaggerated fears of the unknown to justify what are usually higher price points. As you know from reading this book, the attitude of the Offshore Interest Group, with membership of over 30 companies, is that all vendors (India- and U.S.-based) essentially provide excellent quality services. The competition is such that there is very little room for error or customer mismanagement — given the high-level visibility of the corporate customers involved.

This is not to mean that India-based vendors will not walk away from a deal. Most of the top India-based vendors insist on a minimum volume

FTE Offshore in order to be interested in a business relationship. But they also are generally — as a group — so willing to meet whatever it takes to win big contracts away from the U.S.-based vendors that the decision usually comes down to the softer factors such as what "feels" like a good fit. Because Offshore is much longer in terms, and broader in scope, than most vendor relationships, this is a good thing!

Don't: Lock the Firm into Overly Lengthy Contracts

Offshore programs can be very daunting at first. Across the backdrop of sometimes unreasonably strong emotional barriers relative to letting go of Onshore daily application control, there is a legitimate complexity to the successful execution of Offshore. If this is not mastered, the negative impact is not usually reflected on the delivery of application requirements — the Offshore vendors know any high-visibility failure will be their last, and bring out every resource in the world to resolve issues before they become critical. The impact is usually in lowered savings. Usually large firms initiating Offshore programs feel keenly the lack of appropriate IT program control, such as effective management reporting, vendor performance analysis and tracking, legal understanding, and network security architecture. These can make it appear as if the firm will be dependent upon the vendors forever.

Yet, inevitably, usually between year two and year three of Offshore, the reality settles in. The hysteria that all IT jobs are going Offshore subsides. The ease of execution, and improved overall IT methodology and discipline, become evident. "Safety" and application risk are redefined. The organization will want to take these newfound skills and muscle, and flex them. It is important to ensure that the vendor contracts do not lock the organization out of creatively exploring new options. Generally, it is best, no matter how tempting the tactical price points or other offers on the table, or how lengthy and difficult the knowledge transfer or network preparation, to keep Offshore vendor contracts to a maximum of three years (a relative eternity in the business world under any circumstances). Two is better.

8. Risk Management

DO: Choose a Network Security Architect with Flexibility and Mature Leadership Capability

Beyond the hype, one major critical success factor to risk management is the robustness of the network security function, because most firms utilize a Co-Sourcing model in which data and systems reside in the United States. The key to creation of a workable network security architecture is a leader with vision.

Experienced network security architects view security as a continuum, ultimately made up of a series of intelligent compromises. The only 100 percent "secure" computer is one that is unplugged from the network. Once a computer is networked, it can theoretically be compromised. The role of the network security architect is to provide leadership across these myriad possibilities — driven, as always, by the firm's unique business needs and drivers.

Thus, network technology knowledge alone is not enough to embody leadership in this critical arena. This unique leadership role requires the ability to articulate risk fairly and objectively to senior executives, and to outline clearly the options, costs, strengths, and weaknesses across myriad combined process- and technology-based solutions. Careful selection and support of these rare individuals is one critical success factor of Offshore.

DON'T: Let Generalized, U.S.-Centric Thinking Become the Basis for Offshore Risk Strategy

The reality is that there is no difference in risk between consultants sitting in Bangalore, India and those sitting across the street, when both are logging into internal systems over a network. Most large firms have a "Don't ask, don't tell" policy regarding external systems access by consultants, because the written policy says not allowable, yet the organization also pragmatically can't function without it. So there is usually an unrealistically rigid policy alongside a huge list of "exceptions," both official and unofficial.

Offshore often serves as a catalyst to suddenly drive these murky waters into the light of day. It is important that this debate not delay and muddle the program. Separate, early on, the risk issues that are specific to Offshore versus those that are related to all consultants' remote access of internal systems. Otherwise, Offshore may be buried under an endless debate, and remain in limbo attached to broader issues that will never be resolved, with the consequent loss of the myriad advantages it brings.

9. Employee Impact

DO: Set Aside Funds Up Front to Support the Vulnerable Worker Transitions

Offshore is not the decimator of IT departments that the popular press portrays. What the press neglects to point out is that Offshore to date has generally been limited to Fortune 100 firms, and of those, well under 30 percent of applications move Offshore. The factual economic statistics of Offshore underscore that the actual number of displaced IT workers is few compared to those affected by general economic conditions and other factors. The great majority of organizations in the Offshore Interest Group have not experienced any negative employee impact in terms of jobs, choosing instead to eliminate consultants (for an even higher savings) or using other strategies such as not replacing employees who leave due to normal attrition.

However, for those individuals who do find themselves without viable career options, the reassurance of these numbers showing the actual smaller impact of Offshore ring hollow.

We know enough about Offshore to anticipate that those affected by losing their jobs or even their careers are likely to be those most vulnerable of U.S. workers — relatively advanced in years, but not yet of retirement age, with financial responsibilities for children (often requiring college tuition), aging parents (often needing expensive health or nursing home care), and communities (serving as the primary tax base as long-term home owners). Career loss at this phase of life can be devastating, not only to the individual, but also to the wider family minieconomy this individual's salary and benefits represent.

The good news is that, although it is expensive and time consuming to help re-career a long-term, loyal employee, this expense is still a small part of the overall anticipated savings of Offshore. (In "Offshoring: Is it a Win-Win Game,"[1] this cost is estimated at five percent of total corporate savings generated by Offshore.)

In Offshore as in life, ethical behavior is good business. It is pragmatic to avoid alienating most of the current workforce, who understand very deeply (and take personally, as their co-workers and friends) what is at stake in the ethical cost equation of the treatment of the older and loyal worker. The new investor and the potential new recruits are also highly influenced by the ethical track record of the organization. In this day of instant communications, don't believe for a moment that word will not get out — positive or negative — on how these workers are ultimately treated.

DON'T: Leave the Tough Strategic Sourcing Strategy Engendered by Offshore to Be Driven by Default

What appears to separate the organizations truly able to fully leverage the advantages of Offshore from those that dabble, with equally desultory results, is the willingness to mandate change from the top down. Executive mandates are not the most politically popular concept within large firms, legitimately so. IT as a functional discipline within the Fortune 100 is usually dependent upon project-focused, matrix management of cross-functional teams. These are comprised of equals communicating and cooperating in order to achieve complex technical initiatives.

Offshore, with its emphasis on centralized decision making and executive mandates, may appear to be undercutting the fundamental principles of good teaming so critical to the success of complex initiatives.

However, the fundamental challenge of Offshore resides not in the program execution, which although complex and challenging, is relatively (believe it or not) routine. The challenge resides in strategic resourcing, core skills management, and the delicate art and balance of ensuring a new kind of "just-in-time" inventory management of the IT workforce itself. Unless these decisions are recognized and shepherded at the highest levels, they fall by default to the middle-management tier, a group that frequently lacks the authority and information to successfully envisage and deliver.

10. Ethics

DO: Understand That in This Our New Millennium, "What" Cannot Be Separated from "Whom" and "Why"

If the ethics of the business world have been busted open to a new level of focus, concern, and interest, clearly one of the fallouts from the debate is the realization that the era of reported business information as intrinsically neutral, objective, and ethically sound is past. What we understand now is that facts and details have little to no meaning without context — a sort of business world equivalent to the new physics' Heisenberg Uncertainty Principle. This Principle states that an atom changes its very nature in the process of being perceived.

As there are no neutral atoms, there are no neutral facts. Every radio announcer's intoned wisdom, newspaper article, financial audit, and Fortune 100 Annual Report — despite language and settings elaborately structured to the contrary — is written by a human being. It is at our own peril, in this post-Enron world, to be unaware of who is speaking, what their bias is, and how that agenda may affect their particular "atom," intentionally or unintentionally.

The culture of IT in large organizations is, at its best, based upon solid delivery of results — a "show me" of winning confidence one project, one success, at a time. This reputation-based approach to the building and earning of trust will serve these firms utilizing the Offshore model well.

DON'T: Overlook the Ultimate Ethics of Opening Our Job Markets to Offshore Countries

Although this is clearly not the popular view, and as a result is barely mentioned in discussions on Offshore, the truth is that the larger U.S.-based firms have displaced many jobs within Offshore countries in the name of free enterprise.

U.S. soft drinks have taken over or put out of business the local Indian equivalents — we sell our shoes, our clothing, our entertainment/movies, and even our focus on popular culture. American culture is our biggest export worldwide, and few areas of the globe have not been touched by our burgeoning markets. It is with no little satisfaction that many, who track the movement of these global economies, see the chance for us to even the score a bit, and provide good jobs for the hard-working and talented individuals of other cultures. In the process, we all grow and prosper.

We close with a few words from several members of the Offshore Interest Group.

May the wind be at your back!

APPENDICES

A Final Word from Some Members of the Offshore Interest Group

From: Brad Clark[2]
Manager, Global Resourcing at LexisNexis

Don't underestimate cultural issues. As Americans we live in an era of "political correctness" which says that we should treat everyone the same. While that works for American culture, it doesn't work very well when you add an outsourcing company to your staff mix.

What has worked best for our company is to provide cultural training for our staff, as well as the staff of the outsourcing company (that is, if they don't provide themselves). As a result, we have learned to be more open about the differences in our cultures and have embraced them as a way to become stronger partners.

In practice, it's the little things that count. For example, take the onsite staff of your Indian outsourcing company out for lunch to celebrate Diwali (the main Hindu holiday) instead of Christmas. Send emails to your staff about the meaning of Hindu holidays celebrated by your offshore Indian staff. Have a cultural night where your staff and the onsite staff of your outsourcing company learn about customs, food and traditions of each other's culture. Take the onsite staff of your outsourcing company to a sporting event they've never seen (like American football, baseball or ice hockey) and buddy them up [with] your staff so they can ask questions and learn the rules. Budget permitting, take one or more of your first-line development managers with you on your offshore visits so they can overcome the mental hurdles of working with an offshore company.

From: Helen Cousins[3]
Senior Vice President and CIO, Corporate Technology, Cendant Corporation

Exhibit 8.1 outlines the Cendant Offshore methodology.

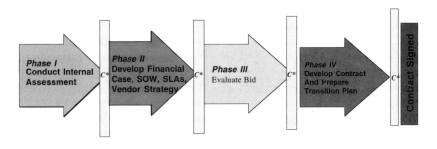

Exhibit 8.1   Cendant Offshore Methodology (High Level)

Offshore Considerations for the IT Executive

- The ability to outsource a key function is becoming a core competency of the IT Executive
- Managing the outsourcing is becoming a "rite of passage" in the IT career
- Outsourcing is a business decision that may lead to feeling a loss of power, control, and autonomy
- You must transition to become a manager of services versus an implementer of systems
- Strong support and leadership are needed to make it successful
- Challenges may come from unexpected places

Challenges of [Offshore] Leadership

- Commit fully to the effort
- Accept ambiguity and uncertainty
- Become a quick change artist
- Be accountable for outcomes
- See yourself as a service center
- Act as if this is your own business
- Manage your own morale
- Don't complain

NOTES

1. McKinsey & Company, August 2003.
2. Brad Clark can be reached at brad.clark@lexisnexis.com.
3. Created by Helen Cousins of Cendant Corporation, 2001.

INDEX

H

H-1B visa, 229–232
HCL Perot Systems, 21
HCL Technologies, 21
Hewlett-Packard, 21
Hexaware, 21
Hiring, 43–52
Honesty, importance of in workplace, 72
Hotline, ethics, 75
Hughes, 21

I

IBM, 21
iFlex, 21
Impact of offshore outsourcing on worker, 14–17, 33–34, 183–204, 243–245
  checklist, to program for displaced employees, 196
  corporate irresponsibility, 203
  employee placement, 196–199
  ethics in, 183–184
  impact on future, 199–201
  logistics, 193–195
  loyalty, 203
  morale, 203
  recommendations, 193–195
  relocation of staff, 203
  70:70:70 rule, 184
  strategic resource management, 188–193
  threat of offshore to information technology workers, 184–188
  value of jobs, 201–203
Impartiality, in workplace, 72
Independent consultants, 52. See also Consultants
India as vendor location, 4, 5, 10, 108–109
  business environment, 115
  educational system, 115
  graduate salary, 115
  infrastructure, 115
  offshore services leadership in, 123–128
  political environment, 115
  software exports, 115
  time difference, 115
  visit to, 51
Indonesia as vendor location, 117, 124
  business environment, 117
  graduate salary, 117

infrastructure, 117
  political environment, 117
Information, security of, 212
Information technology, 3. See also Offshore outsourcing
  stages, onshore, versus offshore locations for, 9
  traditional outsourcing model, 6
Infosys, 10, 21. See also India as vendor location
Infrastructure, offshore, 115–122
  Brazil as vendor location, 122
  China as vendor location, 116
  India as vendor location, 115
  Indonesia as vendor location, 117
  Ireland as vendor location, 121
  Malaysia as vendor location, 118
  ownership of, 98–99
  Philippines as vendor location, 119
  Sri Lanka as vendor location, 120
  Vietnam as vendor location, 117
Initiation of offshore outsourcing program, 29–80
  consultative assistance, 50–52
  measurement of return on investment, 55–58
  network security infrastructure, timetable for upgrade, 60–61
  return on investment, measurement of, 55–58
Insolvency of vendor, risk management, 218
Integrity, importance of in workplace, 72
Intellectual capital
  ownership of, 102
  security of, 212
Internal gatherings, 35
Internal information technology organization, preserving value of, with offshore outsourcing, 11
Investment, focus on, 106
Ireland as vendor location, 120–121, 124
  educational system, 121
  graduate salary, 121
  infrastructure, 121
  managing risk in, 114
  software exports, 121
  time difference, 121
Israel as vendor location, 120
IT. See Information technology